CONTENTS

The Lean Six Sigma Guide to Doing More with Less

The Lean Six Sigma Guide to Doing More with Less

Cut Costs, Reduce Waste, and Lower Your Overhead

MARK O. GEORGE

WILEY

John Wiley & Sons, Inc.

FOREWORD

Though I have now retired from the consulting industry, I spent over 20 years helping companies grow corporate value through process improvement initiatives and business transformation. My work with improvement had begun in the late 1980s, when, upon my return from extended studies in Japan, my colleagues and I pioneered the introduction of what are now known as Lean methods in the United States. Years later, in 2002, my company, George Group Consulting, led another wave of innovation: fully integrating Lean with Six Sigma so that companies could simultaneously improve cost, speed, and quality while tying all process improvement projects to shareholder value.

Lean Six Sigma has subsequently become one of the most popular business improvement methodologies of all time. Our clients reported to the markets that their Lean Six Sigma initiatives have been cost-neutral in less than one year, that they've reduced costs upwards of 20 percent and have improved ROIC and Economic Profit by as much as 10 percent or more by year two of the deployment. The media abounds with examples of companies large and small that have made similar gains.

In the past decade, continuous improvement, including Lean, Six Sigma, and Lean Six Sigma, has reached unprecedented levels of acceptance. In fact, about 50 percent of Fortune 500 companies and over 80 percent of Fortune 100 companies (according to AVR Associates, Ltd, 2009), as well as government entities such as the U.S. Navy, U.S. Army, and multiple federal and state agencies have active Lean Six Sigma or similar programs.

The relevance of Operational Excellence and Lean Six Sigma continues to this day, nearly three years after having sold the George Group to Accenture and seeing it become their Process and Innovation Performance service line.

Yet despite its proliferation, research indicates that many continuous improvement programs are, unfortunately, not delivering the expected business benefits. In late 2008, the Conference Board released the results of its survey of 190 CEOs, chairmen, and company presidents from around the globe. These leaders were asked to list their top 10 challenges, particularly in the time of financial crisis. The top-of-mind concerns among business leaders today may surprise you:

Executive's Leading Concerns During Time of Financial Crisis	Percent of Respondents
Excellence in execution	55.4%
Speed, flexibility, adaptability to change	46.6%
Economic performance	44.6%
Customer loyalty/retention	40.1%
Improving productivity	36.9%

Source: The Conference Board's 2008 CEO Challenges Survey.

Even though continuous improvement programs are resident in organizations of all types and in all geographies, many companies don't seem to be addressing the fundamental issues these methodologies are intended to improve. All of the concerns listed here speak directly to the objectives of Lean Six Sigma, yet many executives don't perceive the business impact. While many companies have claimed hundreds of millions in economic benefit from Lean Six Sigma, just as many others have failed to see the results. Is the methodology not universally applicable, or is it being poorly administered?

Today, my son, Mark George, along with hundreds of my former colleagues, continue to bring the power of George Group's methodologies to Accenture's clients around the globe. They've captured their best practices in this book, *The Lean Six Sigma Guide to Doing More with Less.* Previous books on Lean Six Sigma (including my own), served to *introduce* the concepts to readers who did not understand them or had not seen the benefits of their integration into a single transformation approach. By contrast, this new book helps the reader understand *how the concepts are best applied* in reducing cost and enabling competitive advantage in today's economic climate.

The Lean Six Sigma Guide to Doing More with Less provides an understanding of the difference between Lean Six Sigma deployments that provide incremental reductions in cost and those that enable step-change improvement. In particular, Mark and his contributors present the reader with a practical understanding of how process transformation can deliver not only an operating advantage but also a structural advantage.

Throughout this book, Mark presents case studies from a wide array of engagements that help the reader comprehend the approach for Lean Six Sigma to manage costs, along with the pitfalls, lessons learned, and ways to mitigate risk—it is truly a *how-to* guide.

For those who have toiled away mapping processes, gathering data, and applying tools only to see business outcomes left relatively unchanged, Mark helps readers understand how a holistic Lean Six Sigma approach can enable annual cost reductions of 20 percent or more and improved ROIC and Economic Profit by as much as 10 percent or more. *The Lean Six Sigma Guide to Doing More with Less* is a valuable reference tool for anyone seeking to reduce cost and improve business performance—no matter what degree of impact you seek, what amount of commitment you're willing to make, or how mature your Lean Six Sigma program is.

Michael L. George
Former CEO and Founder of George Group Consulting
(now part of Accenture)

PREFACE

The global economic collapse of 2008–2009 is widely recognized as the most severe crisis of its type since the Great Depression of the 1930s. As of this writing economists and analysts cannot be certain that the crisis has yet reached its profoundest depth; all agree that it will take years, if not decades, to restore the economy to anything near its prior strength and expanse.

No geography, industry, government or socioeconomic group has been spared. As the commercial economies and public sector budgets contract, there is increased pressure for organizations to survive the crisis by reductions in the cost of operation. The rescinded demand for goods and services has revealed that global overcapacity has been evident through rampant increases in unemployment, the total elimination of enterprises, the consolidation of many who remain, widespread shuttering of plants, and the closure of tens of thousands of retail outlets. Following demand and capacity balancing, many organizations have looked to restructuring, outsourcing and the tried-and-true analysis of profit-and-loss (P&L) statements to identify myriad cost reduction opportunities.

In a difficult economic period, people are tempted more than ever to apply quick fixes and ad hoc solutions. Cost reduction activities may be knee-jerk reactions—typically, poorly planned and executed—rather than well-devised strategies. Grasping for solutions is a natural, yet ineffective, reflex. Without careful analysis and understanding of the drivers of cost, reductions may not last, with costs reemerging in the same form or in other manifestations of inefficiency. The outcomes can be hit and miss; some may have benefits that are short-lived, while others may do more harm than good by eroding market share through lack of customer focus and decreased service levels.

We have discovered that the most egregious mistakes organizations make in cost-cutting actually don't show up as total disasters but, instead, as missed opportunities. Organizations will often miss 10 to 50 times the potential savings by succumbing to traditional cost-cutting tactics, scrambling to find cost management solutions at the P&L account level and not at the enterprise level. The solutions often fail to understand the need to rethink operating models and the offering portfolio, and to build in organizational resilience, flexibility, and speed to react to market conditions.

In times of crisis, markets, institutions, and policies quickly evolve; the competitive landscape changes and new consumer trends emerge. In such times, management's decisions can seal their company's fate: do little and join the ranks of others in the struggle to hold market share and diminishing margins, or do something transformational and emerge even stronger than before—best poised to surpass the competition once markets recover and demand resurges.

Organizations must develop near-term strategies to survive the downturn, and longer-term strategies to thrive in the new economy. This book provides a practical understanding of how Lean Six Sigma (LSS) supports both the near-term need to survive by safely and rapidly reducing cost, and the longer-term road to high performance by transforming into a fast and agile enterprise. And while continuous process improvement is typically associated with gradual, incremental performance gains, this book illustrates how a concerted focus on process and execution can enable a structural, operational, and cultural transformation that confers true competitive advantage.

High Performance Business Defined

Thus far, Accenture has studied more than 6,000 companies, including more than 500 that meet our criteria as high performers. As described in *Going the Distance: How the World's Best Companies Achieve High Performance*, Accenture defines high-performance businesses as those that:

- Effectively balance current needs and future opportunities.
- Consistently outperform peers in revenue growth, profitability, and total return to shareholders.
- Sustain their superiority across time, business cycles, industry disruptions, and changes in leadership.

And how do high performers achieve these feats? Our research has identified the "how" as the building blocks of high performance:

- Market Focus and Position results in better decisions.
- Distinctive Capabilities results in better practices.
- Performance Anatomy results in better mindsets.

> High-performance businesses continually balance, align, and renew the three building blocks of high performance, creating their competitive essence through a careful combination of insight and action.

CREATING A HOLISTIC APPROACH TO LEAN SIX SIGMA

How do you avoid knee-jerk reactions and, instead, act like a high-performing organization? What's needed is a holistic approach that focuses on applying Lean Six Sigma at multiple levels and in multiple ways across your organization. Describing that holistic approach to using Lean Six Sigma to reduce costs is the purpose of this book.

"Holistic" Lean Six Sigma addresses all seven of the fundamental requirements for effective operational cost reduction:

1. Alignment of the reduction effort to company strategy and its sense of urgency—be it immediate survival, business as usual, or establishing competitive advantage.
2. Identification of the greatest levers of operational cost reduction opportunity.
3. Understanding of the multiple drivers and root causes of cost (including processes, offerings, customers, suppliers, and distribution channels), as well as their interrelationships and the ultimate cost of complexity they create.
4. Speed-to-results, and the related effort and investment required to realize the cost reduction.
5. Practical and pragmatic implementation: the cost reduction approach must be robust and universal, able to address a wide array of opportunities, environments, and levels of operational maturity.
6. Balance between internal and external forces; ensuring that the cost reduction activity will not adversely affect net overall business performance—especially through any degradation of quality, customer service, and market share.
7. Sustainability of the cost reductions realized.

Each of the preceding seven requirements presents its own set of challenges; yet a concerted operational cost reduction strategy must address all of them. This book will illustrate that when implemented holistically the Lean Six Sigma approach encompasses all of these critical requirements and delivers cost reduction with remarkable speed.

Without consideration of all these elements, the cost reduction effort will fail to rapidly yield its full, sustained potential. Taken together, these elements address the relationship between speed, cost, and the step-change improvement that speed and agility can enable when they become a primary leadership strategy. Process performance and execution excellence can give an enterprise the speed and agility necessary to directly support radical improvements in cost, through changes in organizational structure and operating model.

If your company, division, or department is faced with rising operating costs, reduced budgets, or declining share in a shrinking market, and needs to rapidly reverse these trends, this book is for you. Throughout this text you will learn how dozens of companies have deployed Lean Six Sigma to successfully improve costs and gain a sustainable competitive advantage. Even if you already have a Lean Six Sigma program or other form of continuous process improvement initiative, you will learn how to extract greater returns—migrating from traditional gradual and incremental gains toward truly transformational high performance.

LEAN SIX SIGMA: FAD OR PHENOMENON?

You may relate to one of our clients who recently invited us to view a cabinet he sarcastically termed his "initiative vault." It contained coffee mugs, T-shirts, banners, and training guides branded with slogans of, not one, not two, not three, but four previous improvement initiatives his company had undertaken. All had failed to live up to their promised savings, leaving him understandably cynical of any new potential additions to his "vault." This man's cabinet was littered with previous initiatives that failed to eliminate the underlying process performance maladies, employing only partial solutions that could not simultaneously improve cost, speed, and quality.

This book serves as a practical guide for those who are simply looking to reduce operating costs in an isolated area, as well as those who wish to enable true competitive advantage through enterprise transformation. For both situations, this book illustrates how to identify the root causes of cost and how to rapidly mitigate them with sustained net benefit.

We offer insights into how companies have deployed Lean Six Sigma to reduce costs at the local process level by as much as $2 million or more in 6 to 12 weeks and others who have reduced enterprise costs by $50 to $100 million or more in less than one year. These latter firms regularly look to Lean Six Sigma to provide annual savings equal to 2 to 3 percent of cost of goods sold. The savings are real. The approach applies to most any environment. And this book can help you apply the methods to start reducing costs now.

While individual projects will no doubt improve financial performance, they may fall short of enabling true competitive advantage for the organization. Only through an organized effort that identifies, coordinates, and aligns multiple disparate projects toward common enterprise objectives can true competitive advantage be realized.

We recognize that Lean Six Sigma is not a new phenomenon; thousands of deployments having been launched in the past decade alone. But the approach to *successfully* deploy this methodology and enable rapid yet substantive net returns is not widely understood and practiced. Countless firms claim to have already deployed Lean Six Sigma, but closer examination reveals that their program returns have barely exceeded total costs of deployment in many cases, if they can even be found on the P&L at all. And the time to results has been so slow that many a leadership team has lost faith and no longer sees the initiative as a true enabler of their strategic agenda.

For many firms their Lean Six Sigma journey failed to deliver the full business impact potential owing to missteps in deployment design, management, and, moreover, failure to secure and maintain leadership engagement. This book presents insights and practical approaches to extract the highest returns from your Lean Six Sigma investment—be it a single project or an enterprisewide transformation program.

For those seeking substantive impact, we provide an understanding of the array of elements required for enterprise transformation: from the initial identification of opportunities and the value at stake to the analytical relationships between offerings, process, speed, and agility, to leadership's role in driving and supporting change, all the way to results realization and performance management. Further, we share deployment best practices and lessons learned in having architected and supported hundreds of change initiatives around the globe. We also present new, innovative, and flexible deployment approaches that minimize the time required to deploy Lean Six Sigma, and cost-effective models that allow smaller numbers of resources to be trained with faster speed-to-results.

ACKNOWLEDGMENTS

This book would not have been possible without the significant contributions made by my many collaborators who are cited throughout this book. Their experiences have combined to present Accenture's holistic point of view on enterprise Lean Six Sigma transformation and customer value creation. To assemble and manage such an array of topics and thought capital into a single, seamless treatise was only possible through the industry and expertise of our talented associate writer, Sue Reynard.

I would like to recognize Accenture's leaders, Walt Shill and Matt Reilly, who sponsored and truly enabled this project; whose support I am greatly appreciative.

Over this last year, my wife Irma and my children, Mark Jr. and Paloma have sacrificed countless days to allow me to dedicate myself to this project, over cherished family time. For their patience and understanding, I'm eternally grateful.

Finally, the most important acknowledgment is to my father, Michael George, who set me out on this course of authorship and who has been and shall remain my source of personal, professional, and spiritual inspiration.

CHAPTER 1

WHY USE LEAN SIX SIGMA TO REDUCE COST?

With Michael L. George and Mike Tamilio

Several years ago, a hydraulic hose company that was a Tier 1 supplier of hoses and fittings to the automotive industry found itself barely profitable, generating a negative 2 percent economic profit. A telltale sign: customer order lead time was 14 days when the industry average was 7 days. Yet its leadership, not attuned to the relationship between process velocity and cost, didn't realize that *speed* was a main driver of the company's poor financial performance. In addition to long lead times, the company also suffered from poor quality, and frequently shipped defective brake and steering parts to its primary customers.

In less than two years, the company had made a remarkable turnaround (see Table 1.1).

How were such remarkable results enabled? Through a focus on cost reduction? Partly, but the strategic alignment was around **enterprise speed—**reducing waste *across* and *between* functional units, which brought with it cost reduction and true competitive advantage.

For example, one client was a leading manufacturer of heavy duty trucks. Unlike other customers of this Tier 1 supplier, the truck manufacturer created a high proliferation of end items (mostly low-volume runners) required for its wide variety of truck models. When we helped the hose company complete some complexity analytics (similar to those described in Chapter 10), we discovered that process improvement was *not* its highest opportunity area. Rather, long manufacturing lead times were caused by having to provide the vast number of part numbers for the truck company. Management at the Tier 1 supplier decided to drop the truck company as a client,

1

Table 1.1
Hose Company Results from Lean Six Sigma

Operating Margin	Improved from 5.4% to 13.8%
Capital Turnover	Improved from 2.8 to 3.7
Return on Investment Capital (ROIC)	Improved from 10% to 33%
Enterprise Value (Market Capitalization)	Improved by 225%
EBITDA	Improved by 300%
Economic Profit = ROIC% − WACC%	Improved from (−2%) to +21%
Work-in-Process (WIP) Inventory Turns	Improved from 23 to 67 turns per year
Customer Order Lead Time	From 14 days to 2 days

eliminate the related complexity, and focus on its remaining clients, those with higher volumes and fewer part numbers.

Eliminating that complexity allowed the hose company to focus on the next priority: reduce the number of defective brake and steering components shipped to America's leading automotive companies. So the hose company began an all-out assault on quality, with project identification and selection now prioritized around defect prevention. As shown in Table 1.1, quality improved from 3Sigma to 6Sigma on all critical-to-quality product specifications.

With product quality and consumer safety under control, the company was able to focus attention on Lean speed and flexibility. It launched a series of operations assessments that identified the cause of long process lead times and developed an appropriate mitigation plan that included the synchronized deployment of Lean tools (such as 5S, work cells, process flow improvement, setup reduction, and, eventually, pull systems).

This holistic approach—combining complexity reduction, quality improvement, and the elimination of process waste—delivered remarkable improvements. As noted previously, in less than two years, profit margins had doubled. But a picture is worth a thousand words! Figure 1.1 shows the drop in cost of goods sold as lead times dropped.

Notice that the rate of cost reduction was relatively slow initially, and then accelerated as cycle time was driven down to less than 25 percent of its original value. Based on the initial observations, one would have expected a linear relationship between lead time reduction and its effect on costs. Why did the rate of cost reduction speed up as lead times continued to drop? What was going on?

Figure 1.1
The effects of customer order lead time on manufacturing cost: For the whole company, cost of goods sold fell by 9 percent as the cycle time from the beginning to the end of production was reduced to 35 percent of its original value. At the same time, company profit increased from 7.3 percent on a sales increase of 13.8 percent.

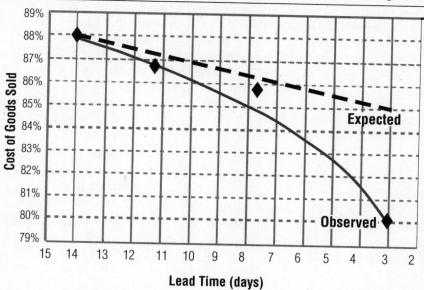

Initially, process improvement projects resulted in reduced cost of poor quality and direct labor cost; savings typically associate with continuous improvement. While these projects were prudent, they yielded *relatively small incremental impact* to the overall business performance; certainly not enough to provide competitive advantage. You will recall that the hose company's manufacturing cycle time was initially 14 days on average, compared to its peer group's cycle time of 7 days (which was also the customer's accepted lead time).

When the hose company's lead time reached the peer-group average of 7 days, costs had been improving gradually. But when the company continued to strive for greater speed and reached a 3-day cycle time, the company's *operating performance enabled a structural advantage.*

There is, in fact, a threshold of cycle time that is needed to dramatically eliminate cost, to make the step-change from a mere operating advantage to a structure advantage. So the question for leaders becomes how much

Customer Dissatisfaction and High Cost Processes Go Hand in Hand

As this hose company's experience demonstrates, slow processes make unhappy customers. We have been working with several clients to drive consistency, speed, and savings in their commercialization processes and in their sales pipeline. It has also become clear that problems with customer-facing processes are responsible for much customer dissatisfaction. Most companies will go to great lengths to please customers when they complain about a product, but ignore the aggravation that inconsistent responsiveness, delayed contracts, and unfriendly agents cause. A strategic project that focuses on the wastes and variability in these areas will achieve a double victory, reducing costs in critical processes while driving up customer satisfaction.

process velocity is required for our operational advantage to enable a structural advantage? Figure 1.2 reminds us that both of these elements are required to enable substantive reductions in cost.

In this case, once cycle time from start to finish was 50 percent less than the lead time demanded by customers, the company was able to close a large warehouse and quality containment facility. Closing the warehouse

Figure 1.2
Where operating advantage becomes structural advantage.

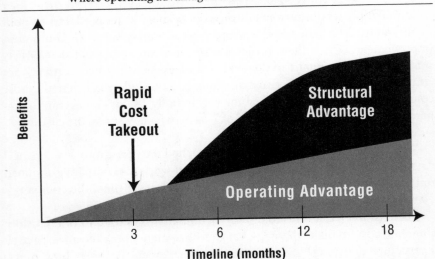

allowed the company to greatly reduce an array of costs frequently referred to as the "hidden factory." These included:

- Inventory
- Capital and equipment
- Energy
- Insurance
- Taxes
- Excess labor
- Transportation
- Handling, product damage

. . . and other costs that added no value from the perspective of the customer.

The correlation between speed and cost—both at a process level and at an enterprise level—is a powerful concept and one that has provided competitive advantage to manufacturing and services companies alike. The lessons we can learn from the hose company are that:

- Process-level speed is important and can confer some operating advantage, but by itself cannot fundamentally shift the cost base of the company.
- Enterprise-level speed and flexibility is where the biggest gains will come from, conveying a structural advantage that will let you supersede your competition, based on both speed and cost (but you can't achieve enterprise speed without process-level speed).

Benefits of Speed and Agility

The hose company just described created a true market advantage when it reduced its lead time by 80 percent across all of its products. The changes needed to achieve that velocity and agility also dramatically dropped costs.

While reducing costs is a good thing in its own right, it is also the case that faster cycle times and the flexibility to rapidly deliver all offerings in your portfolio will win more customers in a financial downturn because customers do not want to tie up their money in inventory; nor, in transactional processes, do they want to wait for new products, faster response, and so on.

TRANSACTIONAL EXAMPLE: LEAN SIX SIGMA TRANSFORMING OUR GOVERNMENT

The opportunity for cost reduction through cycle-time reduction was born in manufacturing but has proven to work just as effectively in nonmanufacturing applications. For example, U.S. Naval Aviation was one of the first government organization to implement process improvement across the enterprise. One example of the ability of cycle-time reduction to generate cost reduction occurred at the Naval International Program Office, which provides proposals to allied governments in response to their request for price, delivery, and specs—on an F/A–18, for example. The response originally required 5.5 man-years of effort and ranged from 30 to 392 days to respond. Customers found significant errors in 91 percent of the proposals. Further, a study of naval weapons systems showed a high correlation between cost overruns and excess cycle time.

Through prioritized project identification and selection and the application of Lean Six Sigma, the average response lead time was reduced to 11 days and the error rate to 8 percent. The overall cost of proposal preparation was reduced by 36 percent, and customer satisfaction dramatically improved. The gains were recognized at the highest levels.

THE ALLOY OF HIGH PERFORMANCE: WHY CHOOSE LEAN SIX SIGMA TO REDUCE COST

The more we have tested and implemented the central tenets, tactics, and tools of the combined Lean Six Sigma methodology, the more convinced we've become that both are essential to rapid and sustainable cost-cutting. The integration of Lean and Six Sigma is one of the most effective methods for consistently improving cost, speed, and quality, with broad successes in service as well as manufacturing functions. Companies have experienced unprecedented cost savings in diverse areas:

- Feeding higher-quality leads into the sales funnel at a fraction of the cost.
- Reducing developmental timelines for new products by 20 to 50 percent while nearly eliminating the high cost of defects.
- Slicing away complexity and variability throughout the supply chain to yield 10 to 30 percent cost savings while shortening process lead time by as much as 80 percent.

These transformations and cost savings are achieved in three- to five-month projects, a timeline made possible by the powerful combination of Lean speed and Six Sigma quality. The true power of the merger of Lean and Six Sigma as a single solution is in its unsurpassed ability to expose the wastes and complexities that are hidden in underlying processes. Cost-cutting measures can then be sequenced for cascading returns at the organizational level.

Lean Six Sigma is the synthesizing agent of business performance improvement that, like an alloy, is the unification of proven tools, methodologies, and concepts, which forms a unique approach to deliver rapid and sustainable cost reduction.

Alloys form new products of high utility from preexisting materials. But, unlike some alloys that lower the purity and value of the source materials, Lean Six Sigma multiplies the additive value of its elements.

- *It's fast*, delivering substantive results literally in a matter of weeks.
- *It's efficient*, delivering exceptional reductions in cost with relatively low investment. Companies featured in this book have realized rates of return at the project level equal to 5 times their investment, and rates of return at the program level 12 times or greater.
- *It's effective*, providing a mechanism to identify, leverage, and replicate best practices in cost reduction across the enterprise.
- *It's practical*, providing fact-based, analytical, straightforward methods used to uncover the root causes of high cost; get waste out of processes; and transform plans into actions.
- *It's game changing*, creating competitive advantage in terms of operational cost, customer quality, and enterprise speed:
  — Reducing direct labor costs.
  — Lowering indirect costs.
  — Improving return on assets.
  — Accelerating customer order lead times.
  — Improving overall customer service levels.
  — Enabling enterprise flexibility—responsiveness to changes in customer needs and market demands and economic conditions.
- *It builds capability*. Whether simple project execution or enterprise transformation, Lean Six Sigma imparts capability to the organization in a blended array of methods, including e-learning, classroom participation, experiential learning, or "just-in-time" project support training.
- *It's transformational*. Resources at all levels are engaged and aligned toward common goals and projects that support business strategy.

Company culture can truly transform as resources are provided with a fact-based improvement methodology and infrastructure that supports and empowers the entire organization to continuously drive toward higher performance.

- *It's sustainable,* linking process metrics with performance management; engaging process owners; and empowering front-line resources by providing them with control mechanisms to sustain gains.

Perhaps the most important advantage of Lean Six Sigma is that it lets you cut fat, not muscle—that is, reduce costs without destroying the ability to meet customer need.

Over the past year, as the world, and in particular the United States and the United Kingdom, have been battling the recession, all companies and many government agencies have been looking at almost any way to reduce costs. However, in many cases, companies in the process of cutting costs have also inadvertently damaged the fabric of the business. They have cut the muscle that is required to effectively serve the needs of their customers in the process of trying to remove the fat that is weighing down the business.

The contraction in demand at the end of 2008 was so severe that many companies had to take drastic action to align their cost base with current and future demand (although that was very difficult to predict, and the forecasting remains challenging). In all businesses or organizations, it is only logical to reduce capacity to meet demand. This can be done fairly safely if the organization knows and understands how the activities in the business react to a drop-off in demand. Where the organization doesn't understand how the business reacts to a drop in demand, or management wants to move beyond "right-sizing," the risk of cutting the muscle rather than the fat becomes more likely.

The problem of not understanding how an organization reacts to a drop in demand is actually surprisingly common, particularly in service industries such as banking and insurance and in government departments. It is in these industries and agencies that we have seen some of the most aggressive but potentially damaging cuts to cost bases.

Companies can't undo decisions made in the past, but they can be more effective in the future, as the need to continuously look at how to cut the cost base and increase productivity will not go away in this highly competitive economic environment.

LEAN SIX SIGMA VERSUS TRADITIONAL COST-CUTTING TACTICS

When working with clients in this and past recessions, the approach to cost-cutting has been dominated by functional cost assessment carried out by the finance function. Our experience has been that upon review of the largest cost areas, senior management either direct where the cuts will be made or provide targets for each function or business to reduce their cost base. While this approach often yields quick results, it tends to have a couple of severe limitations:

- The cost reductions are focused on functions. There is little regard for the impact that reductions could have on the rest of the end-to-end process. Therefore, there can be, and often are, unintended consequences from the actions that are taken.
- The linkages between functions often break down and, as a result, rework and lead times increase and quality of service declines.
- Savings tend to be unsustainable as the core skills required to run the processes are no longer available to execute the processes to the quality required by customers.

So, in effect, the cost-cutting is responsible for breaking the fabric of the processes required to serve customers. An example of the type of confusion this can cause can be witnessed in many of the front, middle and back offices of the world's largest investment banks (Figure 1.3). Here, tremendous reductions in staff have cut out many roles necessary to link processes together across different functions and successfully execute and account for a trade accurately. In one instance, we witnessed 3 different managers at operational risk in a 12-month period, just when the SEC, FSA, and other regulatory bodies had been asking banks to better understand the risks inherent within banking operations.

As you can tell from the title of the book, our focus is on how Lean Six Sigma can help you reduce costs and avoid the pitfalls of traditional cost-cutting approaches (see the sidebar, "Common Pitfalls of Traditional Cost-Cutting Approaches") while delivering lasting efficiencies and savings to the bottom line. Cost reduction, as a term, is most often associated with plant shutdowns and mass layoffs. These truly are slash-and-burn reactions. Such maneuvers, in reality, often hurt the business and the customer by failing to distinguish between what is truly wasteful in the process and what is

Figure 1.3
Functional turmoil caused by ill-thought-out cost reduction can lead to poor execution and low customer satisfaction.

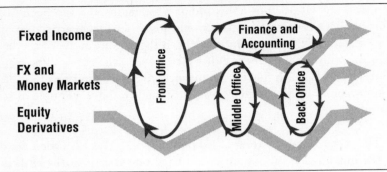

actually valued by the customer. Often, the idea is to cut 10 to 20 percent of the resources and hope the rest will pick up the slack. It never really happens. The slack remains, and it is felt through increasing delays in customer complaints, driving depressed revenues down even further.

These responses to economic pressure fail to position the company with innovative, competitive processes that will outperform the market in recessions and in economic recovery. The crisis may pass, but the choices made during the crisis can persist indefinitely.

Cutting costs via Lean Six Sigma is very different from traditional cost-cutting practices, as outlined in Table 1.2.

In short, Lean Six Sigma cost-cutting is process focused. We have created an analytical method called Prime Value Chain analysis (PVC), described in Chapter 10, that is designed to illustrate how different functions coordinate to deliver the activities that create value. It also illustrates the resources that it takes to deliver the different activities. Using this approach, combined with end-to-end mapping, allows senior managers to see across the value chain to identify where there are excess resources that are not essential to executing the end-to-end process. These are resources that are either surplus to demand (fat) or that can be eliminated via productivity improvements based on process improvements (the equivalent to increasing fitness, to extend the analogy). For it is only through increasing productivity that organizations can do "more with less." Without increasing productivity, reducing staff only enables you to do "less with less." And unlike functional cost-cutting, if the productivity improvements are implemented effectively, they will tend to be far more sustainable. With a strong continuous

Common Pitfalls of Traditional Cost-Cutting Approaches

- *Failure to focus on the process rather than rolling out tools.* Many organizations learn about individual tools and attempt to roll them out. It is not about implementing an individual tool, such as Value Stream maps or 5S, it is about identifying root causes of costs and applying the right tool to close that gap.
- *Lack of understanding of the voice of the customer (VOC).* Therefore, needless complexity and overprocessing encumber the system. Customers determine what is truly "value add." Without understanding VOC, safe and effective waste elimination cannot be achieved.
- *Failure to understand the costs of complexity.* Most organizations fail to recognize that each offering or transaction type introduced into the processes drives higher cost. The relationships between offerings and process are rarely understood.
- *Just doing it,* without sufficient analysis, preparatory work, baseline data, process ownership and accountability, and control plans to sustain improvement efforts.
- *Turning to technology as a solution for every ailment.* If the solution to every business problem begins with IT, and the company has not first considered the process itself, the solution may be suboptimal and costly.

Table 1.2
Comparing Traditional and Lean Six Sigma Cost-Cutting

Traditional Action	Common Pitfalls/Risks	Alternative Lean Six Sigma Approach
Headcount reduction	There was a time when headcount reductions were an easy fix for cost-cutting. Many companies have productivity ratios far below industry leaders, making headcount reductions a necessity for competitiveness. This is no longer true. Most organizations today run on skeleton crews, compared to those bloated years. Further cuts are dangerous if they are not done carefully, and only after eliminating waste. There are well-documented repercussions,	Rapid cost-cutting can be achieved by eliminating wasteful process steps, including many that are overprocessing items. By looking first at the waste in these steps, further capacity can be liberated. As the process is streamlined, there are often many savings captured that can render a headcount reduction unnecessary; or talented individuals can be redeployed to essential activities and other cost-cutting Lean Six Sigma projects.

(*continued*)

Table 1.2 (*continued*)

Traditional Action	Common Pitfalls/Risks	Alternative Lean Six Sigma Approach
	including the demoralization and slowing of the remaining workforce, the ensuing flight of brain power, and the inability to ramp up for future demand.	If excess capacity does exist, Lean Six Sigma can help ensure that customer service levels and quality can remain intact during the capacity re-balance.
Capacity decrease	Mistakes abound in a crisis. Firms are in survival mode. Cuts are dictated across business units, and managers are forced to close down capacity to meet shrinking demand. This is done by eliminating shifts, running shorter batches, or closing down operations. Traditionally, these moves take far too long to achieve, and come with enormous trade-offs in ability to ramp up and maintain market share coming out of a demand slump.	A project focusing on the right capacity levels can ordinarily be completed in less than three months (even for multinational organizations). Capacity levels need to reflect current levels of demand, taking into account statistical considerations for the variability and demand by offering as well as potential impacts on delivery requirements. If ramping production down irritates customers with late deliveries, the cost savings can be minuscule compared to the loss of revenue. Using the Lean Six Sigma toolkit, capacity can often be optimized inexpensively. Then, decisions can be made statistically, on a product-by-product, service-by-service basis. This yields the best balance between cost reduction and demand profiling.
Inventory reduction	Reducing inventory levels in tight times is as old as business. A look at the balance sheet of most companies will reveal that there are still excessive inventory levels. The traditional cost-cutting reflex tends to set a percentage reduction across the board. This is both unwise and unproductive. The inventory levels are often incorrect or muddied by overaged and obsolete material. Reductions come as a large write-off with some cash, but actually negatively hit the balance sheet. Remaining inventory levels still have too much of the wrong items and too few of the right items.	High inventory levels can be a result of waste in a process stemming from poor execution and process performance, ill-conceived policies and procedures, lack of integrated planning and scheduling, inflexibility and low equipment or operator reliability, and so on. Starting with the largest costs and volumes, it is more effective to streamline the processes feeding inventory into the warehouses. Often, pull systems can replace push systems for immediate and permanent reductions in inventory levels, with the advantage of easy ramp-up when demand increases.

Table 1.2 (*continued*)

Traditional Action	Common Pitfalls/Risks	Alternative Lean Six Sigma Approach
		As process speed improves, flexibility increases, and deliveries are made on time with fewer and fewer items in stock.
Price increases	More companies are pursuing the business model of specialization rather than commoditization. It is difficult to find an organization that believes it is something other than a specialist. If customers can be convinced they are receiving specialized items, rather than a commodity, they can be convinced to pay more. One rubber products company recently went into bankruptcy after raising rates for its clients by 20 to 30 percent. It turned out, their customers already knew they were buying a commodity. Words alone will not convince customers that your organization is adding specialized value, and everyone believes they are adding value.	Understanding customers' real needs and identifying value that can be improved, as well as waste that can be removed, allows you to effectively drive cost reductions in existing processes without harming the customer. The Lean Six Sigma toolset defines these needs while making the resulting improvements highly visual. Exploring these solutions together with the customer often leads to agreements for higher prices. At the bare minimum, cost savings are achieved in the resulting processes. Lean Six Sigma can also help develop flexible pricing processes that optimize transaction prices and contractual terms where perceived differentiation and value exists.
Demanding productivity	Companies have often demanded improvements in productivity without using the Lean Six Sigma methodology. Processes will not improve because we ask them to. We cannot expect better performance from people stuck in bad processes.	Companies seek immediate returns using a proven disciplined methodology. A useful productivity metric presented in this book is Process Cycle Efficiency (PCE). Analysis of low PCE can uncover root causes of high cost and low performance and lead to effective mitigation approaches.

improvement culture, productivity improvements can be built upon to create a virtuous cycle of improvement.

Taking a process perspective also gives managers real insight into the impact that making reductions will have elsewhere in the process, so the likelihood of changes having unintended consequences (that is, reducing important muscle from the operation) is dramatically reduced. It also gives a clear picture of where the business should focus to improve its operations in the short to medium term so it can consolidate the gains that have been made and look to how it can create a competitive cost advantage.

Managers need to understand what they are cutting before they get out the meat cleaver to cut costs. Attacking the largest cost areas while providing short-term cost reductions can lead to significant unintended consequences that can be difficult and expensive to fix. We recommend that understanding how an organization executes the processes that deliver value to customers is the first step to being able to cut fat from an organization, rather than the muscle that binds it together.

EMERGING STRONGER THAN EVER

Competitors may try to copy your products and offerings—but it's nearly impossible for them to copy your processes.

—Lou Giuliano, former CEO, ITT Industries

At the same time Lean Six Sigma can support near-term, local, cost reduction opportunities, it also enables transformational change that provides competitive advantage, *beyond cost*, especially once the enterprise emerges from the downturn. Why is this true? This book shows how the Lean Six Sigma approach yields rich visibility into the root causes of operational

Figure 1.4

ROIC of winners versus losers: Winners are those that outperformed others in their industry for the six years following the recession of 1990–1991; losers are those that under-performed others in the industry. Following a recession, winners that view downturn as an opportunity to improve business performance pull away from the competition.

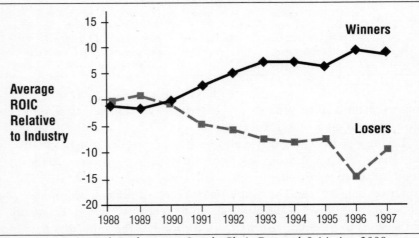

Source: Accenture High Performance Supply Chain Research Initiative, 2008.

cost, and provides an understanding of the dynamic relationships between processes, offerings, people, capital, equipment, suppliers, materials, and—most importantly—the customer.

In its ability to address these elements, the Lean Six Sigma cost reduction approach provides an all-important residual benefit: effective and predictable execution. Lean Six Sigma helps stabilize processes and makes them more predictable; it reduces order lead times and improves fulfillment rates; it uncovers what is truly valued by the customer, and helps deliver that value at the lowest possible cost to the company. We know of no other cost reduction approach that can rapidly drive such increased internal efficiency while at the same time improve the enterprise's ability to dependably serve its customers.

High-performing organizations manage their cost reductions strategically during economic downturns and strengthen their existing positions. These organizations view a downturn as an opportunity to improve business performance, to take market share, and change their competitive position. They make fundamental changes to increase cash flow and to drive sustainable results. They advance their strategic position by building differentiating capabilities, shedding/acquiring assets and businesses, anticipating downturns, and positioning themselves for better performance postrecession (Figure 1.4).

SPOTLIGHT #1

HOW TO USE THIS BOOK

This book has been written and organized to help a wide array of readers address their cost reduction opportunities and strategies by implementing Lean Six Sigma. Some may not be familiar with the methodology and how it can rapidly reduce cost. They may be managers or P&L owners looking for cost reduction alternatives to improve financial performance within a functional area, department, or single facility. Part I of this book is designed specifically for this group of readers. This section, even though it focuses mainly on Lean Six Sigma's *tools of cost reduction,* is not intended to be a do-it-yourself substitute for the requisite skills possessed by trained experts. Instead, it provides an understanding of Lean Six Sigma's practical and rapid cost reduction approach. It helps management understand the method sufficiently so that they may immediately improve local or departmental operating cost by leveraging skilled Lean Six Sigma practitioners, be they internal or external. Other readers may already be familiar with Lean Six Sigma but need to extract greater impact from the methodology across the entire business. These readers may be business leaders, deployment champions, or sponsors of an enterprise program who want to take their initiative to the next level. Perhaps their Lean Six Sigma initiative is no longer relevant to the business, or it needs to evolve, or perhaps their investment has failed to yield its full cost reduction potential.

Parts II and III of the book provide key insights into Lean Six Sigma's *deployment strategies for cost reduction*—not at the individual project level but at the enterprise level. These sections of the book share with the reader insights and lessons we have learned from our experience designing and deploying more than 200 business transformation programs over the past 10 years—techniques that can help the reader understand how Lean Six Sigma results in true competitive advantage.

17

OVERVIEW OF PART I: PROCESS COST REDUCTION—A FOCUS ON THE TOOLS OF WASTE ELIMINATION

Given the state of our global economy, organizations of all types are seeking ways to reduce their operating costs without losing precious market share. Managers are being asked to do more with less—excel in delighting the remaining customers of a contracted market while, at the same time, reducing the costs to serve, in order to maximize margins on seemingly less and less revenue. It is business processes that serve customers, and an understanding of the complex and intertwined relationship between offerings, processes, and customers is the very foundation of how Lean Six Sigma reduces cost.

Part I explains how departmental or functional costs can be improved by means of thorough analysis of the relationship between process and customer. The true cost of a process can be measured in terms of its efficiency to create value for the customer. All activities within a process add cost for the organization. The only costs that can be recovered are those associated with activities that create value for customers. Any other activity is either pure waste or administrative cost.

Part I also explains how to capture the activities within a process so that pure waste and administrative costs can be identified and isolated from "good costs," which drive value for customers and revenue for the business. This *cost intelligence* allows you to systematically eliminate "bad costs" without jeopardizing customer service levels and revenue. Next, Part I presents an approach to identify and categorize waste and value, supplemented by a rapid problem-solving technique that can be used by cross-functional teams to reduce or totally eliminate the waste that drives high cost.

The manifestations of cost can be categorized into its several forms of waste so they can be readily identified and then reduced or eliminated. Identifying and reducing these various forms of waste is considered by many to be the fundamental element of Lean. While it is vital that waste be eliminated in order to reduce cost, it is equally important to understand the activities that may have caused the waste in the first place, in order to prevent reoccurrence and drive even further reductions. As such, Part I provides a general understanding of Six Sigma's root-cause analysis techniques, as well as the adverse effect that variation can have on process cost in terms of its quality, speed, and capacity.

Further insight is given to ensure that the cost reduction project is successful in all measures of effectiveness—that it not only enables the highest rates of (cost reduction) return but does so in the shortest amount of time and ensures that the cost improvements are feasible and sustainable.

OVERVIEW OF PART II: ENTERPRISE COST REDUCTION—A FOCUS ON VALUE, SPEED, AGILITY, AND COMPETITIVE ADVANTAGE

Across the globe each year thousands of Lean Six Sigma practitioners—Green, Black, and Master Black Belts—deliver tens of thousands of continuous improvement projects. Most achieve the project objectives as stated in their charters, using Lean tools to reduce waste, and Six Sigma tools to reduce variation and improve customer quality. Despite the apparent success of so many thousands of individual projects, however, comparatively few organizations have reported that their Lean Six Sigma initiatives have delivered true competitive advantage—the level of advantage typically required to weather a global economic crisis and emerge more resilient and fortified. Why is this?

Certainly, there are examples of organizations that have transformed and enabled step-change improvements in cost through Lean Six Sigma, and Part II explores the characteristics that set these firms apart from the hundreds whose programs have not delivered their full potential. A fundamental difference is that continuous improvement is an integral part of a journey driven by business leadership—and that Lean Six Sigma is a foundational element that leads to effective execution, which is as important to success as the structure and operating model. The transformation journey also recognizes that *Lean means speed*, not just waste elimination. A vast majority of Lean Six Sigma practitioners believe that the ultimate pursuit of Lean is the reduction or elimination of waste. It is our belief, however, that waste elimination is not the goal but rather the means to an end: *Enterprise speed is the true objective* and is the crossroads at which a firm's operating advantage can also enable a structural advantage.

The strategies for enterprise cost reduction presented in Part II also consider the adverse effect that product and service complexity has on the organization's costs. Understanding how the delivery of goods and services traverse the enterprise helps uncover hidden costs of complexity that traditional process maps and analysis may overlook. Further, this holistic view of offerings and their delivery channels helps ensure that costs are not reduced in one area of the business only to be transferred to another. Part II also offers insights into some common impediments to transformation and competitive advantage by illustrating the analytics behind speed and flexibility.

OVERVIEW OF PART III: ACCELERATING DEPLOYMENT RETURNS—GETTING MORE, FASTER, FROM A LEAN SIX SIGMA DEPLOYMENT

Over the years we have had the opportunity to work with many firms that have asked us to help them relaunch or reenergize a legacy Lean Six Sigma program that has failed to deliver its full potential. Part of our assessment approach includes engaging with the client's senior executives. In our interviews, we consistently hear the same complaints about their legacy program: The projects take too long, the returns are too small for the effort required, and they don't have enough resources to dedicate to the program. Do any of these complaints sound familiar? If they do, then Part III of this book may provide the insights you're looking for. None of these issues are unique, and in Part III we present some approaches we've developed to successfully mitigate them.

The complaints we often hear about long project cycle times and low project values are closely interrelated. A characteristic of the firms that have realized step-change improvement in cost reduction is placing rigor and discipline around enterprise project portfolio management. Part III explains this approach, and how, when linked to operations assessments, rigorous project selection cannot only enable enterprise speed but, moreover, drive tangible improvements to shareholder value creation.

The remaining chapters of Part III address other mechanisms you can use to make sure your Lean Six Sigma deployment yields the most tangible results in the shortest amount of time:

- Recognizing that the Lean Six Sigma toolset is only as effective as the projects to which they are applied, and developing a rigor around program management.
- Using communications, readiness assessments, and an understanding of improvement maturity and change management to speed results.
- Exploring new alternatives for reducing the amount of time needed for training, and thus reducing the time to results. The universal concern associated with Lean Six Sigma is resource availability. Organizations seeking alternative ways to reduce cost cannot afford the luxury of

displacing large numbers of resources in classrooms for weeks on end, only to have their first projects completed six to nine months afterward. No, today most organizations that have survived are already "truly lean," without waves of resources on tap to be trained or the patience to wait for results to come two quarters later.

Over the years we have developed flexible, scalable, and rapid deployment models that minimize class time and rapidly mobilize client resources on improvement projects. These alternatives presented in Part III are truly the next generation of Lean Six Sigma, where small numbers of client resources are able to rapidly drive high-impact returns through innovative learning applied to high-value projects.

PART I
PROCESS COST REDUCTION

A Focus on Waste Elimination

INTRODUCTION TO PART I

Your business is a series of processes. Your people work, live, love, and hate those processes, whether or not they are aware of the extent of those processes. To drive out costs and overhead from the business, you must drive it out from the framework of processes that constitute your business. The difficulty for most employees and business leaders is that their day is filled by work that is not focused on improving processes. People are busy thinking in terms of their job requirements, job responsibilities, and job descriptions, in order to keep their jobs. Your people are busy with the steps of the process rather than the costs of the process.

What is the state of your processes? Are they best-in-class or barely functioning? Global business pressures and customer demands—and we all have customers in some way—require more than barely functioning processes. If daily attention is consumed by every sales call that must be closed without ever working on the process to actually get higher-quality leads into the sales funnel, costs and lead times will grow in the absence of control. (This is a case of the third law of thermodynamics, which tells us that chaos will expand.)

Lean Six Sigma Question: What would the impact on your business be if you could cut 30 to 80 percent of wasted time and costs out of your processes?

Answer: When applied holistically to strategic needs such as cost-cutting, the Lean Six Sigma execution methodology provides exponential returns. Even large-scale deployments typically break even within the first year, and cost savings accumulate across the organization in the following months

23

and years. For example, in 2008, Eli Lilly CEO John Lechleiter reported, "In 2007 alone, the financial benefit of projects completed by our Six Sigma team totaled more than $600 million" (see http://www.lilly.com/news/speeches/080924/default.html).

Focusing Lean Six Sigma efforts on a process is a powerful way to identify and combat the wastes that cannot be perceived when efforts are focused on machines, headcounts, departments, or balance sheet accounts. Lean Six Sigma begins by recognizing the waste in each process step, wastes that are responsible for significant costs and losses in organization processes. The costs that are built into the process seem hidden in plain sight: employees so acclimated to the massive efforts it takes to accomplish their tasks, they can't actually see the waste. Additionally, very few people see the process from end to end, unless they are working on a Lean Six Sigma improvement team, much less have accountability for the entire value stream. Only when taking an end-to-end process perspective do wastes become visible.

This fundamental insight focuses the improvement strengths of Lean Six Sigma cost-cutting where it is most effective: the process level. No matter how good the training is, how experienced the Lean Six Sigma leadership is, or how prepared the organization is for change, the real improvement must still be enacted at the process level.

CHAPTER 2

FIND COST REDUCTION OPPORTUNITIES IN WASTE

With Mike Tamilio

Speed is the essence of war.

—Sun Tzu

A consumer goods packaging and container manufacturer was trying to increase the yield of a particular process by 1.5 percent. It focused first on trying to improve the materials forming step, where it's important that the packaging container adheres to strict size tolerances. This company took on several major capital expenses focused on this aspect of the process, only to realize less than a 0.25 percent gain in total product yield.

After the containers were produced, they needed to be packaged. After being packaged, however, often the customer order would change, and the containers would need to be resorted and repackaged—inevitably damaging some containers in the process and adding enormous complexity to the staging area.

In the language of Lean Six Sigma (LSS), the initial forming step is considered value-add, because it contributes to the final container product in a way that customers value. The packaging, unpacking, sorting, and repacking (and consequent damage) is all non-value-add activity. Or, in a word, waste.

Many companies seek incremental improvements to their value-adding steps, while greater savings can be found by looking first at the *waste* in their processes. It became clear to this company, for example, that even had it made a 1.5 percent productivity gain in the value-add step, overall productivity would still have been low because of the waste, complexity, and

25

error in the packaging area. To improve yield and reduce costs in container production, the company needed to focus first on eliminating the reasons for the waste, rather than trying to make the valuable steps more efficient. Applying a suite of Lean Six Sigma methods—process mapping, pull systems, and cellular flow—it achieved a productivity gain of nearly 3 percent, valued at millions of dollars in lower cost and increased revenue, annually.

The experience of this container manufacturer exposes the secret to cutting costs via Lean Six Sigma: The opportunities will be in reducing waste, not in trying to improve the few value-add steps in a process. You need to identify the definite output that customers value from a given process and then cut away anything that does not support the output.

Lean Six Sigma cost-cutting success is based on three fundamental insights about waste:

- Processes are riddled with waste.
- Costs are created at the process level wherever waste exists—*waste generates cost*.
- To reduce costs at the process level, you have to eliminate waste.

In short:

Wastes = Costs = Opportunities

When wastes are properly identified and measured as costs, the appropriate sequence of improvements becomes apparent. Lean Six Sigma counters these process costs with improvements at the root-cause level, focusing on high-cost wastes first.

This chapter is designed to help you recognize process waste: the seven common types of waste spelled out in Lean. We will also demonstrate how all these wastes generate costs that are good first targets for any cost-cutting project.

Using Both Lean and Six Sigma to Eliminate Waste and Control Costs

The promise of LSS cost savings is the targeted and tactful application of the right tools, regardless of whether they originate from Lean methodology or Six Sigma methodology. It is the *combined* tenets, tactics, and tools of Lean and Six Sigma that drive cost savings at the process level and overcome both waste and variability—gains that neither discipline can achieve alone.

- *Lean alone:* Lean methods are very effective at **eliminating process waste and accelerating velocity.** Yet organizations that apply Lean methods only, even with all of its potency for streamlined process improvement, often fail to sustain their gains, or fail to practice the internal habits that drive bottom-line returns and strategic alignment with overarching goals. A goal of Lean is to improve process speed and improve capacity. However, process variation can have enormous adverse impacts on speed and required capacity. Lean depends on low process variability but lacks an effective analysis approach. Six Sigma is well known as a highly effective means to uncover and eliminate the root causes of unknown process variability.
- *Six Sigma alone:* Six Sigma's superior root-cause analysis tools and prescribed infrastructure give companies the power to *eliminate variation* and drive priority improvements across the business. But if they applied Six Sigma only, benefiting from its fact-based, customer-centric statistical decision-making and root-cause identification, companies often struggle to create transformed processes with lower-cost solutions. There is no explicit approach to remove waste and improve speed (other than defect elimination). A pure Six Sigma model may lack rapid improvement events such as Kaizens (see Chapter 7), which can accelerate results and project completion rates. According to one self-reported survey, nearly 40 percent of Six Sigma practitioners claimed their own projects as failed or incomplete (*iSixSigma* magazine survey, November/December, 2008, v4, no.4). Most of these companies also struggle to achieve a payback early enough to compensate for the up-front fees of Six Sigma training requirements. *Without Lean efficiencies and rapid improvement, Six Sigma suffers delayed payback and suboptimized solutions.*

Throughout the supply chain, operations, back office, logistics, and commercialization of products, high costs have persisted and proven resistant to partial solutions—even Lean or Six Sigma are not robust solutions apart from each other. *Having only half of the tools can yield, at best, only half the solution.*

THE SEVEN COMMON FACES OF WASTE: TIMWOOD

Reducing waste increases speed and decreases cost, simultaneously. The seven common faces of waste are fairly well documented, and can be remembered by the acronym TIMWOOD:

Transportation
Inventory
Motion
Waiting
Overproduction
Overprocessing
Defects

This section is meant as a brief refresher on these kinds of waste, in the course of which we'll point out some insights on the relationship between these wastes and the unseen costs they create. Some of these wastes are immediately visible, while others are more difficult to detect, requiring value stream mapping and analysis to unearth.

Waste #1: Transportation

Growing Departments Rather Than Processes   Transportation is the movement of process inputs, work-in-process, or outputs. This waste is ordinarily due to the layout of facilities, but can also depend on the lack of flow between process steps. Ineffective layouts—whether in an office or plant floor—require larger outlays of cash and working capital.

In manufacturing, transportation costs are literally driven by lot size. It is a consequence of process "villages" in the plant layout. For example:

- If the batch sizes in your process are larger than the industry average, you can be sure you have exorbitant costs in transportation waste.
- If your production systems are only economical in large batches of apparel, electronics, equipment, or whatever you produce, the layout of the facility is most likely creating the need for large amounts of transportation from batch step to batch step.

Poor layout means longer lead times, and slower processes are expensive, as work is caught in the system rather than being available to customers. Correcting the layout is an early step toward minimizing costs. With continuous flow between processing steps, transportation waste is minimized, smaller machines can be utilized, and overrunning a machine is avoided.

In service infrastructure and service organizations, transportation is a consequence of departmentalization. As a company grows, it squeezes in service departments wherever they can fit them: a few HR people in one building, legal and finance in another, perhaps information technology splintered among four or five locations. An internal request then has to find its way not only from department to department but often from individual to individual within them, back and forth, getting lost for days in the serpentine maze of buildings and cubicles. Costs result from overstaffing and lost time. Headcount reduction may exacerbate the cost of delays when people inherit unfamiliar work, queues build, customers scream, and processes slow even more.

At one quality department, we strung kite string to walk and measure the flow a quality complaint form would take for typical processing. The 500-foot roll ran out before we could finish walking even half of the process! What does it mean for your organization if every form follows a toiling, winding, cycling pathway for completion? How much time is lost by excess work and rework done (or redone)? In this processing area, we applied the "cellular flow" concept to reorganize the work area over just one weekend, which reduced average processing time by 90 percent. In addition, after a few weeks of cross training, the work originally requiring 10 people could be done with 6, freeing 4 people to work on other needs within the organization. Not only were expenses and time reduced, but this company gained the equivalent of 4 full-time employees without having to hire them!

Lean Six Sigma eliminates transportation wastes through the redesign of processes into cellular layouts and streamlined flows that can reduce batch sizes. Cost-cutting with Lean Six Sigma should start by reducing batch sizes, rather than by maximizing the bottleneck. This is a counterintuitive insight in Lean Six Sigma that may avoid the early expense of other quality programs your organization could attempt. If you seek to create flow in every expensive process, it becomes a guiding light, illuminating waste. Lean Six Sigma cost-cutting teams should create flow wherever they can, then pull between the flows using generic and replenishment pull controls.

Waste #2: Inventory

Mismatches throughout the Supply Chain   In manufacturing, the waste of inventory is often easily recognizable as work-in-process—stacks of raw materials, components, partial assemblies, finished goods, and so on. These costs have become the focus of many Lean initiatives over the years, particularly because the balance sheet makes them blatant.

We have discovered, however, that the much larger inventory waste is somewhat less transparent. It is the result of mismatched demand and supply. Poor understanding of customer needs, irrational forecasting, and attempts to manage production control from enterprise resource planning software packages, and other root causes create this mismatch. Pipelines are filled with pipedreams, unless pull systems respond in real time to customer demand. These wastes are magnified throughout the entire supply chain, and the costs are not immediately obvious until the process is clearly mapped, using value stream mapping or similar tools.

Most companies have excessive inventory throughout their supply chains, and this large cost is a symptom of the mismatch. For example, at a chemicals manufacturer, several product lines were suffering low gross margins. Analysis revealed that contracts were based on unrealistically high estimates of demand volumes. Very little understanding of actual manufacturing costs compounded errors in quotes and loss of profitability. When demand failed to materialize, the company was stuck with excess inventory, and had to face the additional costs of more changeovers, smaller orders, higher raw material levels, and higher finished goods carrying costs. These same costs echoed throughout the supply chain, as suppliers ramped up trying to deliver against the same poor estimates of demand.

A Lean Six Sigma cost-cutting team was able to create visual management tools to prevent these mismatches. Contract language was changed for future orders to allow the transfer of certain costs if demand curbed from the customer. Pull systems were also developed to respond in real time to customer demand, rather than carrying excessive inventories.

The supply chain is still the largest cost contributor for most companies. Lean Six Sigma instills flexible processes to meet ever-changing customer demand, drive continuous flow, and reduce batch sizes, without accumulating inventory. The focus of improvement efforts needs to shift from "How can we optimize the storage of finished goods to meet customer demand?" to "How can we increase flexibility and flow to eliminate the need to carry and pay for finished goods altogether?"

Even companies that have previously reduced inventory levels (sometimes by as much as 80 percent) can have problems with inventory. You'll see symptoms such as late customer deliveries due to changes in product orders, driving up costs of penalties and lost business; or having a lot of inventory around, but not the *right* inventory.

Such problems arise because companies do not understand the patterns in their demand. Only a business that thoroughly understands the sources of variability in its supply chain will be able to carry the right mix of reduced inventory levels. For one client, even after a previous Lean effort, we reduced their total inventory levels (and associated working capital) by nearly 20 percent while increasing on-time deliveries from 89 to 96 percent. Customers today demand both.

Inventory is not just a problem in manufacturing. You'll find "partial products" at many stages in transactional processes. Take a slow collection process, for example. The inventory is the days of outstanding sales waiting to be collected. In reality, all of the wastes are present in these kind of transactional processes, where paperwork travels, waits in queues of inventory, involves excessive work in typing and processing, creates rework and delays, as well as defective bills. The costs of such a process are much higher than one with smooth, rapid flow.

Safety stocks are another area of expense. The reality is that most safety stocks have too much of the wrong stuff, and are oversized and poorly managed. If your stock levels are controlled by maximum and minimum reorder points that were established more than 12 months ago, you can be relatively certain you have high carrying costs and likelihood of stock-outs.

Waste #3: Motion Waste

Busyness versus Business Costs   Motion waste relates to the movement of the people who are performing the operations in the process. This waste is more about people going to things, rather than people moving things. Excessive motion is an underestimated cost in the organization. Unnecessary typing, lifting, walking, and moving are all examples of motion waste that increases delays, opportunities for defects, and eventual employee health deterioration.

Motion has not often been given a priority because it is not tracked to the same level of detail as other wastes. Even if motion waste is tracked in terms of "lost minutes," say, the total will look insignificant compared to transportation or waiting time, which add up to hours, days, months. That's why motion can be easily viewed as insignificant, at first. We have discovered, however, that the true cost of motion waste is crippling for many organizations in the long run. This is the waste that causes injuries, lost time, and health problems for employees. Consider carpal tunnel syndrome alone—a generation of typists and assemblers undergoing expensive surgery, pain, lost time, and loss of productivity. According to an article in *Risk and Insurance* (June 2004) the lifetime cost of every carpal tunnel patient is at least $30,000, plus the extended adverse effects that absenteeism generates. Whatever the exact expense is, excessive motion leads to injuries and long-term health costs.

We recommend tracking not only lost-time incidents and near hits throughout the organization, but diving into the motion waste at the process level. If you follow a worker day to day, you will see his or her work traces a different path every time, filled with wild goose hunts, strange body positions, bending, poor posture, injury-prone environments, and so on. Lean Six Sigma counters with cellular flow that includes standard walking paths, operating procedures that are optimized and balanced, as well as ergonomic body positioning. Take steps today to avoid long-term costs and employee suffering while reaping immediate efficiency and cost improvement. Putting safety first will help to inspire employees who may otherwise resist your efforts.

Waste #4: Waiting

Costs Accumulate at Every Interruption in Process Flow   There is an old joke that considers dining out at a restaurant. Your evening often begins by waiting in the car for the rest of the family to join you. At the restaurant, you will wait in line to find out how long the wait will be before you are seated. Once you are called, you wait to be served. After placing the order, you will wait until it arrives—often repeating the process for dessert. Finally, you will wait to get the check. And they have the nerve to call the person who presides over this process the "waiter."

Many business processes are similar, and the people continually waiting are your customers. A study of the wait time in one mortgage application department demonstrated this life cycle of waiting. A customer calls and waits on hold. Once connected, the customer answers all of the personal financial questions. Then the real waiting begins, for several weeks, to determine an approval or disapproval. Afterward, the customer waits some more to determine the exact amount and receive the necessary paperwork. The application itself spent 99 percent of its time waiting to be processed at various desks, in backlogs, or just plain old lost.

The wait time in this mortgage application process was measured in weeks, while the value-added time was measured in seconds! The costs of this process are not just the added resources, but also the lost business because customers are often time sensitive. A Lean Six Sigma cost-cutting team identified several causes of delays, eliminating unnecessary steps and controlling work-in-process levels, to reduce process lead time by over 80 percent while increasing capacity with no additional costs.

Waiting strangles process flow. Interrupted and constrained processes are expensive. Like clogged arteries, they force the organization to work harder until it simply cannot pump any more work out. We have seen that 95 percent of time is spent waiting in most business processes, manufacturing and service processes included. In fact, service processes are guilty of larger costs due to waiting because they typically have not received the same amount of improvement attention as manufacturing operations, and they are "opaque" in nature—activities, flow, defects, workarounds, queues, capacity, and work-in-process go largely unseen in service environments.

After reducing and controlling work in process, Lean Six Sigma cost cutting teams can achieve dramatic wait time reductions by looking to constraining steps in the process. Constraints are any step in the process that cannot meet customer demand. These steps become apparent using value stream mapping and comparing process capabilities to customer demand rates. If your organization measures lead time in weeks but only adds value in minutes or seconds, you should focus cost-cutting efforts on eradicating the wait time throughout core processes.

Take the example of one emergency room manager who was faced with wait times that typically exceeded 90 minutes. This manager collected data and realized the wait times were extremely variable. The solution the company planned to incorporate was to add beds so patients could get to a bed sooner. Would that have solved the problem of long wait times? The constraint in this case was the availability of doctors and nurses to see patients. Moving patients from the waiting room to the beds, in essence, only created another place for waiting. It would also require further dividing of the limiting resource: doctor and nurse availability. This solution would actually have added delays and costs! The same effect would be to increase the number of chairs in the waiting room.

A Lean Six Sigma cost-cutting team analyzed the actual work that nurses and doctors performed throughout a shift. Many opportunities to cut costs and time were unveiled, while servicing patients faster. Standard work and pull signals, as well as more consistent triaging and simplifying of paperwork yielded further improvements. (To link back to the opening of this chapter, notice that the cost and time savings here were *not* focused on improving the few minutes of diagnostics and treatment actually spent with a patient. Those minutes are the precious value-added patient time. Rather, the bulk of the opportunity was again in the wasted time between patients. Waste = opportunities!)

Waste #5: Overproduction

Creating and Ordering More Than Necessary   Overproduction is usually clear in a manufacturing environment for the same reason the waste of inventory seems obvious: things accumulate between processing steps. In transactional processes, overproduction may go undetected and cost the organization much higher sums. As companies search for opportunities to claim returns to the bottom line, they are often leaking potential margin gains away every day through uncontrolled indirect spend.

Overproduction shows up in terms of (avoidable) expediting fees, special orders that fail to leverage economies of scale, overpayments, early payments, and so on. Overproduction is also accountable for high service fees for legal, accounting, auditing, and so on. These processes tend to accumulate costs if they are not carefully designed and controlled. Lean Six Sigma projects focused on indirect spend often achieve cost savings of 3 to 10 percent in working capital. A multinational provider of insurance recently discovered over $50 million (USD) in avoidable losses from indirect spend, working capital that is scarce during periods of low demand.

Here are other not-so-obvious examples of overproduction:

- Managers at one of our clients were often paying legal fees to consult third-party lawyers at $350 per request, while their in-house attorneys possessed standard policy solutions for most requests that were essentially free. They were ordering more of a service than needed, mainly because of a lack of communication, protocol, and management attention.
- In continuous-processing industries, the plant will fill large containers until they are, basically, filled. The notion of what is absolutely needed is only vaguely factored into the amount of production. If a bin is empty, maybe it should stay empty for a while, until demand pulls production to fill it. Does your organization track overaged inventory or the length of time material sits idly waiting for demand to catch up?
- Likewise, a lack of spares management can be a source of savings. Parts are purchased because personnel cannot find the parts they already purchased. This overpurchasing is just another untracked source of overproduction.

If your organization does not manage these processes tightly, you may want to focus a Lean Six Sigma cost-cutting team to capture savings and avoid future expenses.

Waste #6: Overprocessing

Adding More Value Than Needed Is Not Adding Value at All   Overprocessing is delivering *more* of something than the customer wants (and wants to pay for). Overprocessing, by definition, adds cost to a process because you are doing work and investing time and materials that you cannot expect a payback on.

The cost of overprocessing arises more from the numbers or types of steps in a process than from the number of people in the process. Starting Lean Six Sigma cost-cutting projects with the voice of the customer is essential to determine the value of the ultimate product or service. An interesting insight is that the customer determines not only the ultimate value but actually the value of every single step in the process. Overprocessing is cost at every single step, not just in the final product.

To avoid overprocessing, you need to have a good understanding of customer needs along the entire value stream, from order to delivery, from concept to production. What could be more expensive than designing, planning, purchasing, manufacturing, and delivering components of a service or product that are unnecessary and undesirable to the customer? (We'll go into more detail about how to understand customer needs in Chapter 3.)

Attack the Original Designs, If Possible

Making sure your products and services are designed *not* to overdeliver is a great opportunity for long-term cost savings that are exponentially larger than the incremental gains achievable *after* a design is created. If your organization is not utilizing Design for Lean Six Sigma (DFLSS) or Fast Innovation practices, engineering workflows will require immediate attention to ensure your future competitiveness. Using these design approaches to overhaul the research and development functions, companies have designed products that outperform competitors with built-in quality and ease of manufacturability, all while spending less time and money on the development effort.

Waste #7: Defects

Making Errors in the Products or Services Intended for Customers   Defects per million opportunities (DPMO) has been a standard metric in Six Sigma since the discipline was invented. Though an excellent metric, it has suffered abuse in some Six Sigma deployments. Much effort in the past has gone into calculating the DPMO for every process in a misguided attempt to bring all processes up to a 3.4 DPMO level, six sigma quality. This is time-consuming, and cost-cutting teams have no time to waste (pun intended).

A better approach to rapid cost-cutting is to focus on high cost areas of scrap, rework, repair, or customer escapes, instead of trying to raise quality levels in your value-add process steps. Also, focus on areas requiring expensive overinspection. Prioritize around costs rather than any other metric such as DPMO scores. Why? Because Waste = Costs = Opportunities. *We pay to fix defects, but don't forget, we pay to make defects, too.*

The Lean Six Sigma synergy comes to life most vividly in eliminating costly defects in a process or product. There are many statistical tools embedded in the Lean Six Sigma toolkit—such as the basic define, measure, analyze, improve, and control (DMAIC) tools; analysis of variance (ANOVA); hypothesis testing; regression; tests for special causes of variation; and so on—that can help you debunk long-held beliefs, revealing factors that are truly significant in causing defects. Better process controls eliminate these confirmed causes using Lean tools.

These kinds of tools and insights are not restricted to manufacturing, either. The telesales function at one of our clients ran a Lean Six Sigma project to increase sales and lower costs. It was a cherished belief that the two most important aspects of sales performance were years of experience of the salesperson and amount of time on the phone with a customer. More minutes should mean higher sales. This belief was demolished by running a designed experiment, a statistical test of various factors at various settings. It turned out that the years of experience and the length of time on the phone did not have any correlation to higher sales. The factors that did drive higher sales were following standard scripts, asking for a close from the customer, and use of flexible pricing.

If defects seem to haunt your process, causing customer complaints despite your best efforts to catch them, your Lean Six Sigma cost-cutting project should focus on this waste. Likewise, if your inspection costs are higher than similar processes in your industry, defects are likely built into your processes due to faulty equipment, instructions, design, or beliefs. These are excellent opportunities for cost-cutting, as eliminating defects saves the scrap, rework, and repair costs while increasing yields and customer satisfaction.

The Eighth—and Perhaps Costliest—Waste: Capital

The seven forms of waste covered in this chapter stem from waste at a process level. While each is an insidious drain on productivity and efficiency, there is an eighth form of waste that may have a much greater impact on cost than all of these forms combined: the waste of capital. Exploring capital waste is beyond the scope of this book, but we urge you to look at how your investments in financial, personnel, and equipment capital are being spent.

USING THE FULL LSS TOOLKIT TO DRIVE COST REDUCTION

We recently worked with a multibillion dollar freight-haul transporter. The most cost-intensive asset is the truck utilization, costs represented in hours per delivery. This client had an urgent need for cash and turned to LSS to help focus on priority areas and liberate working capital. With our guidance, the client discovered that the truck utilization process was rife with waste.

The first wave of projects achieved $15 million in working capital reduction. The targeted implementation was not necessarily designed to instill large-scale cultural change, rather to drive immediate cost savings. However, early projects like these plant the seeds of change and help answer employees' silent question: "Will this really work?"

It's unlikely that any single Lean Six Sigma project will generate $15 million in cost reduction. But no matter what the scale of improvement you want to achieve, the first step is learning to recognize the waste around you so you can target those areas with strategically selected projects. This freight hauler, for example, discovered the following forms of waste in its processes:

- *Transportation* for a freight hauler is arguably a value-add activity; but every additional mile beyond absolutely necessary is wasted fuel, time, and money. A Lean Six Sigma cost-cutting team determined that poor routing decisions were the result of inadequate process controls and faulty data integrity. Even zip code files for driver and customer locations were mistaken for 10 percent of all entries. The team enacted mistake proofing and streamlined routing decisions, greatly reducing excess mileage, saving fuel expenses, and liberating capacity.

- *Inventory, motion, and waiting* went hand in hand for this client. Inventory in excess trailers was a staggering waste, with thousand of dollars in disrepair or lost in terminals and client locations across the continent. Drivers spent hours searching and waiting at these terminals, looking for their containers and trailers (excess motion). Since the dispatchers, planners, purchasers, and driver managers were all working with the same faulty data, they had learned to pad their plans by 10 to 20 percent every day to compensate. It was "just the way things were" for decades. When the team used a DMAIC approach to eliminate variability in the data inputs, driver delivery variability dropped from hours to minutes. Accurate data allowed them to reduce inventory needs, driver wait time, and uncompetitive costs. A separate team focused on the terminal layouts, using 5S, standard work, and streamlined flow, and driver wait time was further reduced.

- *Overproduction*, in terms of excessive truck and trailer purchases, were runaway costs. The previous improvements delivered hidden capacity without hiring more drivers or making further asset acquisitions. A large contract for new trailers was postponed and later reduced as the standardized flow accelerated processing of existing trailers to meet customer demand.

The Lean Six Sigma cost-cutting team mapped driver requirements and data inputs, finding that the majority of signals sent back and forth were non-value-add. This *overprocessing* only increased variability, while causing further delays for drivers (infuriating them in the process).

Finally, the greater accuracy in customer delivery times and locations greatly reduced the company's costliest *defects*: wrong deliveries, late deliveries, and early deliveries. Arriving in a more precise delivery timeframe avoids the customer fines imposed for early or late deliveries. Accuracy in routing and simplified decision making avoids wrong deliveries, which carry further costs of driver time, fuel, and delays.

The $15 million USD in working capital, as well as millions more in avoided costs, was accomplished in under four months. The key to rapid cost savings was focusing on high cost wastes rather than on the value-add steps themselves.

The wastes revealed costs, the costs revealed opportunities. And that brings us back to where we started this chapter:

Wastes = Costs = Opportunities.

SPOTLIGHT #2

SPECIAL TIPS FOR NONMANUFACTURING PROCESSES

With Robert Gettys and Michael Mueller

Process improvement or operational excellence in general, and Lean Six Sigma in particular, are most widely accepted and most easily understood in a manufacturing environment. This is often cited as an excuse for not deploying Lean Six Sigma into service- or retail-specific businesses or service or transactional areas of a business. In fact, the effectiveness of Lean Six Sigma in service and retail can be just as strong as in manufacturing, if you understand and accept the unique characteristics of these environments and respond accordingly.

What are the unique characteristics of service or retail environments?

- A high number of customer-facing transactions
- A large number of locations in which the transaction (retail or service) takes place
- High variability in the customer-facing workforce (due to either high turnover or the use of seasonal workers aligned with the business cycle)

High Variability = High Cost

Higher costs are created when there is variability in either the end product/service or in the perceived quality of the overall customer experience associated with that product or service. In addition, higher costs can be driven by variability in those costs, to create, maintain, or deliver the product or service (inventory, turnover and training, facilities, service or product delivery, and so on).

Perhaps more importantly, the service or retail *experience* plays a big role in determining customer's perception of value. That is, the output of a manufacturing process is a product that will be used by the customer, and the perception of value and satisfaction comes from how well that product meets the customer's specific requirement. "That bolt really works well" or "My dishes have never been so clean" are expressions of how well the product met the customer requirement.

However, in service or retail environments, it is a combination of the product or service and the customer experience that drives the customer's perception of value and satisfaction. "Yes, my brakes work, but now there is a grease stain on my carpet"; or "I got the markers my child needed for school but they were hard to find and I waited too long in checkout." These examples illustrate that it is not just the end result, the quality of the product or service that drives customer's perceptions. *Therefore, when focusing on cost-out in these environments, the quality of the product or service needs to be balanced with the quality of the customer experience.*

KEY SUCCESS FACTORS IN REDUCING COSTS IN SERVICES AND RETAIL

There are five key success factors in reducing costs in services and retail:

1. Involve the people who actually do the work.
2. Focus on identifying and eliminating the non-value-add (NVA) work that they do so that they can spend more of their time focusing on the customer.
3. Understand that in both services and retail there are best practices that can be turned into repeatable processes (regardless of how many people are independently doing the work).
4. Don't forget the infrastructure required to support the value-add, client-facing processes (it may represent cost-cutting opportunities).
5. Recognize the interfaces with technology—process analysis must include the systems on which processes rely.

Involve the People Who Do the Work

In services and retail, there are typically lots of people doing similar tasks but using slightly different processes. Not only are these people the most familiar with the actual processes, they are most familiar with and impacted by the waste and inefficiencies in those processes. You can bet as well that they have come up with ways to make the processes easier or less prone to create defects.

Teach employees to see their work in terms of a process and how to see the waste in their process. The latter point is very important: *Teach people to see the waste in their process*. In a traditional manufacturing process, this is easy. A pile of scrap or defective units requiring rework is an obvious and tangible source of waste. In a service or retail environment, waste is typically an activity that consumes time or resources but either does not deliver value to the customer or is inefficient in the way that it does. You need to involve the people who do the work on process improvement teams; and when you do, make sure that you listen to them. Home office may set the standard operating procedure (SOP) but it's the people in the field who interpret it, execute it, and are closest to the customer.

Teaching people to see the waste in their process begins with an understanding of the seven sources of waste described in Chapter 2—transportation, inventory, movement, overproduction, overprocessing, and defects (TIMWOOD). You can add to that list "people." Not that people are waste, but management should be asking if they have people who could be delivering productive, value-add work but who are in fact wasted by being consumed in non-value-add activities.

Focus on Identifying and Eliminating Non-Value-Add Work People Do

This follows on the first factor. Instruct the people who do the work to map out the steps of their tasks. Determine which ones truly add value and which do not. Eliminate the non-value-add steps. This not only allows the people in the process to focus more on the customer but in fact increases capacity so that you can do more with the same number of people. Too often, when faced with attempting to take costs out of service or retail processes, management takes the simple expedient of "cutting heads." This may be a viable alternative when you possess capacity in excess of demand, but it is hardly a basis for long-term growth.

Look for and Formalize Best Practices and Turn Them into Repeatable Processes

As we mentioned earlier, in service and retail environments, there are typically many people, often out of sight of management, executing identical processes but based on their own interpretation of how the processes should be completed. Yet when analysis of performance is examined, there is, in fact, considerable variation between individuals or locations. Same processes, but some do it better and some do it worse. It is generally not the case that this is the fault of the individuals executing the process. To quote Dr. W. Edwards Deming as he originally stated his belief: "Eighty to 85 percent of problems are with the system. Only 15 to 20 percent are with the workers. . . . (In later life, Dr. Deming changed his mind; he said it was more likely that more than 90 percent of problems we see are built into a process.)

Take the time to do some internal benchmarking, identify the best performing individuals, groups, or locations, and document what they do. It may surprise you that they are executing the process in a manner that is not wholly consistent with management's higher-level perception of how the process should be executed. But remember, they are continually adapting to the market and customer requirements (which at times they may see much more quickly than management) and, consciously or not, adjusting the process to deliver value to the customer and minimize unnecessary work for themselves.

Often, it can be as simple as bringing these people together, mapping their processes, and determining an overall best practice. This is also a great opportunity to take it a step farther and apply the TIMWOOD approach to eliminate or at least minimize remaining non-value-add steps.

Look for Opportunities for Cost Reduction in the Infrastructure

The case is very much the same in traditional manufacturing as it is in services or retail. When a business is growing, the focus is on the front end. In manufacturing, it is generally on the cost, quality, and utility of the product being produced. In services and retail, it is on the end result of the service or the provision of the products that the customer is trying to purchase, as well as the overall experience of the customer during the service or transaction. In all cases, we focus on the front end and often miss the growth of infrastructure required to deliver the service or retail transaction.

That is not to say, of course, that these back-end processes are not required. It is simply that they often can provide substantial opportunities for improvement in both efficiency and effectiveness. In the military, this is referred to as the "tooth-to-tail ratio"—the ratio of both personnel and resource consumption between the combat troops (in our case, those people directly dealing with the customer) and the service and supply troops (those people in the infrastructure processes). Management should be particularly sensitive to providing the service or retail experience with the minimum of infrastructure required. It is important from time to time to rethink your infrastructure requirements. Does the existing infrastructure support or burden your ability to service the customer?

Recognize Interfaces with Technology

Unlike manufacturing environments, transactional or services processes tend to be opaque; it's difficult to immediately recognize where work-in-process (WIP) is piling up, where queue times are growing, where capacity bottlenecks reside, where defects exist, and where rework is taking place—all of which create waste and drive high cost. Unlike manufacturing, there is limited structure or process governance in services, mainly owing to less capital equipment and tangible output. In order to provide a level of structure and governance, some transactional or service processes rely greatly on technology. When applying the tools of Lean Six Sigma to improve these processes and reduce cost, it is critical that relevant interfaces with technology are recognized and IT resources are included on the projects as extended team members. Value stream maps, SIPOC diagrams, and other process analysis tools must recognize the intersections of technology and how the process relies upon it. In service environments, such as banking and insurance, technology is frequently the greatest determinant of the ability to transform the process—and IT resource capacity can become an impediment to results. When selecting and prioritizing services projects, it is, therefore, important to identify potential demand on IT resources, their availability, and the impact on project completion rates.

Tips for Using Lean Six Sigma in Services

- *Make the case for Lean Six Sigma in your specific environment:* Be ready to specifically respond to the inevitable comments that it will work fine in manufacturing but won't work here. Make sure that you thoroughly investigate any potential firms that you plan on partnering with to help you with your implementation. There are a lot of firms that claim to have experience in service and retail, when in fact their experience is limited or nonexistent—just papered-over manufacturing examples and content in disguise. Nothing will damage an implementation faster than allowing the naysayers to gain credence because those associated with the implementation are not truly experienced in working in service or retail environments.
- *Focus on creating customer value:* Taking cost out is a critical result, but not at the cost of destroying customer value or competitive

advantage. Take the time to collect current and comprehensive voice of the customer. Do not rely on VOC that is dated or anecdotal. Lean Six Sigma activities should be concentrated on improving customer value (value-add) and reducing or eliminating non-value-add.

- *Teach people to see their work as a process and to see the waste in their processes.* Provide an understanding of the seven sources of waste, as described earlier. Also, help people to view their activities as a process through value stream mapping, and analyze the value stream maps to identify the non-value-add activities.
- *Pick the right projects and provide the right support and leadership to the project teams:* Projects need to be clearly linked back to critical voice of customer, external or internal; but in the final analysis, external is the more important. You can do projects and take out costs, but if you don't meet or exceed customer requirements, it doesn't matter how efficiently you fail.

SPOTLIGHT #3

DESIGN A SUCCESSFUL LEAN SIX SIGMA PROJECT OR PILOT

With Darrel Whiteley, Danny Glidden, Chris Kennedy, and Shane White

WHICH METHODOLOGY IS RIGHT FOR YOUR PROJECT?

Lean Six Sigma is a powerful problem-solving methodology, but it is not suitable for all types of problems in all situations. In general, Lean Six Sigma methods and tools are not designed to help you answer strategic questions such as whether you're in the right markets or offering the right products, or whether you should consider shutting down a factory or combine two offices.

If, however, you are faced with the need to cut costs by improving the effectiveness or efficiency of your operations, then Lean Six Sigma should be able to help. Just which aspect of the broad toolset is most appropriate will take some careful assessment. Figure SP3.1 shows that, in general, the decision about which approach to use is based on how much you know about likely causes and solutions ahead of time.

When to Use Lean Six Sigma

- You have a challenging goal to reach or issue to solve.
- The goal/issue is linked to your business unit strategy/priorities.
- The issues are valuable for the business unit to resolve—that is, people will notice that the problem has been solved.

Figure SP3.1
Problem-solving approaches.

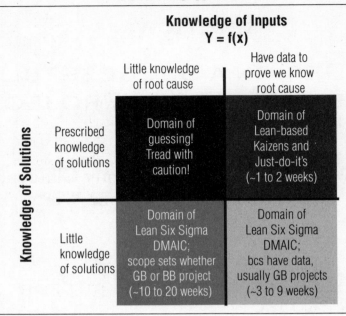

- The problem is thorny and the solution is not clear.
- The problem has "stood the test of time" (in other words, has resisted previous attempts to solve it).
- The causes of the problem are unknown or unclear.
- The solution to the problem is not obvious.
- You are willing to commit people to identify and resolve the issue.
- You want a more robust solution than traditional methods can provide.
- You want to encourage the upward flow of ideas and build team spirit.
- You want group ownership of a course of action.

When Not to Use Lean Six Sigma

- There is no specific challenge or clear issue to solve. (Lean Six Sigma projects must have a clear definition of the problem.)
- You are reasonably certain about a potential solution and course of action (in which case, launch a quick "do it" project that focuses on

the implementing the known solution, but be sure to gather data to verify that it worked).

- You don't have a process to improve.
- The organizational patience to follow the rigors of the Lean Six Sigma method is lacking.

IDENTIFYING THE PLAYERS AND THEIR ROLES

Projects happen through people. And many projects go off-course because the roles of those people are not clearly defined up front. Since cost reduction projects are generally driven by a business need to generate results quickly, having all the standard players in place—and clearly defining their roles—is especially critical. The basic roles are summarized in Table SP3.1.

Table SP3.1
Standard Project Roles

Role	Responsibilities
Sponsor	Leadership position *accountable for business* results being addressed by the defined Lean Six Sigma project.
	Plays a key role in identifying business gap/opportunity, initiating potential projects, and identifying team resources to lead the project; involved in clearly defining the project.
	Responsible for the project direction, execution, ongoing reviews/ inspection of project progress, removing barriers, providing resources, and implementing process improvements.
	Responsible for capturing and *sustaining* improvement results.
Team leaders	Charged with utilizing resources, planning, organizing, coordination, building relationships, processing information, making sure decisions made on time, analyzing data.
Team members	Perform team tasks (collect data, prepare charts, conduct background research), contribute ideas, participate in meetings, suggest methods the team can use to get its work done, and participate in decision making.
Expert coach or advisor	A person with expert knowledge in Lean Six Sigma, project management, change management, and so on.
Other stakeholders	In a cost reduction project, you will want a direct connection with someone from your accounting or finance office, so he or she can help you quantify and verify different types of benefits.

Defining Roles in a Cost Reduction Project

In every project, you want to clearly identify who is responsible for what, otherwise your project can be delayed when critical steps are missed, or you can waste time via duplication of effort.

Typical team roles and their responsibilities are covered in many other resources, and the instructions you find in them should serve you well. A generally favored tool is a RACI chart, a table that lists every player (team members, sponsors, team coaches, other stakeholders) down (or across) one side, with anticipated team tasks listed across (or down) the other. For each task and each player, you either leave the space blank or indicate whether he or she has one of the following roles:

Responsible—the person(s) who actually do the task.

Accountable—the person who has ownership, who ensures that the specific task is completed.

Consulted—person(s) who provide input before a task is completed.

Informed—person(s) who receive a status update on the activity of a task.

Tips: Must-Haves for Rapid and Sustainable Cost Reduction

Projects are complex beasts. A lot of factors have to come together before a project achieves (or exceeds) the cost reduction goal in the time frame set by your company: Here is our top-10 list of success factors:

1. Strong engagement between the project sponsor and the team:
    - Communicate, communicate, communicate (see Chapter 13). Hold regular meetings with the team leader and/or the full team; keep them informed of relevant business developments; ask them to alert you to barriers they encounter.
    - Consistency in reinforcing the larger context of the project (why the project is important, how it contributes to a broader goal).
    - Regular review meetings between the sponsor and the team.
2. Connection with the rest of the organization:
    - Clear direction from department or senior management, to make sure the project is important to the business.
    - Method of communicating project progress with department management.

3. A written project charter that clearly identifies the what, when, where, and impacts an issue.
   - Clear objectives/goals.
   - Clear business case.
4. Commitment to data-based problem solving:
   - Review historical or recent data that quantifies the gap between current and desired performance levels.
   - Collect new data to make decisions about where to focus the projects, which actions are best, and so on.
   - Test *all* assumptions.
5. LSS subject-matter experts who can provide training, guidance, and coaching, as needed. (If you have an existing Lean Six Sigma deployment in your company, this would likely take the form of Black Belts or Master Black Belts.)
6. A well-respected and strong project facilitator (change agent).
7. A project leader who has been trained in project management skills.
8. Reasonable and well-defined project milestones.
9. Access to necessary tools, knowledge, and resources.
10. Sufficient allocation of staff time to the project (50 to 100 percent for the project leader; perhaps less for other team members).
    - Only the smallest projects can get done quickly if people have to add project work onto a full workload; and small projects are unlikely to be important enough to do in the first place.

CHAPTER 3

USE THE VOICE OF THE CUSTOMER TO IDENTIFY COST-CUTTING OPPORTUNITIES

With Ken Feldman

A pharmaceutical manufacturer was required to provide production samples to a regulatory agency in order to gain certification of a certain manufacturing line. The company decided to provide 100 samples, taken hourly over the course of one week. After doing this a number of times, one employee got the idea to actually question the regulatory agency as to what the company needed to submit. The regulatory agency had no intention of specifying a particular sample size or sampling scheme. It only wanted statistically valid proof that the product was safe.

A Master Black Belt then calculated what would constitute a statistically valid approach and discovered that the manufacturer could significantly reduce its sampling plan—and significantly cut the cost of sampling, as well as reduce the time to validation so the product could get to market sooner. Direct dollar savings through reduced quality assurance (QA) lab costs was $125,000 annually. (The company didn't calculate the value of getting the product to market earlier as a result, but obviously it could realize earning earlier.)

As with this pharmaceutical company, it's likely that your company is rife with cost-cutting opportunities with respect to many of your customers. The key is making sure that the steps you take to cut costs don't harm your customers and, ultimately, your business. Throughout Part 1 of this book we focus on eliminating waste to reduce cost and retaining that which is *customer value-add*, in order to preserve quality, service levels, and market share. In this chapter, we discuss how to understand what customers truly value. Without this we cannot safely improve processes, nor can we fully eliminate waste.

Over the past few decades, businesses have embraced the philosophy that "quality begins and ends with the customer"—meaning that only customers know what they really need and whether or not the business has met or exceeded those needs. Never is that notion more important than when you're engaged in a project to reduce costs. Knowledge of customers is essential to make sure your resources are focused on delivering what they need, and that when making changes to reduce costs, you don't inadvertently cut something that will hurt you in the long run (via customer dissatisfaction).

In the parlance of Lean Six Sigma, gathering information from customers directly is called listening to the voice of the customer (VOC). In this chapter, we'll do a quick review of the three basic types of customers and present a useful model for classifying their needs, then review different ways to gather VOC data and how that data can help you become very specific about what you need to do to meet customer needs.

CUSTOMER TYPES AND THEIR NEEDS

All organizational processes have customers. For the purpose of a cost-cutting project, it's helpful to know which type(s) of customers are relevant:

- *External customers:* The people outside your organization who pay your bills by purchasing your products or services. They are the ultimate arbiters of "quality" in the products and services you sell. These people will take their business elsewhere if you fail to meet their needs, or, conversely, will become loyal advocates of your products or services if your company demonstrates a deep understanding of their needs.
- *Internal customers:* The internal function that receives the output (product or service) of your process. There are almost always ways to "Lean out" internal processes to reduce the "cost" of moving a product from one function to the next. Though internal customers can't take their business elsewhere, understanding their needs is still critical to ensuring you don't make your processes too expensive by under- or overdelivering on their needs. Interestingly enough, some organizations have given their manufacturing sites the option of continuing to receive intermediate product from the company's own plants or to purchase it outside if the price is lower and the quality better.

- *Regulatory customers:* While we usually have no choice but to comply with regulatory requirements, we often interpret regulations to be more restrictive than they are really intended, and thus incur unnecessary costs of providing the required information, documents, and other forms of compliance (like the pharmaceutical company at the opening of this chapter). Conformance to regulatory requirements is often paper-intensive, so truly understanding what these customers want will often help us cut costs by not providing more than they really need.

When you talk to customers in the course of your project, the odds are good that they will voice a number of needs and want. But there are two principles to keep in mind:

1. Customers will not be able to voice all of their needs.
2. Not all needs are created equal.

COLLECTING DATA ON CUSTOMER NEEDS

There are many, many ways to collect data about customer needs, and many, many resources for learning the how-to's for each method. Here we provide an overall framework for understanding the basic options you'll face, and discuss how to choose those methods that will work best for your project.

What Are VOC Collection Tools?

There are many ways to collect customer information. Some are **passive**, meaning they come at us whether we want it or not. These are useful as indicators of what's important to the customer but rarely are specific or definable enough to be of much use. There are also **active** methods of gathering VOC, requiring us to seek out customers. Figure 3.1 summarizes some of the most common forms of both passive and active sources of customer information.

Why Use VOC Collection Tools for a Cost Reduction Project?

There are several ways a process, product, or service can be more expensive than it needs to be with respect to customer needs:

1. Providing something a customer doesn't value (a feature the customer doesn't want, too much of a feature, more expensive materials or components than the customer wants, and so on).

Figure 3.1
Where to find information about customers.

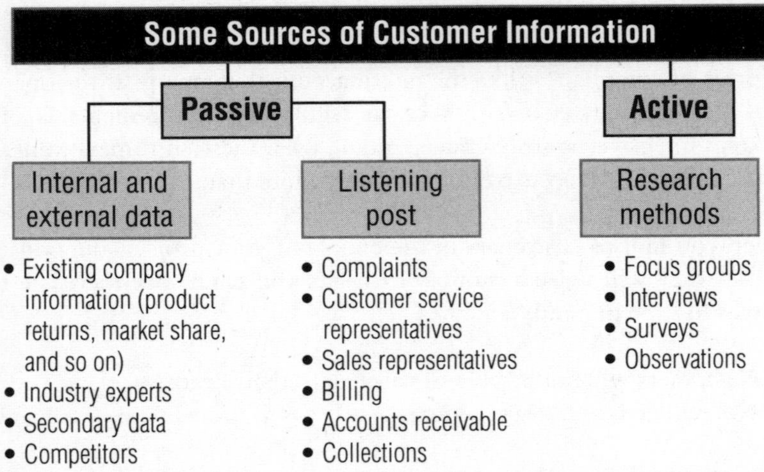

Some Sources of Customer Information

Passive

Active

Internal and external data

Listening post

Research methods

- Existing company information (product returns, market share, and so on)
- Industry experts
- Secondary data
- Competitors

- Complaints
- Customer service representatives
- Sales representatives
- Billing
- Accounts receivable
- Collections

- Focus groups
- Interviews
- Surveys
- Observations

2. Providing something a customer does value, but in a way that is time-consuming and costly.

Either way, when deciding what can and cannot be changed in a product, service, or process, you need to know what customers value and how much they value it.

Which VOC Collection Tools Are Best for a Cost Reduction Project?

While it can be useful to review any existing customer data your company has (either passive data it currently collects or the results of former active methods) to get a lay of the land, you need *specific* and *current* data when working on a cost reduction project. The active methods will help you identify the specific VOC needs that should serve as the focus of what is important to customers, as well as where you will have the best opportunities to reduce costs.

The different methods of active VOC collection vary in their purpose and expense (in terms of time and cost), so we can't be prescriptive about what combination of methods will be best for your project, but Table 3.1 provides a brief review of the methods and their appropriate uses.

Table 3.1
Methods for Collecting VOC Data

Tool/Method	Description	When to Use It in a Cost Reduction Project
Focus group	A small number of customers (typically 7 to 13) are brought together and led through a discussion around selected topics. You get detailed feedback and comments from a representative group.	Use when you have something physical for customers to explore (such as simulations of a changed process or service, prototype of a revised product).
Interviews	One-on-one or small group conversations (either in person or over the phone).	Use early in the investigation if you lack *valid* data on existing customer needs.
		Suitable at any point when you need to explore customer perceptions in some detail to root out subtleties.
Surveys	A large selection of customers are asked to provide answers to carefully selection questions (often with limited potential answers).	If you need to verify needs across a broader range of customers.
Ethnographic studies	Customers are observed as they interact with your product, service, or process, in real-world settings. Provides insights into customer behaviors that cannot be exposed via any other methods.	To gather ideas on which options/features can be cut from existing products/services because customer's don't use them.

To help demonstrate the uses of these various methods, here are a few case studies illustrating how the concepts have been used in cost reduction projects:

- *Combining multiple VOC methods:* An HR team at a large food manufacturer was troubled by high expected employee turnover. Not only did it represent a brain drain for the company, but hiring and retraining new employees is very costly. To stop the drain and save the company money, the team first conducted a *focus group* with key employees to determine which factors affected their job satisfaction. They then *interviewed* a broader selection of employees to compile a more detailed list. Finally, they did a *survey* of all current employees to gather detailed feedback. The company identified several basic management practices that added no direct costs, while improving employee satisfaction. (This avoided the preconceived notion that salary increases would be necessary to stem the flow of people leaving the organization.)

- *Ethnography example:* A large electronics company observed how customers removed the product from the packaging, utilized the product inserts and instructions, and eventually used the product. Those observations led to the conclusion that they were "overengineering" the packaging and some elements of the product, which led to a simplification and a reduction of costs of approximately $1.3 million. A traditional approach to VOC would not have revealed this information.
- *Focus group example:* A major pharmaceutical manufacturer used focus groups regularly to provide a foundation for decisions about marketing strategy. For example, one focus group identified trust as a key attribute they wanted in their interactions with sales representatives. More probing through interviews and surveys identified specific behaviors that the representatives could be trained on that would help build trust (such as "respect their time," "understand their patient mix," and "not to try to sell them a product they can't use in their practice"). In another example, a focus group was used to evaluate the effectiveness of promotional program. The group's feedback helped the company reduce the yearly spend on one brand from $27 million to $700 thousand once it became clear that the original spend was not providing any greater access or success.
- *Focus group example:* A major breakfast cereal manufacturer thought it needed to improve the quality of a specific cereal. This cereal underwent a baking/toasting step in the process, which gave the product a general slightly brown toast color. Unfortunately, a few pieces of cereal, due to air currents in the oven, would be blown back upstream and receive too much heat, becoming very dark. In very rare cases, the cereal pieces were almost burnt. There was a known engineering fix to the problem, but the cost of the change was over $2 million dollars in each manufacturing plant (five plants).

Before the engineering work was undertaken, focus groups were used to assess the perception of quality in the eyes of the consumer. Focus groups were conducted in three cities across the United States. The focus groups consisted of 5 to 10 individuals who routinely purchase breakfast cereal. Focus group sessions lasted for one to two hours and were conducted by an independent moderator. During the focus groups, the moderator directed the discussion about cereal quality, using sample bowls of cereal. Some of these bowls had the "defects" (burnt pieces) as perceived by the manufacturer.

What the cereal manufacturer considered defects, the consumers did not worry about. The key finding in focus group after focus group was that the consumer was not overly concerned about the burnt pieces. The usual comment was that they simply picked the burnt pieces out of their bowls.

This information from the focus groups allowed the manufacturer to forgo the cost of a substantial engineering change to the ovens in their plants, saving $2 million per plant in capital expense.

Collecting VOC Data in a Cost Reduction Project

The general procedures for collecting VOC data is the same for a cost reduction project as for any other project.

1. Identify all the outputs of the process you're studying (products, services, reports, data, and so on).
2. Identify or confirm the customers:
   - Any person, function, department, or organization that directly receives one of the outputs you identified
3. Review any existing passive data on hand that is relevant to the output.
4. Gather customer perceptions of all the outputs:
   - What do they like or not like?
   - Are all the outputs needed? (Is there a feature they don't use? A report no one looks at?)

If you have a large customer base, you may want to "stratify" the customers by dividing or segmenting them into subgroups of shared characteristics. By identifying and stratifying customers based on their value to the company, you will be able to discover which needs, wants, and expectations should be the focus of your efforts. Avoid the "squeaky wheel" syndrome and try not to focus merely on the noisiest and most vocal customer.

GETTING SPECIFIC ABOUT CUSTOMER NEEDS

VOC is a term that is given a lot of lip service these days. People commonly say they desire to exceed expectations, they desire to delight the customer, and so on. All of this is meaningless chatter unless voice-of-the-customer methods are used to distill customer feedback and priorities down to critical requirements that can be succinctly stated as metrics. One hotel chain sought to reduce complaints of customers that check-in times "take too long!" The question became, "What is too long?" Careful polling of customers revealed that 3 minutes was an acceptable target and 5 minutes or more was clearly too long to stand in line or work through the check-in. Now the hotel had a genuine target. "Too long" doesn't mean anything until it can be described in minutes.

Collecting VOC data is just a first step. The next step is interpreting that data to decide specifically what is and is not important to customers. Generically, we describe this process as developing statements about Critical Customer Requirements (CCRs).

What Is a Critical Customer Requirement?

A Critical Customer Requirement is a statement that translates a customer need into something measurable. To be useful, a Critical Customer Requirement statement should:

- Be specific and measurable (and the method of measurement is specific).
- Be related directly to an attribute of the product or service.
- Not present alternatives; not bias decisions.
- Be complete and unambiguous.
- Describe what, not how.

The transition from customer statement to useful CCR is illustrated in Figure 3.2.

Why Develop CCRs for a Cost Reduction Project?

The VOC data you collect in its raw form is unlikely to be actionable, in the sense that what customers say will be too vague or imprecise to enable you to make decisions about whether you are or are not meeting the customer need. To get to that point, you first need to reach a point where you can define the customer need with some precision.

How to Develop CCRs for a Cost Reduction Project

The basic principle behind developing Critical Customer Requirement statements is to take something general and add specificity.

Figure 3.2
Converting customer statements into CCRs.

Customer Statement	Performance Need	Product/Service Requirement
"This mower should be easy to start."	→ Wants the mower to start quickly and painlessly. →	Mower has electric start and starts on one push of the starter button, every time.
"I want to talk to the right person and don't want to wait on hold too long."	→ Wants to quickly reach the person who can solve their issue. →	Customer reaches correct person the first time, within 30 seconds.
"You have poor delivery of your alloy."	→ Customer receives product too early or too late. →	Reliable lead time from order to delivery receipt is 8 days ± 1 day.

The foundation of all CCRs is an *operational definition*: a description of process, product, or service characteristic written in sufficient detail to ensure it will be interpreted consistently by everyone involved in the process. Unless both you and the customer define what is important in the same way, you may be delivering product and service that does not provide the value the customer wants and needs.

Sometimes, just developing an operational definition can lead to cost savings. For example, a large food company was always complaining that it was discovering defects in its supplier's products during incoming inspection. The supplier was insistent that its quality control department was releasing only good product. This conflict was costing a food company close to $800,000 per year because of returns, rework, and replacements. The local Black Belt did a quick analysis and discovered that a food company and its supplier were conducting the quality checks by different methods. This inconsistency in method turned out to be the heart of the problem. Once a food company and its supplier agreed to a common operational definition of the desired characteristic and how to measure it, the defect rate dropped to nearly nothing, thus saving both companies considerable money.

Depending on your situation, you may need to use more specific methodologies, such as:

- *Key Buying Factor Analysis:* This is a method of comparing your delivery on various customer requirements against customer perceptions of both you and competitors (see Figure 3.3).

  The bars show relative importance of key buying factors to customers, based on their rating of those characteristics. The solid line rates the company's performance against those factors; other lines rate competitors' performance. Is this company wasting money? How can it cut costs? From the graph, we can conclude that the company is doing better on everything that isn't important to customers (the solid line is above the bars toward the right of the graph) and poorly on the things that customers value (delivery on the leftmost bars does not match the importance that customers place on those features.)

  If this company is spending money to maintain dominance in the relatively unimportant factors, it is wasting money and can immediately reduce costs by not trying so hard in those areas. On the other hand, it may transfer some of the savings and try to upgrade its performance in those areas where its competitors are doing well and it is not. Or, it may concede the position to its competitor, if it appears that there is not sufficient benefit in spending the money required to compete.

- *Quality Function Deployment (QFD):* This is a structured and iterative approach for converting statements of customer needs into specific definable characteristics—and, ultimately, a complete design—of a product or service.

- *Design of Experiments (DOE):* This is a statistical method that lets you quickly discover what combinations of features or characteristics will best satisfy customer needs. DOEs are very good at helping you find where it will benefit you to spend more money on particular features, and were you can cut production or delivery costs. (DOE is discussed in greater detail in Chapter 6.)

AVOIDING MISINTERPRETATIONS

The simple way to frame this issue is: *Can you believe what your data is telling you?* Can you be confident that your internal measurement systems are accurate in telling you how you're doing relative to customer needs? The Lean Six Sigma tool used to answer questions like this is Measure

Figure 3.3
Key buying factor analysis.

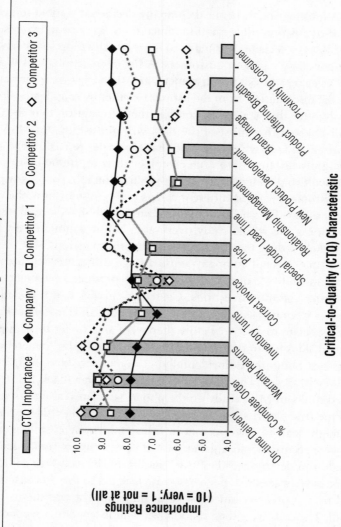

CTQ Importance ◆ Company □ Competitor 1 ○ Competitor 2 ◇ Competitor 3

Critical-to-Quality (CTQ) Characteristic

Importance Ratings
(10 = very; 1 = not at all)

10.0
9.0
8.0
7.0
6.0
5.0
4.0

On-time Delivery
% Complete Order
Warranty Returns
Inventory Turns
Correct Invoice
Price
Special Order Lead Time
Relationship Management
New Product Development
Brand Image
Product Offering Breadth
Proximity to Consumer

System Analysis (MSA). You can find instructions for performing an MSA in many good references; here are some cases that illustrate its application to understanding customer needs in a cost reduction project.

Case #1: A multinational chemical company decided it wanted to update its voice-of-customer information. Since there were so many customers to talk to, a decision was made to have 20 sales representatives call on the company's biggest customers. A list of questions was written for the sales reps to ask the customers, and then they were sent out to gather the information from the list put together by sales leadership. It was only after they started to compile the information that the company discovered that most of the data was not useful. An MSA was done, after the fact, which revealed that each sales rep asked the questions slightly differently to each customer (low reproducibility), so it was difficult to distinguish whether the variation in responses was because customers wanted different things or because of how the question was asked. The chemical manufacturer could have eliminated the cost of doing the whole study over again had it conducted an MSA study to help reduce the variation in asking the questions.

Case #2: A major retail company staffs a large call center so customers can call in and ask questions about their products, payments, and many other common questions. Customer surveys had revealed that customers were not happy with the number of call transfers from one phone associate to another before they were able to get their question answered. This frustration resulted in "abandoned calls," whereby customers just hung up. Coincidentally, customer satisfaction started to slip; likewise, sales. The company's internal Master Black Belt (MBB) decided to do an MSA study on the phone associates' ability to understand the true nature of the customers' questions when they called in. This might lead to fewer errors in transfers. Thirty customer phone calls were recorded and a group of call center supervisors listened to the calls and determined the "true" nature of the call. Five call center associates were selected. Each associate listened to the 30 calls and selected from a predetermined list what they thought was the nature of the call. The calls were then randomized and listened to a second time. The MBB then did an MSA and computed how often each associate agreed with him-/herself between the first and second trial and how often the five associates agreed with each other on a call, and, finally, how often the five associates agreed with the supervisors. As suspected, there was a good deal of variation between the associates. An effort was made to provide better operational definitions, along with some enhanced training and practice in identifying types of issues. As a result, the customer satisfaction score attributable to transfers increased 1.7 percent, which translated to $2.5 million in annual sales.

Case #3: A major full-service bank was concerned about an increase in the amount of documentation being reported as defective by one of its major customers. The bank did an extensive final audit and validation on critical documents, which its customer used to deliver its service to its customers. Because of the critical nature of the documents, the customer also did an incoming audit of the documents upon arrival at its service center. It was noted that for the past quarter, customer complaints and rejections had increased 11 percent. This increase in rejections was estimated to add an annual additional $1,500,000 to processing costs.

Before approaching its customer, the bank decided to do an MSA on its audit process. It was found to be well within acceptable parameters. The company then asked if it could be given data regarding the MSA capability of the customer's inspection process. It also turned out to be well within acceptable parameters. A combined team of company and customer audit personnel, led by one of the company's Black Belts, did an examination of the respective standard operating procedures for doing the audits. In theory, they were supposed to be the same. Upon analysis, it was discovered that there were two steps in the process that varied, as did the criteria for acceptance or rejection. When an MSA was done on the combined process, the results revealed a significant problem with the operational definitions of what a defect was. It turned out that the audit process had been revised but the company had not been advised or consulted.

The use of MSAs enables organizations to understand whether they are seeing the truth of what is going on, or not. In this case, both the customer and the company had adequate systems in place to minimize reproducibility and repeatability problems, the two major issues addressed by an MSA. Unfortunately, a failure to communicate changes between the customer and company, along with the slight changes in procedures and operational definitions, put the two audit systems in conflict. The matter was resolved during a two-hour meeting, and agreement was reached as to the "standard" process for auditing the documents.

The small changes in process resulted in a cost savings of approximately $1,500,000, plus the renewed customer satisfaction.

CONCLUSION

Chapter 2 made the point that the biggest opportunities for cutting costs lie in eliminating waste from your processes, products, and services. To make that call, you first have to know what it is that customers value, and how much they value it. That's the only way to make sure that your cost reduction measures don't inadvertently make your products or services less attractive to customers—and is the reason that a deep understanding of customer needs should be the foundation of every cost reduction project.

CHAPTER 4

MAKE PROCESSES TRANSPARENT TO EXPOSE WASTE

With Tim Williams, Lisa Custer, and Chris Kennedy

It's hard to be aggressive when you don't know who to hit.

—Vince Lombardi

If you know the enemy and know yourself, your victory will not stand in doubt.

—Sun Tzu, *The Art of War*

Chances are good that the project you've selected involves a process that raises one or both of the following questions: Why does it take so long? and Why does it cost so much?

A global IT support company we recently worked with was in just that situation. After a recent merger, turnover in the sales force topped 15 percent, and even long-term the company anticipated having 1000-plus new hires per year. Rapid onboarding was a priority, yet "provisioning" of new employees—getting them linked in to all the systems and equipment they needed to be productive, such as computers, cell phone, network access, business credit cards, and so on—often took more than two weeks. The company estimated that these "lost" weeks were costing $400,000 annually.

To solve this problem, we helped this company bring together a cross-functional team of people involved in hiring and onboarding. The team painstakingly traced the process step by step, creating a map on the wall of their conference room as they went. They documented the information that was requested in each step, printing out electronic forms, then tacking them up at the appropriate step.

Throughout this exercise, the team identified patterns of repeated hand-offs, including one particular piece of information that was requested again and again—11 times in all throughout the process. They saw that some steps currently being done in sequence could be done in parallel.

In short order, the team made a number of relatively minor changes that sped up the process to less than one day. That included a 60 percent reduction in e-mail traffic, a 100 percent reduction in "waiting for approval e-mail" (meaning there were no longer any delays), and a 50 percent reduction in data elements requested. Employee reactions have been universally positive, and a process that was once considered a major hassle is now something they don't have to think about at all.

Articulating those processes—documenting what actually happens day to day, in detail—often uncovers new information and identifies waste that you didn't realize was there. This IT company, for example, took work that is normally hidden from sight—e-mails, attachments, online forms, decisions, conversations—and created a visual map that helped everyone involved see the complete process from end to end. In doing so, they discovered duplicated effort, places where departments stumbled over each other, areas where useless delays were built-in standard procedures. Having a visual representation of a process that everyone can look at and analyze is what we call "process transparency."

Creating this process transparency often brings about surprise and disbelief from the management team: "How could our process have become so inefficient and cumbersome?" The short answer is that, "Our processes have grown organically over time; we've expanded the process, added more and different types of work to be done." We created workarounds to allow the process to keep functioning, given the new workload and different types of work being processed. And as we "bolt on" new steps and functions, add new capabilities and workflows, we usually don't step back and understand how this process should really be designed to run efficiently and effectively, given all the changes that have occurred over the years. So we end up with a process that asks for the same information 11 different times and inherently drives up the cost of running that process.

Making processes transparent is a prerequisite for sustainable and real cost reduction, because real, sustainable reductions can come about only through process change. Had the IT support company leadership stopped at exhorting people to "work harder," staff would never have been able to discover exactly where, how, and why time (and therefore cost) was built into their current way of working.

Compounding this problem of process "opaqueness" (being hidden from sight) is that there are generally three versions of every process:

- What management "thinks" is going on.
- Which official processes are documented in some reference manual or system.
- What actually happens and is executed at the working level.

Typically, all three of these versions disagree with each other! It will require effort to get past what people "know" and drive toward what is really happening and bring the process into the light of day, so you can see where waste and cost are being generated.

The purpose of process transparency is to let our processes speak to us, to capture what we call the "voice of the process." In this chapter, we'll talk about what that means, then cover two steps we recommend for achieving that goal:

1. Using a supplier-input-process-output-customer (SIPOC) map to help scope the effort.
2. Creating a value stream map (VSM) to capture the workflow in detail, along with relevant process data.

How to Define the Boundaries through SIPOC Diagrams

One purpose in making a process transparent is to develop a *shared* understanding of that process—where it stops and starts, what's coming into the process, what's going out, what happens to the work in between. A simple way to capture that basic information is through a SIPOC diagram.

What Is a SIPOC Diagram

A SIPOC diagram captures the basic components of a process (Figure 4.1):

Suppliers: The people, departments, and companies that provide the information and material needed to perform the process work (they provide the inputs).

Figure 4.1
SIPOC diagram.

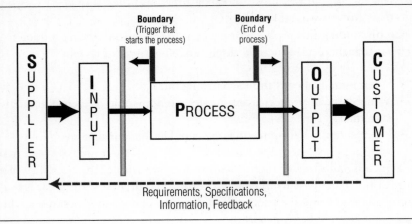

Requirements, Specifications,
Information, Feedback

Inputs: The information, material, and so on that is required of the process to produce the output.

Process: The actions taken to convert the inputs to outputs.

Outputs: The product of the process that is delivered to the customer (internal or external).

Customers: The organization, function, or person that requires/needs the output.

Why Use SIPOC in a Cost Reduction Project?

A SIPOC chart is used early in a project to create a shared understanding of the process boundaries to be studied in the process. Everyone involved in the project—the sponsor, leaders, team members, other stakeholders—will have the same definition of the start and end points. A SIPOC chart defines the "playing field"—what the team needs to investigate in terms of suppliers, inputs, and the process to drive sustainable cost reductions.

If you haven't already identified customers and their needs (see Chapter 3), a SIPOC diagram will help you identify the process output(s) and the customers of that output that you should consider when making decisions about what to change and not change in a process, product, or service.

How to Use a SIPOC Map in a Cost Reduction Project

The basic steps for creating a SIPOC map are the same for any project:

1. Start by identifying the starting and ending points of the process. Make sure that everyone involved in the project (sponsor, leader, team members, stakeholders) agree on these points.
2. Identify the high-level steps that identify the full scope of work you will include. (Do *not* get caught up in detail.)
3. Identify the outputs of the process and key customers (users/purchasers/regulators) of that output. Conduct research to identify what is important to those customers. Identify how you measure the outputs, and in turn, customer requirements.
4. Identify the key inputs and the providers of those inputs (suppliers). The inputs could be raw materials, instructions, a previous step in the process, and so on.

For a cost reduction project, there are a few special considerations:

- Remember that understanding customer needs and requirements is key to making cost reduction decisions.
- Therefore, when you identify important requirements for the process, include both customer requirements (features, quality levels) and business requirements (reduced input, increased throughput, faster speed, reduced cost).
- If you want, you can divide the expectations into three categories: Customer CTQs (critical to quality), CTDs (critical to delivery), and CTCs (critical to cost).

Example SIPOC

The process for responding to a request received at a Congressional office is shown in Figure 4.2. The figure also includes a table showing the metrics that staff could monitor to evaluate how well this process was working.

USING VALUE STREAM MAPS TO ACHIEVE TRANSPARENCY

Once the boundaries and basic elements of the process are clear, the next step is to develop a picture of the process details that captures the kinds of information that will help you identify and select improvement actions. You can think of these pictures as "flowcharts with data"—also known as *value stream maps* (VSM).

Figure 4.2
Example of a SIPOC diagram.

Suppliers	Inputs	Process	Outputs	Customers
• Congress-people • Congr. staffers	• Letters	Review Requirement ▼ Determine Action Office ▼ Forward to Action Office ▼ Action Office develops response ▼ Action Office forwards response ▼ Review response ▼ Approve response ▼ Deliver response	• Responses	• Constituents • Congress-people

	Input Metrics	Process Metrics	Output Metrics
Quality	• Quality of request • Accuracy of database information • Staff experience	• % rework at each step	• Response accuracy and tone
Speed	• Time to receive request	• # of process steps • Time to complete steps • Time to deliver response • Delay time between steps • Response cycle time w/in 7 days	• Response cycle time w/in 15 days

---

A Broader Look at Value Stream Maps

In this chapter, we focus on the use of VSMs in the context of an identified project. However, they are also extremely useful when used to capture the overall flow of work in an entire business unit or company. Such high-level VSMs will help you identify waste in your core business processes.

What Is a Value Stream Map?

Value stream maps are part flowchart, part data capture form. (See Figure 4.3.) They depict both the sequence of actions in a process plus data on other types of relevant information: material flow, information flow, inventories, processing times, setup times, delays, and so on.

Value stream maps come in different formats. Three of the most common are described here.

Traditional Value Stream Map   Figure 4.3 depicts the form of a basic value stream map. As you can see, it captures the main steps in a process (including inputs and outputs), plus the flow of material and information.

The boxes that depict each step will be used to capture important process data (see Figure 4.4). Typical data includes:

- Elapsed time for that step
- Amount of work-in-progress

Figure 4.3
Schematic of a traditional value stream map.

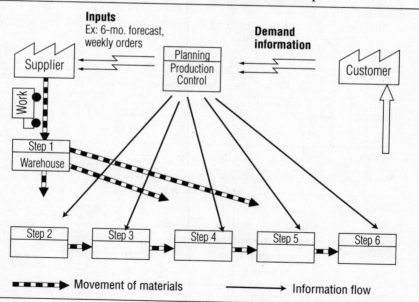

Figure 4.4
Data captured for each step.

Process Step 2	
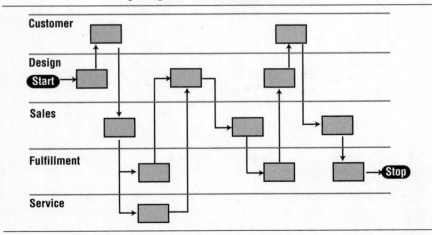	4/shift, 2x9 hr shifts
Processing Time = 18 sec/pc	
Setup Time = 7 min	
Uptime = 85%	
Batch size = 50 pcs	
Yield = 98%	
Efficiency = 60%	

1400 pcs

Inventory for this step (the # of orders, parts, etc., waiting to be worked on)

Swim-lane Value Stream Map A swim-lane VSM (Figure 4.5) captures the same kind of data as a traditional map; the only difference is that the action steps are sorted into rows (or columns) depending on who does the work (which person or group).

In this schematic shown in Figure 4.5, the process flow goes *across* the chart, from left to right. (An alternative format is to have the action flowing *down* the page, with columns instead of rows showing the division between

Figure 4.5
Depicting actions in a swim-lane format.

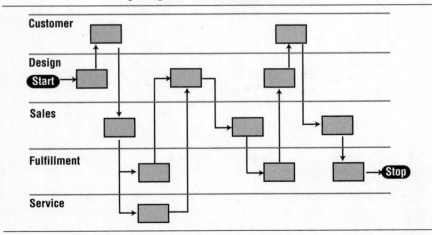

people or groups). This format highlights handoffs between groups. The same type of data for each process step is captured as in a traditional value stream map.

Shingo-Style Value Stream Map This format is named after Shigeo Shingo, who was instrumental in development of the Toyota Production System. Shingo-style value stream maps also capture process data, like a traditional VSM, but the format is much more reminiscent of a SIPOC map. The main actions are captured as, perhaps, 3 to 7 "process steps" that flow across the top of the page. The actions required to perform the process steps are labeled "operation steps"; they are shown in vertical columns below the process steps (see Figure 4.6).

Figure 4.6
Schematic of the Shingo format.

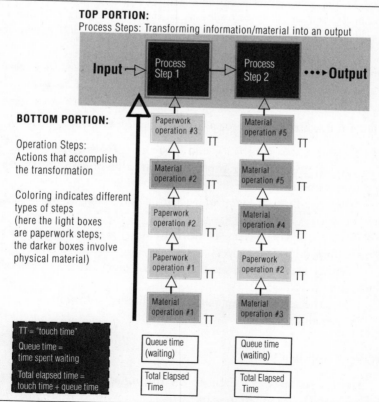

Picking a VSM Format

Each of the VSM formats have strengths and weaknesses, and we offer some tips here on how to choose between them. But the main message is: You will learn something no matter which format you use, so don't spend too much time on the decision. Go with your gut, or ask an expert for advice. If you find that the format you've chosen doesn't let you capture information you need, you can either redraw it in a different format or layer the extra information onto your original form.

- The traditional format does a good job of capturing the flow of materials and information in a process, and is easily adapted to many situations.
- The swim-lane style is most often used in transactional/service environments because the handoff between groups is often a major issue in those processes.
- The Shingo style captures process actions in greater detail than is normally used for either the traditional or swim-lane format. That detail is helpful in tracking down the source of defects that are adding time and cost to a process.

You can find two several examples of value stream maps on the previous pages.

Why Do a Value Stream Map for a Cost Reduction Project?

- To *see* and *measure* the *value* and *waste* in a process. VSMs:
  — Provide greater *depth* into the process, allowing discovery of more waste and variation.
  — Illustrate flow of *material and information across machines,* and *people.*
  — Give a true visual representation of how the *work transforms input to output* inside a process.
- To identify ways to improve the process—quick wins and project opportunities. VSMs:
  — Give the team greater *velocity* to discern solutions to eliminate waste and variation.

Analyzing Value on a VSM

The activities so far have focused on the *mapping* aspect of a VSM. Once you have a completed map, attention turns to the *value* aspect.

As we've discussed before, the whole basis of being able to cut costs without harming customers is understanding which parts of a process add value and which don't. So this analysis of what creates and what destroys or hinders value in a process is the critical step for identifying waste (in terms of time and dollars) in a process and identifying cost reduction opportunities.

Identifying value is also a prerequisite for calculating the *Process Cycle Efficiency* (PCE), a key process metric that lets you gauge the amount of waste in a process. (PCE is discussed in more detail in Chapter 5.)

Therefore, as you construct the VSM, or after it is completed, you need to examine what actually happens in each step and determine what adds value (see the instructions to come), and determine the PCE for your process.

Identifying Value-Add and Non-Value-Add Steps Each activity in a process should be labeled according to whether it adds value or is waste (non-value-add). There are three categories:

1. *Value-add (VA)/customer value-add (CVA):* Any activity in a process that is essential to deliver a service to the customer. It:
   - Must be performed to meet customer needs.
   - Adds form, feature, and/or function to the service or product (enhances service quality, enables on-time or more competitive delivery, or has a positive impact on price competition).
   - Includes those tasks for which the customer would be willing to pay if he or she knew you were doing it (that is, has value to the customer).
2. *Business value-add (BVA):* Activities that allow greater effectiveness or efficiency in a process. These are activities that are required by the business but add no real value from a customer standpoint (e.g., obtain the order, provide a bill, safety activities, regulatory compliance activities). Ask yourself:
   Does this task reduce owner financial risk?
   Does this task support financial reporting requirements?
   Is this task required by law or regulation?
3. *Non-value-add (NVA) activities are those that:*
   - Are not customer value-add or business value-add, meaning they are not required to meet or exceed customer needs and are not required by the business.
   - Include the seven types of waste discussed in Chapter 2.

Post the definitions given here of CVA, BVA, and NVA prominently; you will need to refer back to them often.

Just because a process step is labeled as NVA does not mean that the step is not critical to the process *as it functions today*. Often, NVA process steps are very critical to how the process operates—but only because that's how it is designed to operate. For example, a process today may require us to move a raw material from one location to another so that processing can occur. If we stopped doing that movement today, without any other process changes, our process would break down; the processing step would eventually run out of things to work on as no new material is brought to it. This "transportation" is a critical process step in our current process design, but the customer does not care how we move material around within our process. So this step, even though critical, is still NVA.

There are several ways to visually capture the separation of value-add and non-value-add steps on a value stream map. You can write the designations on the process step, or flag them using different colors of self-stick notes or colored dots (for example, green for CVA, blue for BVA, red for NVA).

Calculating PCE Based on CVA Time

Identifying CVA is a prerequisite for calculating an important process metric called **Process Cycle Efficiency (PCE)**. This metric compares the amount of value-add time to non-value-add time and is a key indicator of waste (and, therefore, trapped costs) in a process. See Chapter 5 for more on PCE.

Planning a Path Forward   Figure 4.7 summarizes the decisions that will lead you to identify the priorities as you move forward:

1. Start by trying to eliminate all NVA steps. This will automatically generate time (and, often, cost) savings.
2. Then improve BVA tasks as much as you can. Make sure each activity is truly necessary for the business. Remove waste from these process steps.
3. Finally, optimize the VA steps. This will include removing all forms of waste, fixing problems so errors and defects do not occur, reducing variation, and so on.

Figure 4.7
Analyzing steps in a value stream map: As you analyze waste and value in your VSM, the path forward would be to (1) eliminate NVA first, (2) reduce BVA activities, then (3) work to improve/optimize any CVA steps.

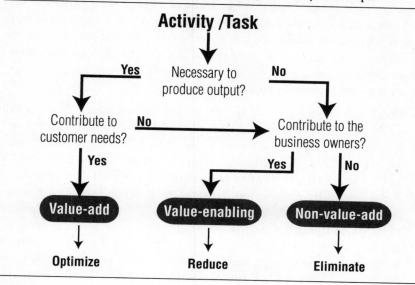

Value Determinations Can Be Tricky

Though the definitions of customer value-add, business value-add, and non-value-add seem straightforward, distinguishing between them is sometimes much harder in practice than it may sound.

For one thing, *fewer activities are CVA than you'd think*. Our data on hundreds of processes show that it's not unusual for the value-add time to be less than 5 percent in many processes, and even less than 1 percent in paperwork processes. So the majority of time—and activities—will be something other than CVA.

Second, the natural attitude is to believe that an activity that has always been part of a process *must* be "needed"—and therefore value-add. That is not the case.

Third, you may run into sensitive territory if you have to tell some staff that the majority of their time is spent on non-value-add activities. Recognize that value-add is determined from the customer's perspective—not what is currently required to do the job. It helps if you consciously separate the activity from the person doing the activity/job: The job may be critical;

however, if it doesn't transform the product or provide a new feature/service, and the customer isn't willing to pay for it, then the *activity* is non-value-add.

Fourth, most process steps will be some combination of value-add and non-value-add. Filling out a form, for example, may have elements of both VA and NVA in the step. If so, it is often best to label the process with the vast majority of the activity—perhaps noting a small increment of value-add activity.

Here are some tips to get you started:

- Make a decision and move on. We guarantee that there will be lots of easily identified NVA work in your process the first time you go through this activity. If there are some activities where it's not clear whether they are NVA or BVA, just make a decision and move on. Even if you label it as BVA for now, you may find you can reduce or eliminate it later on.
- If you anticipate running into sensitive areas around what is or is not considered value-add, consider having a good facilitator (experienced in VSMs, too!) run the session.
- If you end up labeling a lot of steps as BVA, then consider using a Shingo-style (and its added level of detail) so that you can identify the specific part that is BVA and those that are NVA. In this way, the waste can become more visible.

VSM Examples

Here are two examples of value stream maps.

Example #1: New Hire Onboarding   Remember the case study showcased at the beginning of this chapter? Figure 4.8 shows the basic flow of the work involved (in a swim-lane format, since the company wanted to highlight handoffs). The crossed-out steps will no longer be needed because the team identified ways to capture more of the required information just once, much earlier in the process.

Example #2: Maintenance Operation   The current cycle time in a maintenance operation was 10 days for the repair of parts. A team created the value stream map of their current maintenance repair process (Figure 4.9) and identified categories of waste to improve (highlighted with the starbursts in the figure).

They made changes to address those forms of waste (see Figure 4.10) and succeeded in reducing cycle time from 10 days to 1 day. Increased

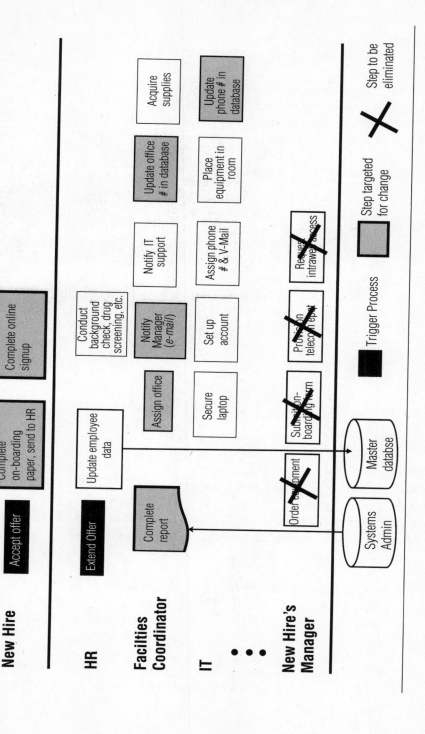

Figure 4.8
New hire onboarding VSM.

Figure 4.9
As-is VSM.

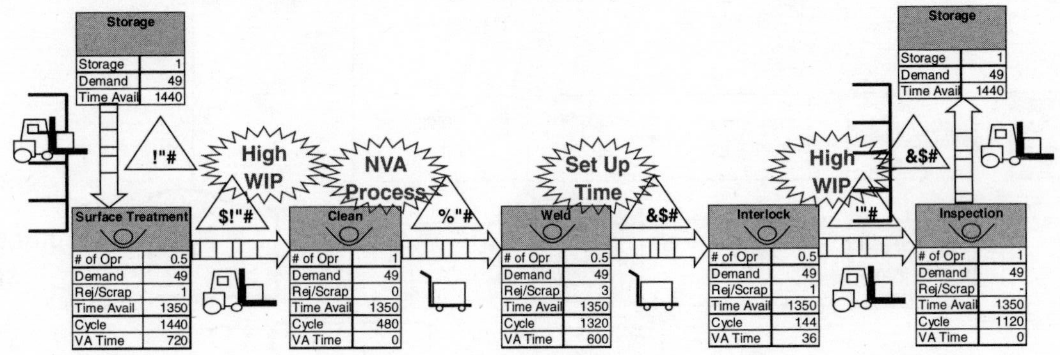

Storage	
Storage	1
Demand	49
Time Avail	1440

Surface Treatment	
# of Opr	0.5
Demand	49
Rej/Scrap	1
Time Avail	1350
Cycle	1440
VA Time	720

Clean	
# of Opr	1
Demand	49
Rej/Scrap	0
Time Avail	1350
Cycle	480
VA Time	0

Weld	
# of Opr	0.5
Demand	49
Rej/Scrap	3
Time Avail	1350
Cycle	1320
VA Time	600

Interlock	
# of Opr	0.5
Demand	49
Rej/Scrap	1
Time Avail	1350
Cycle	144
VA Time	36

Inspection	
# of Opr	1
Demand	49
Rej/Scrap	-
Time Avail	1350
Cycle	1120
VA Time	0

Storage	
Storage	1
Demand	49
Time Avail	1440

Kaizen bursts: High WIP !"# · NVA Process %"# · Set Up Time &$# · High WIP !"# · &$#

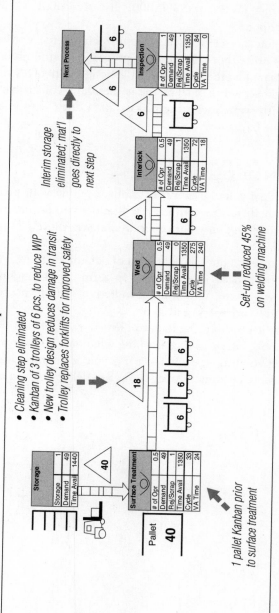

Figure 4.10
Improved flow.

- Cleaning step eliminated
- Kanban of 3 trolleys of 6 pcs. to reduce WIP
- New trolley design reduces damage in transit
- Trolley replaces forklifts for improved safety

Interim storage
eliminated; mat'l
goes directly to
next step

Set-up reduced 45%
on welding machine

1 pallet Kanban prior
to surface treatment

Storage	
Storage	1
Demand	49
Time Avail	1440

Surface Treatment	
# of Opr	0.5
Demand	49
Rej/Scrap	1
Time Avail	1350
Cycle	33
VA Time	24

Weld	
# of Opr	0.5
Demand	49
Rej/Scrap	0
Time Avail	1350
Cycle	275
VA Time	240

Interlock	
# of Opr	0.5
Demand	49
Rej/Scrap	1
Time Avail	1350
Cycle	72
VA Time	18

Inspection	
# of Opr	1
Demand	49
Rej/Scrap	-
Time Avail	1350
Cycle	84
VA Time	0

Pallet 40

40

18

6   6   6

6

6

6

6

6

Next Process

throughput of the weld process by >40 percent was achieved by reducing the setup time. The team generated a one-time benefit in reduction of work-in-process (WIP) of $380,000, plus $245,000 savings in the increased throughput.

As you can see from this example, completed VSMs can be visually complex because they capture both process flow and process data. But don't be intimidated by the final product. Though it involves some effort to agree on the right sequence of steps and gather data, constructing a VSM is relatively straightforward, with the process data dealt with in sequence and layered onto the basic flow.

CONCLUSION

Creating a value stream map is one way that your process can speak to you about reality. The map itself will allow you to understand which activities are happening, in what order, and at what levels of performance from end to end.

By investing in the right kind of data monitoring, you will also be able to evaluate process performance in terms of throughput, cycle time, setup time, wait time, WIP waiting to be worked on, process downtime/uptime, defect/rework rates, and so on.

The details of using data to "listen" to a process are beyond the scope of this book, but in essence learning what data to collect and how to analyze it will let you monitor whatever it is you deem important about your process: cost levels, customer satisfaction, and delivery speed or quality.

CHAPTER 5

MEASURE PROCESS
EFFICIENCY

Finding the Levers of Waste Reduction

With Stephen Clarke

An e-commerce website was starting to feel drowned by the creative burden of producing new ads each week. From start to finish, the process took about 4 months. At any given moment, there were about 180 unique ads in development, with about 45 new ads required each month.

One of the first lessons this company learned after adopting Lean Six Sigma was that slow processes were expensive processes. So company managers had to ask themselves whether there was a way to cut time—and cost—from this process.

The first clue came when they constructed a value stream map (as described in Chapter 4) and completed the value-add analysis portion of the procedure. The company realized that there were only 15 days of value-add work in the 120-day process. In other words, 105 days of the cycle time (just under 90 percent) was wasted time from the clients' perspective. They approached the task of improving the efficiency in stages, and over a period of 6 months had cut the lead time to just 60 days—and cut the cost to run the process the equivalent of $350,000 annually.

This company was in a common position. It had a process that *felt* like it took forever to complete and was unnecessarily complicated. With the tools described in this chapter, it was able to convert that feeling into data and discover a relatively simple way to cut process time in half—which led to dramatic cost savings as well.

In this chapter, we will explore the two primary process efficiency metrics—called Process Cycle Efficiency (PCE) and Process Lead Time (PLT), and one important relationship, Little's Law—and show how they can be used to expose significant time and cost-saving opportunities, including a simple six-step method for achieving quick wins.

Other Advantages of a Quicker Process

Fast, efficient processes are not just less costly than slow processes. They have other benefits:

- Faster feedback on process performance (increased learning cycles).
- Improved first-pass yield (results in improved productivity—less time and cost due to rework).
- Improved process stability (results in improved throughput).
- Discovery of process deficiencies (forces problem resolution).
- Less work-in-process (reduced risk, reduced spoilage or damage).
- Improved customer satisfaction (flexibility and responsiveness).
- Increased business as customers find value in that improved responsiveness.

PROCESS CYCLE EFFICIENCY: THE KEY METRIC OF PROCESS TIME AND PROCESS COST

When starting any process improvement project, one of the questions is, "Just how bad is the process?" Answering that question requires that you have a metric that tells you something meaningful about the process performance.

One of the best metrics for that purpose is called Process Cycle Efficiency (PCE), a measure of how much value-add time is present in a process compared to overall process time. The evaluation of value is based on the perception of the customer (as described in Chapter 4). Process Cycle Efficiency quantifies the percentage of time in a process that is value-add. In essence, PCE provides an understanding of how efficiently an organization is able to create value for its customers.

Why Calculate PCE for a Cost Reduction Project?

At its most basic, the higher the PCE, the lower the costs to operate. Or, on the flipside, a low PCE number means there is a lot more non-value-add (NVA) time in a process than value-add time. Knowing the PCE for any process tells you just how much waste there is in the project. Calculating PCE before and after process changes lets you quantify the improvement in use of process time—and, as you'll find, there will almost always be a direct connection between time saved and dollars saved.

How to Calculate PCE   The formula for calculating PCE is quite simple.

$$PCE = 100 \times (\text{Value-Add Time}) \div PLT$$

where:

> Value-add time is the amount of value-add time in the process.
> PLT = Process Lead Time, the total amount of time that an item spends in a process.
> The "100×" converts the fraction to a percentage.

The values for value-add time and Process Lead Time should have been calculated when you constructed a value stream map (see Chapter 4).

Let's look at the production of a box of cereal. For simplicity, consider the beginning of the process to be the arrival of the necessary ingredients at the manufacturing plant. The end of the process is when the finished box of cereal is placed on the shelf at your local grocery store. For this process:

Process Lead Time = 95 days
Value-add time is 2 days (it takes 2 days to produce and package this cereal)

Process Cycle Efficiency is therefore:

$$PCE = 100 \times (2 \div 95) = 2.1\%$$

You might be wondering why we're not including the time to ship the product across the country to your local grocery store, or the time it sits in inventory in a warehouse as value-add time. Aren't those steps necessary to get the product to the customers? Perhaps from a functional standpoint it is, but in the eyes of the customer, nothing good happens to a box of cereal while it sits in a warehouse or is traveling across country. Only bad things, like damage, staleness, and so on. Therefore, steps like transport and storage are forms of waste in the eyes of the customer. They should be treated as NVA and minimized or eliminated.

How Reducing NVA Time Reduces Costs

We've stated that faster processes are less expensive processes. What justifies that statement? Think for a moment about the cereal production example just described. The time the finished product sits in a warehouse (as inventory) is considered waste. How does reducing the inventory (and thus the amount of time any single box of cereal sits in that warehouse) lower costs? If there are fewer products in warehouses, fewer warehouses are needed. This reduces warehousing costs. Fewer boxes of cereal get damaged in the movement process, which reduces the number of boxes of cereal that are thrown away, further bringing down costs. Fewer boxes of cereal become stale (and nonsaleable). All of these will reduce the total cost of that box of cereal. Thus the direct cost of the cereal is decreased.

Here's another example, this time in a service/transactional situation. A company that processes home mortgages is looking at the time it takes to approve applications.

Process Lead Time (PLT) = 59 days
VA time = 1 day (from the customer's perspective; the rest of the time is just wait time)
PCE = $100 \times (1 \div 59) = 1.7\%$

Interpreting PCE Numbers

You might be surprised at how low these PCE values are: a manufacturing process with only a 2.1 percent efficiency, and a service process with a 1.7 percent PCE. Trust us, they are typical of nonimproved processes, and we often see much worse.

Consider, for example, an employee of a large firm who calls the IT help desk for assistance with a password reset issue. The first-line help desk personnel are located off shore, and because of the difference in time zones (and a backlog of requests), the help desk staff do not call the employee back until the following day. The average total cycle time to close a case (that is, what we have defined as process lead time, or PLT) is 17.5 hours (1050 minutes). It takes the help desk personnel 6.5 minutes of value-add activity to reset the password and close the case. What is the PCE for this process?

PLT = 17.5 hours = 1050 minutes
VA time = 6.5 minutes
PCE = $100 \times (6.5 \div 1050) = 0.6\%$

Note that to perform the calculation, the units of measure for PLT and VA time need to be the same. So, in this case, PLT was converted from hours to minutes.

You might think that the PCE values in these three examples—2.1 percent, 1.7 percent, and an even worse 0.6 percent—sound too low. But in our experience, based on hundreds of processes in businesses of every kind, they are typical for processes that have not been the focus of improvement (see Table 5.1).

What do you do with a low PCE number? First, as we mentioned previously, a low PCE number means that there is a lot more NVA time in a process than VA time. So your biggest opportunity for making a significant impact on PCE will be to focus on reducing overall process lead time. Consider two scenarios for the IT help desk:

1. Developing standards that let the help desk staff reset passwords in half the time (cut the 6.5 minutes down to 3.25 minutes). PCE becomes:

$$PCE = 100 \times (3.25 \div 1050) = 0.3\%$$

Lesson Learned: Improving VA time but leaving the waste in a process just means you have even less VA time compared to NVA time.

Table 5.1
Typical PCE Values

Application	Typical PCE Values	Typical First-Round Improvement Target	High-End PCE Goal (World-Class Levels)
Manufacturing	<5%	15% (batch) 30% (single-piece flow)	35% (batch processing) 80% (single-piece flow)
Service/ transactional	<5%	10%	50%
Creative/ cognitive		5%	25%

2. Removing non-value-add delays in the process so the overall cycle time is cut in half (from 1050 minutes to 525 minutes). PCE in this scenario becomes:

$$PCE = 100 \times (6.5 \div 525) = 1.2\%$$

Lesson learned: Cutting wasted time is the only effective way to improve process efficiency.

The path forward, therefore, has to focus on removing waste (NVA time) from the process. Addressing waste directly is one pathway to accomplish those goals—via using Lean Six Sigma tools on the types of process waste introduced in Chapter 2. There is another pathway, opened to you by understanding Little's Law (covered next), to see if there are some quick wins.

LITTLE'S LAW: UNDERSTANDING THE LEVERS FOR IMPROVING PROCESS SPEED

Just as there is a simple formula for determining overall process efficiency, there is another that lets us estimate Process Lead Time. The equation is called Little's Law (Figure 5.1).

Process Lead Time = Work-in-Process ÷ Exit Rate (or, PLT = WIP ÷ ER)

where:

Work-in-Process (WIP) = the number of "things" in the process. Those things could be anything: reports, orders, components, batches, requests, designs, widgets, and so on.

Figure 5.1
Little's Law concept and equation.

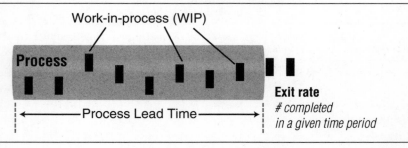

Exit Rate (ER), also called "completion rate" = the number of things that leave the process within a given time period.

How to Calculate Process Lead Time Using Little's Law

Here is a simple example: If there are 10 people standing in front of you at a movie theater, and it takes 1 minute to complete each purchase, you will wait 10 minutes before your turn comes to buy a ticket.

$$PLT = 10 \text{ "people in process"} \div 1 \text{ person per minute} = 10 \text{ minutes}$$

Here is another example for a loan approval process:

WIP = 47 (there are currently 47 loan applications under review)
ER = the work group can complete 5 applications per day

Therefore:

$$PLT = 47 \div 5 = 9.4 \text{ days}$$

The best way to think about PLT is that the next loan application to arrive will be completed in 9.4 days

Why Calculate Little's Law for a Cost Reduction Project?

There are two implications of this relationship defined by Little's law:

1. The longer the movie ticket line (= the more WIP), the longer the wait (and remember, waiting is a form of waste). In other words, cutting WIP is usually the fastest and least-expensive way to improve process lead time. (Note: As we'll demonstrate later in the chapter, cutting WIP *does not* affect how much work is completed—so there is no negative impact on the customers of the process.)
2. You could try to improve PLT by increasing exit rate, but that would mean changing the capacity of the process. For example, if the movie theater were to open a second ticket window, it could double the exit rate—but this approach requires investment of resources, which is usually expensive.

How Reducing WIP Lowers Cost

If Process Lead Time is reduced by decreasing WIP, there is a smaller risk of producing something the customer does not want. (Long lead times in the car market, for example, are why many dealers have historically held end-of-year sales events to clear unwanted inventory.) Alternatively, in other industries, the act of decreasing WIP or inventory results in less rework (another form of waste). This happens when the inventory becomes outdated and work must be performed to bring it back to a saleable condition. And reducing WIP (think about standing in line) decreases the likelihood that customers will go somewhere else to buy the goods or services they require.

THE WIP CAP METHOD: HOW LIMITING WIP CAN INCREASE PROCESS SPEED AND REDUCE COSTS

There is a systematic approach to implementing a quick improvement, based on Little's Law and the basic PCE calculation. We call it the WIP Cap method because it's based on limiting—or putting a cap on—the amount of work-in-process you allow in a process.

What Is WIP Cap?

WIP Cap is a method for determining the level of WIP you can have in a process in order to achieve a desired PCE level (and a desired PLT). It is one form of what's known as a *pull system*—the name implying that work is *pulled* into a process based on customer or business demand. (In most processes, work is pushed into a process based on the exit rate from the previous process.) Pull systems reduce the cost of operating a process by making it more stable and predictable (see Figure 5.2).

A pull system has a number of benefits:

- *Efficiency:* A pull system can attain the same throughput as a push system with less average WIP (and, therefore, a shorter cycle time).
- *Productivity:* Less WIP means less "stuff" to get in the way, and thus more time spent adding value to the process.
- *Ease of control:* Pull systems rely on setting easily controllable WIP levels, creating a much more manageable process.

Figure 5.2
Impact of WIP Caps.

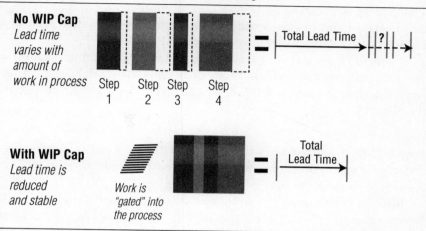

- *Quality improvement:* Low WIP (and associated cycle time) systems are more sensitive to quality (and, therefore, force problem resolution) and facilitate it (by improving feedback and learning cycles).

Why Use WIP Cap in a Cost Reduction Project?

The best argument for using WIP Cap is that it is, by far, the fastest and easiest method for improving process speed—and seeing an immediate impact on process cost. It's fast because you just need to crunch a few numbers; it's easy because setting up the method to limit process WIP requires very little investment in resources and you don't have to make any changes to the core process.

Think of calculating WIP Cap as a good *first step* to take at the beginning of any effort to improve service level or lower costs. It is unlikely to be the only step. This reduces the PLT, and also (very importantly) reduces the variation in Process Lead Time, thus allowing the process improvement team to gain insight into what really drives the process. (Variation in PLT is just as "evil" as other forms of variation, to use Jack Welch's term. From a process improvement perspective, variation hides the real root causes of problems, making it more difficult to make improvements. So, reducing variation makes it easier to see the real critical issues and work on the right ones.)

Determining WIP Cap in a Cost Reduction Project

The guiding principle to using WIP Cap to improve Process Lead Time is that Starts = Exits. In other words, nothing enters a process until something else has been completed and leaves, or exits the process.

The method, then, is built around establishing the maximum number of items that can be in the process at any one time—based on the exit rate. By keeping to that amount of WIP, the Process Lead Time can be controlled to the desired level.

Step 1: Determine the Current Process Lead Time   You can do this either directly or via Little's Law, where you need to know the exit rate and amount of work-in-process.

Advertising Example: The web-based retail advertiser introduced at the beginning of this chapter knew that its WIP (the number of unique advertisements currently being worked on at any one time) was approximately 180. It had an exit rate of about 45 ads/month (about 1.5 ads per business day). PLT is therefore:

$$\text{PLT} = 180 \text{ ads} \div 1.5 \text{ ads per day} = 120 \text{ days}$$

Step 2: Determine PCE   Use process data to determine what is value-add time in the process and what is non-value-add. Add together the time required for the value-add steps.

Advertising example: Once the web advertiser had completed a value stream map, it had data that showed value-add time was 15 days. We know from step 1 that PLT was 120 days. So:

$$\text{PCE} = 100 \times 15 \div 120 = 12.5\%$$

Step 3: Identify a Target PCE   You can refer to Table 5.1 for world-class PCE levels—though we suggest you not try to get to those levels at one time! But pick what seems to be a reasonable level between your current PCE and a world-class level.

For example, in the ad process that had a PCE of 12.5 percent, a reasonable target PCE would be 25 or 40 percent.

Step 4: Calculate the Needed PLT to Achieve the Target PCE Level   You can reverse the PCE equation to "solve" for PLT instead of PCE.

$$\text{Standard equation: PCE} = 100 \times \text{Value Add} \div \text{PLT}$$

$$\text{Reformatted equation: PLT} = 100 \times \text{Value Add} \div \text{PCE}$$

Then plug in the target PCE value and the known value-add time to solve for the ideal process lead time.

Web advertiser example: The new target PCE is 30 percent and VA time is still 15 days, so the target PLT is:

$$PLT = (100 \times 15) \div 25 = 60 \text{ days}$$

Step 5: Calculate WIP Cap This is the maximum amount of work-in-process (WIP) that will let you achieve the target PCE. Remember that the guiding principle is that Starts = Exits, so we want to find the amount of WIP that will let us balance the exit rate. We just need to flip the Little's Law equation to solve for WIP rather than lead time.

Web advertising example:

$$PLT = 60 = WIP \div ER$$
$$ER = 1.5$$

so:

$$WIP = PLT \times ER = 60 \times 1.5, \text{ or } 90 \text{ advertisements}$$

Step 6: Gate Work into the Process to Match the WIP Cap In a WIP Cap system, you need to create a method for gating work items—deciding which items to release into the process, in which order, and in what amounts. The process is similar to the triage procedures you may have seen in an emergency room (or on any television hospital drama show). You need to develop guidelines to determine which patients are most critical and how many patients you can handle at any given time.

Tip: Phase In the New WIP Cap Levels and Target PCEs

Typically, it's difficult to make drastic cuts to WIP in one fell swoop, both from a practical standpoint and a cultural one (people won't believe that the process can operate with lower levels of work-in-process). Therefore, we recommend "stepping down" to the targets through several iterations.

For example, in the ad creation process just described, because the staff was used to working on a 4-month (120-day) cycle, the first step took them to 90 days—meaning that instead of using a 120-day deadline for submission of new ads, they reset their schedules for a 90-day deadline. After a few months, they dropped to 75 days. Finally, after another few months, they dropped to 60 days.

(continued)

(continued)

In part, the months it took to implement this decrease was to give the people working the process the confidence to achieve the goal. After six months, they saw no drop-off of the number of ads created, and yet the customers saw their ads on the website in 60 days instead of 120 days. In the eyes of the customer, they saw a 50 percent improvement in the time it took to get their ads on the Internet.

Linking Waste Time to Costs

The web advertising company dropped overall process lead time by 50 percent—improvements achieved solely by eliminating wait times between value-add steps in the process—not by adding staff, limiting clients, or any other kind of change. How did that lead to reduced cost? By:

- Reducing the chance that critical information would be lost and, thus, have to be re-created or retrieved from the advertising customer again.
- Reducing the chance that customers would change their minds and either cancel their ads or require costly rework (reshoot the photo, amend the price or terms, etc.).

The second bullet point is very important: The longer the lead time for an item, the more likely that external events will impact the decision maker. In the case of the ads, by shortening the lead time from 120 days to 60 days, the web company experienced a reduction in the number of cancelled ads, as well as a decrease in the number of changes (price especially) that were caused due to the competitive environment. Also, clients appreciated having a shorter cycle time, because it allows them to better time their ads based on consumer needs.

Summary of Impact of WIP Cap

One attractive feature of installing a WIP Cap is that the system can be quickly achieved. Using the advertisement example, stop for a moment and consider this: How many ads were not implemented originally because the website's process took too long? How many advertisers wanted to wait 4 (or say 120 days if you prefer) months to see their ad in place?

But you might surmise that because the company dropped the number of items it was working on from 180 to 90, it might have suffered a drop in performance. But look again at the descriptions. The company did *not* reduce the number of ads placed on the website. It did *not* change the exit rate. So the firm still creates, on average, 1.5 ads per day. Only now, it just makes the advertisers wait half the time (from 120 days of waiting to 60 days) to see their ads make it to the website. As we mentioned several times before in this book, the key to success is to recognize the various wastes inherent in a process and eliminate them, not to focus on the value-add steps in the process.

Recap of the WIP Cap Process

1. Estimate current PLT, WIP, and ER.
2. Estimate current PCE.
3. Establish target/desired PCE.
4. Back-calculate from target PCE to target PLT.
5. Back-calculate from target PLT to target WIP Cap.
6. Institute a gating system for release of work into the process.

USING PCE AND LITTLE'S LAW TO DRIVE COST REDUCTION

Applying the concept of WIP Cap is one way to drive time and cost reductions in any kind of process. The method basically targets one particular type of waste: waiting time. A more comprehensive approach is to reduce waste in all of its forms, as described in other chapters in this book. For example, think about reducing defects (one form of waste): Do so and Process Lead Time improves because the process will need less time for extra inspections or rework to fix the defective items. As mentioned with the ad process, shortening the lead time meant fewer changes (defects) in the work product. Here, using the WIP Cap method lead to both less wait time and fewer defects.

Regardless of which approach is taken, the calculation of PCE can assist in providing a measure of how much improvement has been achieved.

CHAPTER 6

IMPROVE YOUR ANALYSIS SKILLS

How Understanding Variation, Root Causes, and Factor Relationships Can Help You Cut Costs While Improving Quality

With Jeff Howard, John Smith, and Ken Feldman

A few years back, the transportation department of a modest-sized Midwest city began to wonder if there were ways to save money and gain greater flexibility around expenditures. Once funds from its budget—about $3 million at the time—were committed to a project, those funds were "locked up" and could not be spent other than on the project. The department created a team that studied the contracting process, and their data showed significant differences between the bid price and the actual price of most jobs: While some projects came in right on budget, many were below the bid price (by as much as 23 percent) and others came in way over the bid (by as much as 22 percent).

While the public would not benefit in a direct monetary sense from cost savings in this process, clearly the differences did carry a cost. If projects came in below the bid, funds that could be spent on increasing services were tied up and unavailable; if projects came in over the bid, the city had to scramble to find the extra money.

The team set to work and was able to significantly improve the bid-to-actual costs. As a result of the team's data analysis, the city was able to free up nearly half a million dollars. In the public sector, that translated into additional service for residents. In the private sector, it would have been counted as $500,000 in cost cuts.

Collecting and analyzing data is, of course, the hallmark of Lean Six Sigma and other improvement practices. The topic is very broad, but in this chapter we are going to focus on three ways in which developing stronger analytical skills can drive sustained cost reductions.

ANALYSIS SKILL #1: LEARNING TO "READ" VARIATION

You don't need to collect data to have an intuitive understanding about variation. The time it takes to download a 3-megabyte file can vary by seconds or minutes, depending on how busy your web server is. Some days it takes you longer to commute to work than others. Your golf scores, bridge scores, batting average, will change from one day to the next. One day you get served in a restaurant in 15 minutes; another day, it might take twice as long.

Everything has variation in it. The questions are how much variation there is, what that variation can tell you about the process, and how you can use information about variation to reduce costs. In this section, we'll look at the relationship between variation and cost, then at "capability analysis," just one of several improvement tools that converts data on variation into information you can use to reduce process costs.

The Relationship between Variation, Lead Time, Capacity, and Cost

Variation in a process impacts cycle time (how long your process takes to complete), and both factors affect capacity (how much work your process can handle).

- *Variation:* Think about variation as if you were throwing darts at a dart board, trying to hit the target. The further the dart is from the bull's-eye, the more likely it is to be considered a defect. As you throw the darts, there typically is some difference in the dart pattern on the board: sometimes the hits will cluster together (left side of Figure 6.1) and sometimes they will be far apart (right side of Figure 6.1).
- *Lead time, or cycle time:* Lead time (often called cycle time) is defined as the total time a process takes from start to finish. From a customer's perspective, that would include everything from when the order is

Figure 6.1
Envisioning variation.

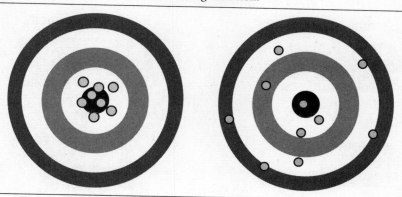

placed until it is delivered. Internally, cycle time would be the time it takes any item of work to make it through any portion of the process from start to finish. Cycle time includes all the process times, rework, delay time, and so on, and is common in every process.

- *Capacity:* Capacity is the maximum output from a process in a given time period. An example would be an order entry process that has a capacity (maximum output) of 120 processed orders per day.

Variation, cycle time, and capacity affect each other, and in turn affect costs. For example:

- A process with less variation will have fewer defects (which means lower costs because you will have less rework) and will be more predictable (which leads to lower costs because scheduling, inventory, delivery times, and so on, are more reliable).
- Think about trying to operate a process where the inputs varied like the right side of Figure 6.1 (highly unpredictable). That would make your cycle time unpredictable (and longer on average compared to a process with less variation), which in turn would frustrate both the people working on the process and customers. Unpredictable processes are costly processes: manufacturers may need to keep extra inventory on hand to make sure they can make the customer delivery dates; service provides may need to work overtime (or pay for idle capacity).

As we reduce variation we are better able to predict cycle times. For example, if the customer delivery expectation is five days, but the process

Figure 6.2
Impact of reduced lead time and increased capacity.

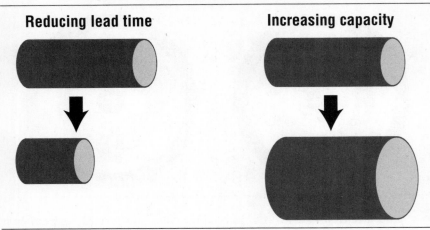

has high variability (plus/minus four days), then presenting an exact delivery date is difficult. If the process variation is low (plus/minus 0.5 days), then customer deliveries are consistent. As you reduce the cycle time and eliminate the steps that cause the longest delays, you are increasing the capacity (maximum output of the process). Furthermore, with more capacity you could reduce such costs as overtime, thereby reducing overall costs and increasing profit. Many cost reduction products, therefore, will be stated in terms of reducing variation (left side of Figure 6.1), reducing cycle time (left side of Figure 6.2), and/or increasing capacity (right side of Figure 6.2).

To illustrate these key concepts, let's take an order entry process that has a current cycle time of five days, process variation of plus/minus one day, and a capacity of 120 orders per day (completed/processed orders). The goal is to meet customer demand. If the customer is asking for an order within three days, then the cycle time has to be reduced by taking out most of the waste in a process (transportation, inventory, motion, waiting, over-processing, overproduction, and defects). After you reduce the cycle time to three days, you still have a customer issue due to the process variation. The order can still be late by one day (three days plus one day of variation). The variation is analyzed using control charts, process capability, and other tools to determine the root cause. Also, the customer is asking for 150 orders per day. This, of course, is a capacity issue, which will have to be addressed separately. All of these process issues are typically dedicated projects that require the DMAIC methodology to resolve.

Figure 6.3
High variation centered on target cycle time.

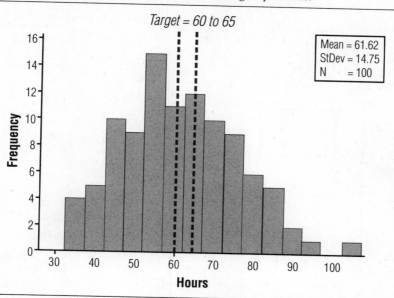

To understand the impact of variation and cycle time, consider Figure 6.3, which shows a process that has acceptable performance—*if you focus only on the average.* The average cycle time is on target (60 to 65 hours), but when you look at the spread, you can see that actual cycle times vary from just over 30 hours to about 105 hours—a 75-hour difference.

Improvement experts who look at charts like the one in Figure 6.3 interpret this pattern—with a lot of data very far off the average—as a process that costs too much to deliver what customers want. For example, suppose the cycle time was measuring time to deliver a customer order. Orders that go over the target of 65 hours probably involve expedited shipping costs. Or if orders are ready too soon, the company might need to take up storage space so as to not interfere with the customer's systems by delivering early.

Now contrast the "on target but too much variation" pattern to that shown in Figure 6.4. Here, there is very little variation or spread in the data (just over 2 hours) but the cycle time is nearly 100 hours beyond the target (which is still 60 to 65 hours).

Whether this is a customer delivery process as we imagined here or any process inside your organization, a pattern like this means, minimally, that you have a lot of very unhappy customers—and, quite possibly, you'll be

Figure 6.4
Low variation, but not centered on target.

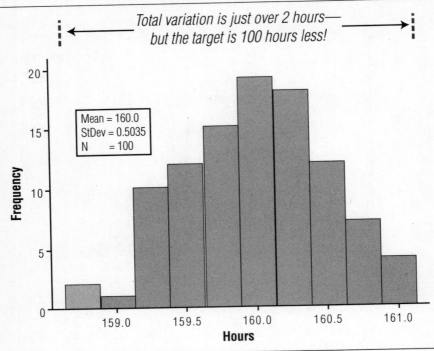

Total variation is just over 2 hours—
but the target is 100 hours less!

Mean = 160.0
StDev = 0.5035
N = 100

spending money on extra shifts or expediting the work to make sure you don't go even further past the target.

In summary, there is a correlation between long cycle times, high variation, and insufficient capacity to operating costs and lost revenue.

- If the process has a long cycle time, the product is experiencing more handling, processing, and labor than necessary. Also, the customer lead time expectation may or may not be met.
- If the process is impacted by high variation, the costs are not predictable.
- If there is insufficient capacity, the customer demand is not being fulfilled and driving lost revenue.

Using Data on Variation to Evaluate Process Capability

Process capability analysis is a tool that tells you whether your process is "capable" of meeting the targets or specifications determined by the

Variation and Lead Time Case Study

Though variation is often thought of in terms of manufacturing processes where there are easily measured product characteristics, variation impacts cost and time in all kinds of processes. For example, a company that produced parts used in ATMs had a lot of variation in its order processing system. Data showed it could take anywhere from 1 to 10 days to place, process, and ship orders. (Customers who got the longer delivery times were very unhappy.) A Lean Six Sigma team tracked down the source of the variation, discovering that:

1. There was not a streamlined processing path for the customer orders. There were a lot of handoffs in the process (>30), each of which varied in duration and which, cumulatively, caused most of the variation in delivery times. Many orders would get stuck along the way due to lack of training/skills or sense of urgency or just poor tools to get the job done. An order could be sitting on someone's desk for days without anyone taking notice.
2. The organizational structure was causing delays. There were many approvals (signatures) that were required due to financial considerations. The majority of the approvals were non-value-add. Some people would sign the order immediately and others would take days, for no apparent reason—contributing to delays and increasing the variation in delivery times.

By tackling these causes head-on, the team reduced the variation in delivery times substantially. The order entry and shipping processes were redesigned to eliminate all the excessive handoffs (down from more than 30 to just 5) and the TIMWOOD wastes (see Chapter 2). As a result, virtually all orders go out within one day. The process is faster and more predictable, customers are happier, and it costs less to process their orders.

customer. That determination is made by comparing the variation in data collected on the process characteristics to the specification limits.

For example, suppose your company makes specialty products for the medical field. In talking to customers, you've determined that the ideal cycle time is 50 days, but they will be satisfied if you deliver the materials within 3 days of that target (so your target range is 47 to 53 days). That quantification of customer needs determines the upper and lower bounds of

Figure 6.5

A "capable" process: Data from this process shows the typical bell-curve shape. All but the extreme "tails" of the distribution of data fall between the specification limits, so the process is considered "capable."

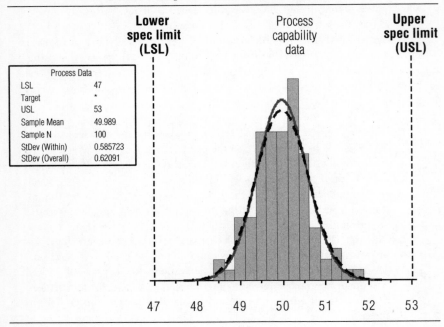

Process Data	
LSL	47
Target	*
USL	53
Sample Mean	49.989
Sample N	100
StDev (Within)	0.585723
StDev (Overall)	0.62091

"acceptable performance," what is commonly labeled as "specification limits" (or "spec limits").

If you collected data on actual delivery times and the results look like those shown in Figure 6.5, then your process is capable because all but a tiny fraction of materials are delivered within the specification limits.

However, if your data looked more like those depicted in Figure 6.6—where only part of the distribution falls inside the specification limits—you may be in trouble. This process would be considered "not capable."

Why Use Process Capability Calculations in a Cost Reduction Project?   If you are producing more quality than your customer expects, or are producing less quality than they need, you are likely wasting money. A process that is not capable of meeting customer expectations and specs will often require costly inspection, separation, culling, and rework to provide customers what they want. On the other hand, if you are spending money to greatly

Figure 6.6
A "not capable" process: In this chart, much of the process data falls outside
the specification limits, so the process (as represented by the distribution of data)
is not capable of delivering what customers want (as represented by the
specification limits).

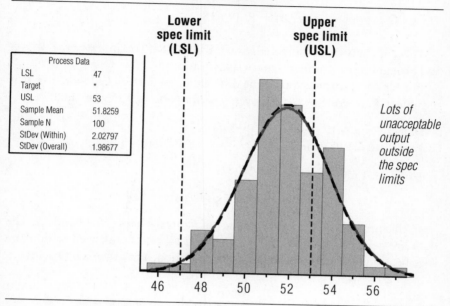

Process Data	
LSL	47
Target	*
USL	53
Sample Mean	51.8259
Sample N	100
StDev (Within)	2.02797
StDev (Overall)	1.98677

Lower spec limit (LSL)

Upper spec limit (USL)

Lots of unacceptable output outside the spec limits

exceed your customers' expectations, then you may also be needlessly incurring costs that can be reduced.

A process capability analysis can therefore help determine whether your process is costing too much because of over- or underdelivery. A too-capable process would be one in which the process distribution is small with respect to the specification limits. In other words, there is plenty of room for the distribution to move from side to side and still be capable. The impact of a too-capable process is the amount of time and money spent on improving the process when the customer requirements have been satisfied.

You can also use process capability data to determine the **Cost of Poor Quality** (COPQ). Consider, for example, a manufacturing process where defects are measured in parts per million (ppm). Process data (using procedures we'll talk about later) show that the "expected overall performance" is 1698.09 ppm—meaning the company expects that nearly 1700 out of all 1 million parts will have a defect.

Defectives = 1698.09 ppm
Part Cost = $200/part

Based on 1 million parts:

COPQ = ppm × Cost/Part = $339,618

This company could potentially save $339,618 if it eliminated the defects and brought more products within specifications.

Just for comparison, suppose the distribution of data looked more like that in Figure 6.7, where the expected overall performance is 0.17 ppm. In this case:

Defectives = 0.17 ppm
Part Cost = $200/part

Based on 1 million parts:

$$COPQ = ppm \times Cost/part = \$34$$

In this process, the acceptable range of figures is between 45 and 55. The data are centered around the average, and all points fall well within the specification boundaries because of low variation. Thus the COPQ is low.

Figure 6.7
Low variation around target equals low cost of poor quality.

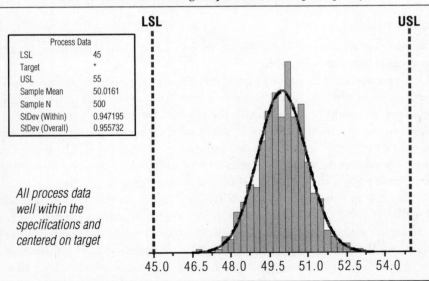

Process capability can be:

- Performed on new equipment as part of the qualification and approval process. The cost reduction is making sure the new equipment does not produce defective parts.
- Carried out on existing processes as a means of establishing a baseline of current operations (so it's possible to tell when improvement has occurred). This is critical in improvement projects like cost reduction. Did the project achieve the results?
- Done periodically as a means of monitoring wear and tear on equipment, and deterioration of a process for whatever reason (material, personnel, environment, and so on).
- Conducted on any process that has specifications established, and has a capable measuring system (needed for valid data).

ANALYSIS SKILL #2: DIGGING OUT ROOT CAUSES

Knowing the true root cause is different from "feeling" you know. There are a number of simple tools that allow you to identify the potential root causes of variation in your process, and thereby provide you information as to where you can reduce costs. An array of sophisticated statistical tools also exists that allow you to ferret out the sources of variation in your process. These analytical tools point to your sources of variation and needless cost.

One goal of any process improvement initiative is to determine what is really impacting the process or output of the process. A number of nonstatistical tools are available for root cause analysis. The most common ones, described in Table 6.1, are brainstorming, cause-and-effect matrix, cause-and-effect diagram, Pareto chart, and process constraint identification.

The power of these tools—and, in fact, the full Lean Six Sigma toolkit—has been well documented in many places. If you have not seen them in use, however, here is a quick example that will show the role each of the tools plays in helping companies uncover root causes of problems that are adding time, cost, and waste:

Each week, around 55,000 invoices at a utility company were stopped and held back due to a number of issues, termed "exceptions," that arose because either the customer accounts failed predefined rules built into the billing system or there were user errors in processing. A team used the full Lean Six Sigma toolset to fix the problem. They identified 142 types of exceptions, and then used Pareto charts to identify the most frequent and most costly. This

Table 6.1
Example Tools Used in Root-Cause Analysis

Tool Name	Description	Use in Root-Cause Analysis
Brainstorming	Team members are guided in generating numerous ideas.	Root causes often lie hidden, so it helps to widen your net very broadly at first. That's what brainstorming does: it gives you a large pool of *potential* causes to investigate.
Cause-and-effect matrix		Correlates process steps to process outputs, which are based on customer requirements and ranked by importance. Understanding how the steps relate to outputs enables you to prioritize.
Cause-and-effect diagram		A structured way to represent the relationship between an effect (problem) and potential causes. In a cost reduction project, for example, the "head" of the fish (the problem) could be stated either in terms of excess cost (or an outcome like "delays" that you know contributes to costs). The "bones" would help you logically sort through factors that contribute to that problem.
Pareto chart		Because it sorts data by frequency or impact, a Pareto chart is one of the simplest tools to use to focus on which factors are contributing the most to costs. It helps you identify which of your problems are most significant, so you can focus improvement efforts on areas where the largest gains can be made.
Control charts		Patterns of variation and/or the appearance of data points beyond the expected range of variation (as defined by the so-called control limits) are giant red flags that something is wrong in a process. Investigating what happens when the patterns or outside points appear will help you eliminate causes that are increasing variation and, thus, costs.

helped them isolate the top six types of errors. The team sorted out root causes and investigated the rules behind these six specific billing exceptions. Subsequent changes to the process helped them reduce the volume of these top six errors by 30 percent. Based on the company's standard accounting practices, the savings amounted to about $1.5 million per year. The results extended beyond the fact that invoices that were on hold could now be collected. Fewer exceptions also meant less labor involved to resolve exceptions, and a dramatic reduction in phone call inquiries from customers complaining about not receiving their bills.

ANALYSIS SKILL #3: ESTABLISHING RELATIONSHIPS BETWEEN FACTORS

Much of the Lean Six Sigma toolbox allows you to study only one process factor, product/service characteristic, or output measure at a time. There are a few tools, however, that let you explore relationships between process inputs (factors) and a key output.

Perhaps the most common of these tools is called *regression analysis*, where you plot data points that are determined by two measurements: one on a potential cause and the other on the outcome of interest. But an even more powerful "relationship" tool in the Lean Six Sigma toolkit is called *Design of Experiments* (DOE). With this tool, you can investigate the interactions between *multiple* factors *at the same time*. In fact, you can quantify the degree to which changes in one factor will affect another factor. This is an extremely powerful capability when your goal is to minimize costs, because it allows you to:

- Establish whether changes in one factor may drive up the cost of some other factor.
- Determine the most optimal *combination* of factors—such as the least-costly process configuration that delivers the required level of quality.
- Identify factors that *do not* affect the output, and therefore can be "set" at the least expensive settings.

Arguably, DOE may be one of the most powerful and underutilized tools in our cost reduction and process improvement arsenal. While often feared and perceived as too advanced or complicated to apply in many situations, the opposite can be true most of the time. Let's look at some basics about DOE.

What Is Design of Experiments?

Designed experimentation is the manipulation of controllable factors (independent variables; aka, Xs) at different settings/levels to see their effect on some response (dependent variable; aka Ys). By comparison, linear regression uses historical data to establish a relationship and correlation between independent and dependent variables. Regression establishes correlation but not causation. DOE will establish causation by the controlled application of the factors and the observation of the change in response.

Benefits from using DOE include:

- *Determining how multiple input variables interact to affect results:* There are very few things in life that *aren't* affected by everything else going on around it. For example, the efficacy of your medications will depend on factors such as what other medications you are on and your overall health. The height of a baked cake will depend on the temperature of the oven, the proportion of ingredients used, and atmospheric pressure. DOE is one of the few statistical tools that allows you to mimic real life by looking at multiple factors at the same time.
- *Focusing more quickly on factors that matter:* Traditional experimentation can be characterized as "hunt and peck." Because you are testing multiple factors at once, DOE lets you screen out unimportant factors very quickly.
- *You will* always *learn something!* A designed experiment produces a mathematical model that captures the relationship between the input variables and responses. That means you will always be able to draw a conclusion (though sometimes it may be that none of the factors you're investigating is the cause of excess cost—in which case, you can stop wasting time on those factors and go back to the drawing board to find other factors to explore).
- *Finding optimal combinations of factor settings:* Trial-and-error experimentation may result in a fruitless search for the best combination and the optimal levels of factors. (For example, what combination of temperature settings, pH, and curing time delivers the best product? What combination of sales scripts, incentives, and payment plans results in the highest sales?) The statistics behind DOE allows for an efficient method to quickly narrow in on the significant factors and the best settings for them to optimize your desired outcomes. You will know when you are done searching.

- *Gaining high level of confidence in the results:* DOE is a statistical method—it relies on actual data from your actual process—and will let you determine the "significance" (in a statistical sense) of the results, which can give you a high degree of confidence in your conclusions.

When designing your experiment, you may want not only to seek to understand the effects of the inputs (Xs) on the average result (Y) but also on the *range* of values of Y (its variation). As we have stated a number of times, reducing variation is a key element in understanding your process and reducing costs. DOE is a way of actually showing how to reduce variation by altering the settings of the Xs.

How DOE Works: A Sales Process Case Study

To illustrate how DOE works, let's look at an example for controlling costs—while maximizing customer satisfaction—in a sales process. Figure 6.8 captures the key inputs and outputs the company wanted to investigate.

Figure 6.8
Inputs (factors) and outputs (responses).

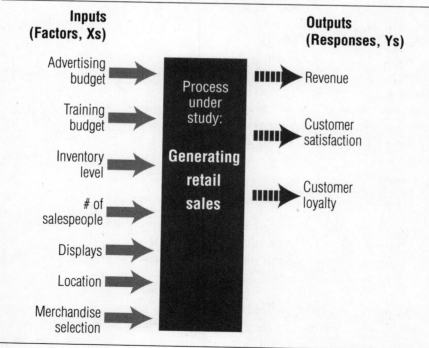

Note that there are a number of Xs and a few Ys. The questions we seek to answer are: Which of the Xs impact the Y? and What is the optimal setting for them?

In most designed experiments, you "set" the factors at two levels. In this case, the company decided that the initial settings for the input variables were as follows:

Advertising budget: $100,000 and $300,000
Training budget: $200/person and $400/person
Inventory level: $500,000 and $1,500,000
Number of salespeople: 50 and 100
Displays: 20 and 50
Location: 5 and 15
Merchandise selection: 250 SKUs and 500 SKUs

Given the number of variables and our budget, the company decided to run what is known as a "fractional factorial design"—this is a DOE method that lets you test a particular subset of the many possible combinations of factors. In this scenario, for example, testing *all* combinations of seven factors with two levels would require 2^7 or 132 trials (runs). This company chose to test half of those combinations (a very carefully selected half), resulting in a need to run 64 trials.

We won't go into the details of the analysis of the results from the 64 trials, but we will show you a few key graphics that capture the key lessons. Figure 6.9 shows a small graph for each of the seven factors tested. The only thing you need to know to interpret the chart is that *the steeper the line, the stronger the relationship* between the factor and the outcome (in this case, customer satisfaction). Before reading on, check out the graph and determine which of the factors you think have a big influence on customer satisfaction.

In this case, it appears that:

- Advertising budget, training budget, inventory level, and number of salespeople may have an effect.
- Displays, location, and merchandise selection do *not* seem to affect customer satisfaction.

As part of the DOE analysis, these visual conclusions would be verified with statistical analysis. In fact, here it turns out that the advertising budget is *not* statistically significant. That left the company with the knowledge

Figure 6.9

Sample plots from DOE analysis: The seven minigraphs show each of the seven variables being tested. There are two points for each factor, because we tested them at two levels. The Y, or vertical axis, is the scale we used to measure customer satisfaction. The slope of the lines represents the degree of effect that each factor has on the response (customer satisfaction). The more severe the slope, the stronger the effect of the factor.

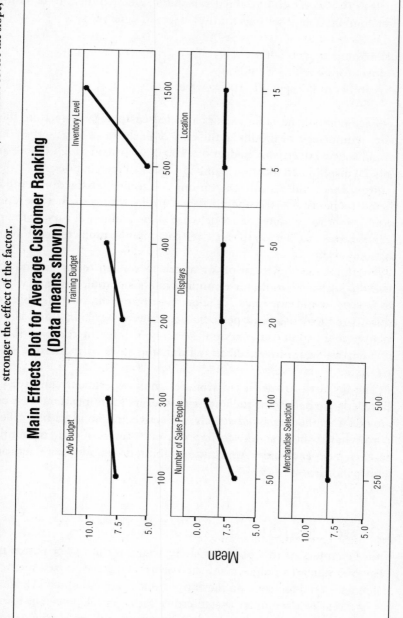

Main Effects Plot for Average Customer Ranking
(Data means shown)

that three factors had the biggest impact on customer satisfaction. Further analysis (we won't go into the details here), enabled them to determine the best combination of settings for these factors, which was:

Training budget: $400
Inventory level: $1.5 million
Number of salespeople: 100 salespeople

Since none of the other factors affected customer satisfaction, the company would seek to minimize the cost of each. In this case, the company would use an advertising budget of $100,000, instead of $300,000, and use only 20 displays, 15 locations, and 250 SKUs of merchandise.

From this combination, the optimal customer satisfaction score is predicted to be 12.59—compared to a current rating of 8. (The company would want to validate the model with some additional runs at the recommended levels to be sure the changes generate the predicted customer satisfaction score.)

The final recommendation of which factors to focus on and at what levels to set them would have resulted in considerable savings, which trial and error would not have revealed. By optimizing our variables we are able to reduce costs and perform at a higher level. In this case, it was relative to customer satisfaction. Possibly a different combination would result if we were interested in maximizing sales or increasing customer loyalty.

The insight provided by a well-designed experiment can give you the knowledge to determine the lowest-cost levers for improvement. It can also provide a method to avoid strictly subjective and nondata-based decisions as to what is the best way to improve performance while preventing unnecessary expenditures. Applications abound in both manufacturing and service industries.

CONCLUSION

Other chapters of this book highlight some of the newer trends in using Lean Six Sigma to reduce cost, such as applying the Kaizen methodology (Chapter 7) and focusing on the entire value chain (Chapter 11). This chapter is given as a reminder that there is still a lot of power in using what might be considered tried-and-true components of Lean Six Sigma to reduce costs.

- Developing the skills to understand variation, for example, will help you make sure you're not overspending by providing value that doesn't make a difference to customers, and by reducing the waste of producing products or services that fall outside target limits.
- The basic analytical tools can help you discover the root causes of problems that are adding time and cost to your processes, products, and services.
- Designed experiments are one of the most effective—and most underused—tools in the Lean Six Sigma kit. They are one of only a few tools that let you investigate the relationships *between* factors, which allows you to determine optimal *combinations* of factors and settings that maximize performance and minimize costs.

Obviously, we hope that you'll find some new ideas for reducing costs by reading through the rest of this book. But as you continue your quest, don't forget the basics. They will serve you well.

CHAPTER 7

MAKE RAPID IMPROVEMENTS THROUGH KAIZENS

With John Smith

When you're working in a high-volume, continuous process environment, like a paper mill, very small percentages of waste can add up to big dollars quickly. When staff at one mill saw that waste on one machine had increased steadily three months in a row, they had to make a change quickly or costs would continue to mount.

Knowing that even the best traditional DMAIC projects can take months to complete, the mill was looking for a different approach that could generate results more quickly. So they turned to the Kaizen (pronounced KYE-zen) project model, where a team works full-time on solving a problem for a concentrated period of time (typically, a full week).

Mill management allocated seven employees to participate in the Kaizen to study and solve the waste problem. There was one limitation given to the team: no capital expenditure. During the week-long event, the team completed all of the DMAIC steps: defining the problem, brainstorming improvement ideas, doing root-cause analysis, identifying quick-hit actions, establishing new operating procedures that would prevent the root causes of waste, and setting up a database metric so they could monitor ongoing performance.

Actions that came out of that week saved the company $2.75 million annually in waste.

Many companies we work with have never heard of the Kaizen project model before. Others associate it with much smaller gains: "We tried a few Kaizens and saved $20,000. It wasn't worth the effort." Whether you are new to the notion of completing a project in one week, or have tried and dismissed Kaizens, we urge you to take a deeper look because they are an incredibly powerful tool for driving big cost reductions, quickly. Most importantly, they drive cost reduction the right way—by cutting waste and improving speed and quality. Those are the kinds of changes that bring immediate gain, set you up for continued performance gains in the future, and allow you to, minimally, maintain service levels to customers, and usually even enhance them.

What kind of gains are we talking about? Typical results we've seen range from tens of thousands of dollars to several million dollars. For example, a sister plant mill to the one just described went through a similar effort and saved $1.25 million. And don't get the wrong idea: gains like these are *not* restricted to manufacturing processes. Kaizens work equally well in service environments. Here are a few quick transactional examples to show the broad application and power of Kaizens:

- A Kaizen team in an IT department of a Fortune 500 company studied an issue with some automation that reset employee security, resulting in unnecessary security changes even though no functional changes occurred. Developing new work standards led to an *estimated annual financial benefit of $200,000*, and reduced nonvalued time (rework and overprocessing) by 60 percent.
- Agents at a national insurance company wanted increased underwriting flexibility and improved responsiveness. A Kaizen team looked at the underwriting process and made changes that reduced the underwriting lead time by 78 percent (from 56 hours to about 12.5 hours). *The estimated annual financial benefit was over $830,000.*
- The billing process at one company was very cumbersome. Through changes identified in a Kaizen, the company improved productivity—and therefore increased capacity. The firm estimated annual financial benefit of *approximately $300,000 per year*, achieved via headcount reduction in the billing area (management will not have to fill open positions because current staff can now handle the full workload).
- A bank realized that the process of "exceptions" in its retail lockbox functions (used to handle big deposits) represented 28.5 percent of the total monthly hours in that work group but generated only 15 percent of the volume. The Kaizen team identified changes that led to an annualized savings of $124,000 Type 1 benefits and estimated annualized savings of nearly $42,000 Type 2 benefits—plus eliminated the unnecessary printing of 14,560 pages of reports! (See definitions of benefit types in Chapter 12.)

As you can see, the Kaizen project model changes how quickly you can make gains, which are not only substantial but sustainable. A Kaizen event is all about *rapid improvement*: how to impact cost reduction and get sustainable results. Kaizens have a number of other desirable attributes as well:

- There is a standard structure that simplifies planning.
- The typical improvement tools used are not overly sophisticated.
- The model can be used in any environment (manufacturing or service; plant floor to back offices to store front).
- Kaizens foster collaboration, which gives employees a sense of ownership over the results and pride in their accomplishments.

In this chapter, we'll discuss how Kaizens work and when they should and should not be used, describe the Kaizen process, and give you some tips on making your Kaizens successful.

QUICK OVERVIEW: THE KAIZEN APPROACH

As demonstrated in the opening case study, a Kaizen (aka, "rapid DMAIC") differs from traditional Lean Six Sigma projects in that the team comes together for intensive project work, usually lasting all or most of a week. There is also a requirement for preplanning before the event, and follow-up to implement the actions and control plans the team establishes. Still, that puts the overall timeline for a Kaizen project at four to seven weeks, as shown in Table 7.1.

There are three key types of participants in a Kaizen:

- *Project sponsor:* The manager who has authority over the work area where the event will take place. He or she helps write the project charter, interfaces with the management team, approves the budget, and has the final word on potential issues and decisions.
- *Event facilitator:* The facilitator is responsible for the preparation and final results of the event, and manages the agenda during the event.
- *Team members:* Typically, these include people who work with the process every day, plus "outside" experts (meaning people from another work area or someone with a particular technical expertise). Collectively, the team members should have the process knowledge and ability (with facilitation) to improve the process.

Table 7.1
Typical Kaizen Timeline

Duration	Preevent Planning 1–2 Weeks	Kaizen Event 1 Week	Event Follow-Up 3–4 Weeks
Description	Complete Define phase: 1. Develop and refine project charter. 2. Identify participants. 3. Define roles and responsibilities. 4. Develop process map (if possible). 5. Collect and chart data.	Complete Measure, Analyze, and Improve phases; develop control plans: 1. Refine or develop process map. 2. Gather and analyze data. 3. Brainstorm and select solutions. 4. Perform pilot tests. 5. Develop/revise process documentation that describes new standards. 6. Develop plans to sustain the change.	Complete implementation and control: 1. Implement final changes. 2. Make final changes to documentation and training. 3. Hand off control to process owner(s). 4. Validate results at a future date.

WHEN SHOULD YOU USE KAIZENS IN COST REDUCTION PROJECTS?

The short answer is that because of its ability to generate results quickly, the Kaizen model should be the first option you consider when you want to make immediate cost reductions the right way (by solving problems, not by arbitrarily making cuts that could potentially harm your customers). That said, the Kaizen model is not appropriate for all situations.

One common method we advocate for using identifying projects is by generating a lot of ideas, completing some initial scoping work on the best candidates, then creating a benefit/effort matrix that rates each project based on the amount of effort it will take to complete and the anticipated benefit from that effort. (Instructions for this method are in Chapter 12.) If the benefits are stated in terms of cost savings, the benefit/effort matrix becomes an ideal tool for selecting good candidates for Kaizen cost-cutting

Figure 7.1
Benefit/Effort Matrix

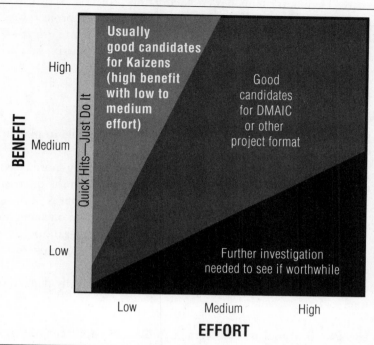

projects. Once the project ideas are rated, they are plotted on a matrix like that shown in Figure 7.1.

Having gone through this selection process hundreds of time and seeing what works and what doesn't, we know that:

- The *medium-* to *low-effort/high-impact* area makes ideal Kaizen cost reduction projects.
- The *low-effort/low-impact* area is reserved for "quick hits" (just do it).
- Projects that fall into the middle ground—medium effort/medium to high impact, is for more complex projects, possibly requiring longer time frames to solve (typically, four to six months).
- Many times the *high-effort/low-impact* projects are eliminated because you have to work hard for minimal payback. They should be included, however, if they are needed to lay the groundwork for higher-benefit projects in the future.

Companies generally want cost reduction projects to generate results right away. They don't launch a cost reduction project so they can see results a year or more from now. Therefore cost reduction projects are often narrowly scoped to begin with, requiring low to moderate effort—which places them toward the upper left on the benefit/effort matrix, precisely the prime target for Kaizens.

Comparing Kaizens to Traditional Projects

Both Kaizens and the traditional project model have a role to play in your Lean Six Sigma toolkit. In Table 7.2 we compare the uses.

As noted in the table, the majority of Kaizen events rely more heavily on Lean tools than on Six Sigma tools. Why? The clue lies in the discussion of value-add versus non-value-add work described in Chapter 5. As you may recall, in most processes, the vast majority of time is spent on some form of waste (the TIMWOOD wastes described in Chapter 2). Lean tools are specifically designed to *remove waste* from a process, whereas many Six Sigma tools are targeted at *problem solving*.

That said, the choice of tools and methods will naturally depend on the situation:

- The statistical tools of Six Sigma can play an important role during a Kaizen *if you have the available data.* For example, one of our clients used a Kaizen to improve process stability on a high-volume machine. The effort required the use of various control charts and graphical tools like box plots and histograms. One of the best tools used on the Kaizen was process capability analysis (discussed in Chapter 6). This tool quickly compared the process variation to the customer specification limits. The graphic tools and capability analysis let the team better understand the issues and develop solutions, all within the confines of the one-week event.
- Many times the Kaizen is limited to the subject matter expert knowledge because there is not much data available, and gathering data would take too much time and could be rather costly. When that's the case, the Kaizen should focus on using the typical Lean tools. A Kaizen that was performed on reducing the response time to production issues used a value stream map, brainstorming, fishbone analysis, and idea prioritization to solve the problem. The Kaizen was very successful without all the statistical tools and only limited data available.

Table 7.2
Comparing Kaizen to Traditional Lean Six Sigma Projects

	Traditional Project Model	Kaizen Project Model	Comments
How quickly results are needed	2–6 months	1–2 months	Rapid gains are possible because of the narrow project scope and intense cycling through DMAIC.
Goal	Major improvement	Incremental improvements	
Scope	Variable	Must be narrowly scoped	
Type of problem	Challenging, intractable problem that has resisted prior attempts to solve it (meaning it will likely need extensive root-cause analysis)	Clearly defined; focus is likely removing waste; also good for safety issues	Because of the compressed time frame, the Kaizen model is best used on problems you define very clearly.
Toolset	Emphasis on Six Sigma	Emphasis on Lean	Both toolsets are typically used in both kinds of projects, but Kaizens typically emphasize quick hits via using Lean tools for waste reduction.
Data issues	Useful for all types of data	Ideally, the process cycles rapidly so outcome data can be collected quickly when new solutions are being tested.	To have tested solutions at the end of a Kaizen, you have to be able to collect data rapidly. If you have a process that cycles slowly (meaning data about process changes won't be known for days or weeks), you will have to adjust the Kaizen plan around confirming the effectiveness of solutions during the follow-up phase.
Project pace	Project lead may be full-time (if a Black Belt); team generally meets once or twice a week over a period of months.	Project lead and all team members must be available full-time during the week-long event.	

SEVEN KEYS TO KAIZEN SUCCESS

Kaizens are not just a powerful tool for driving rapid improvement. Collectively, many successful Kaizens can have a dramatic impact on overall morale and attitudes toward improvement. To get both types of results, pay close attention to seven key ingredients of a successful Kaizen:

1. Sponsor involvement
2. A good facilitator
3. Workplace preparation
4. Appropriate scoping/targets
5. Development of new work standards
6. Emphasis on visual tools/management
7. Celebrating and publicizing accomplishments

Sponsor Involvement

Kaizens are most effective when the sponsor is highly involved in all aspects of the event. This is critical in some cultures, especially those where there is stiff resistance to change; such environments will require a high degree of barrier resolution along the way. A Kaizen recently performed in a production area was faced with a strong resistance to change, but because the sponsor was totally engaged, the event was not only successful, but started to change the culture. The sponsor paved the way for the team.

Having a highly involved sponsor is critical if you want to generate results that are important to the business, and complete the project on time and on budget. That's why the Kaizen model specifies a number of points of contact with the team and sponsor:

- The Kaizen facilitator should discuss any changes to the charter with the sponsor prior to the kickoff.
- The week starts with a meeting between the facilitator and sponsor to review the plans for the week.
- The sponsor kicks off the event by welcoming the team, reviewing the charter, and explaining the goals of the project and the importance of the improvements. The team needs to understand the power of a dedicated, high-performance team to solve problems and make changes that in the past have been difficult to do and maintain.
- The facilitator provides daily team updates to the sponsor to report on the progress made and remove roadblocks for change. This accelerated interaction with management to discuss and decide on concrete

changes based on observations and data is the basis for the success of the Kaizen project.

- There is sometimes a midweek review between the sponsor and the entire team as a directional check.
- The sponsor is the primary audience for the final presentation.

A Good Facilitator

Effective Kaizens happen only when there is a good facilitator—someone who understands the possibilities and limitations of the methods, who can encourage good brainstorming, and who will keep the team focused. The facilitator should be good at managing team members (people skills), able to assign roles and responsibilities and deal with the issues, and know the appropriate set of tools for the event.

You may find it curious that we have *not* said the facilitator needs to understand the process being studied during the Kaizen. That is true. The expertise needed to improve the process will come from the team members. Certainly, it's fine if the facilitator knows the work area, but the more important requirement is that he or she can get the most from the team members during the week.

Workplace Preparation

You also need to identify what you will need to do to prepare the team to be out in the workplace—especially, if they do not normally work in the area.

- Confirm any safety procedures that will need to be followed. Will team members need training on those procedures?
- When working in a production environment, let the production schedulers know in advance if any machine downtime will be required during the Kaizen event week—for example, to test a new setup reduction process or relocate a machine as part of a 5S or process flow improvement event. This will allow schedulers to either build up necessary inventory ahead of time or find alternate machines that can be utilized during the event.
- Coordinate with equipment maintenance to ensure that required machines will be available to the event team, and are not scheduled for maintenance during the Kaizen event. Also, if any equipment moves are expected, this will give them a head's-up. (Meet at the machine(s) to make sure the team understands all utilities involved.)

- Whether in a service or manufacturing environment, be sure to connect with the process owner, work area supervisor, or manager if that person is not the project sponsor. Clarify the kinds of disruptions that are allowable.
- If a union is present, meet with the union steward to discuss the event and any potential issues/barriers. One issue that may arise concerns salary versus hourly job roles and responsibilities. Get approval from the union if salaried employees will be performing any work that is typically done by hourly employees—for example during a 5S event.

Appropriate Scoping/Targets

Another major consideration is how to properly define the project. Too broad a scope and the team will find it impossible to complete the work within a week. Too narrow and you risk investing a lot of time and effort for very little payback. To avoid these problems:

- Discuss the project scope with your sponsor. Clarify what issues, work areas, solutions, and so on, can be included in the project and what is beyond the scope. You want to know what topics the team should and, equally importantly, should *not* work on.
- If you envision a series of projects, each building on the others, use multigeneration project planning so you can keep the scope of this one project narrow, even though there are more ambitious goals overall.
- Seek advice from the Kaizen facilitator, Lean Master, or Master Black Belt. Since there are no cut-and-dried rules that novices can apply ahead of time to know whether they are under- or overscoping, experience is often the best resource.

As part of scoping the project, you should identify two to three (at most) key metrics to measure the impact of the event, and specify for each the level of improvement you want to see by the end of the week (for example, a certain level of cost reduction or time savings).

For certain types of improvements, it may be difficult to calculate targets. A good example of this is a setup reduction event where setting a target of accomplishing a changeover in a "single minute" (as in "Single Minute Exchange of Die") is not a realistic target. In such cases, remember that it is likely that the process is 90 percent (or more) waste. Be ambitious and set a target to cut that waste by at least a quarter, or even a half.

Development of New Work Standards

The basis of change in a Kaizen project is the adoption of the new standard work developed by the team through trials and experimentation, and sustained using visual controls to quickly detect any deviations from the improved process.

In service organizations with long cycle times and many people working separately in isolation, it is common to find that a standard is not in place and that deviations are the norm (and frequently accepted and rewarded). Change is very difficult under those conditions (since there are too many accepted ways to do the work). When teams find these conditions, creating a standard is the initial step prior to making any improvements.

Getting people to agree on what is important and how the work is done is a significant step in a Kaizen project. Value stream mapping (VSM) and other graphical tools are used to find a common ground between separate groups.

Once the standard is defined, time should be given to test and train people on the use of the standard: the steps, the sequence of steps, the tools used to do the work, and the time to perform each step.

Using the standard as the baseline process, value-add analysis can be done on a VSM to eliminate waste and variation in the process, and to document and pilot the improved standard work.

Emphasis on Visual Tools/Visual Management

In Chapter 4, we emphasized the importance of making workflow visible because it helps people truly grasp how work gets done and where and why problems appear. Kaizens, too, deliberately have a very strong visual component, which we strongly urge you to adopt:

- Prominently post the value stream map your team creates in the meeting room.
- Take before-and-after photos of the workspace.
- Use the visual tricks and controls embedded in methods like 5S.
- When documenting new standards and control plans, incorporate visual elements as much as possible.
- Display results from the event via Production, Takt, or 5S boards, or other data charts. (Often, follow-up meetings will take place around these boards.)

Consider ordering several whiteboards prior to the event; they are a very effective communication tool, and it seems like there are never enough to satisfy the team.

Celebrating and Publicizing Accomplishments

Successful Kaizen events play an important role in changing the culture of an organization. Participants experience the power of Lean Six Sigma tools firsthand. Their success and confidence often spills over to coworkers.

Celebrating the event with the team and publicizing their results to the broader organization are actions that help drive this cultural change. Invite the event sponsor and other VIPs to attend a team celebration after the final report-out. If time and budget allow, hold a celebratory meal off-site, though bringing in lunch/dinner is more common. Along with awarding team member certificates, this is a way of expressing to the team the importance of the event.

After the event, post the results in a prominent place, and publish a brief summary in a newsletter or on an internal website.

Tips on Running a Successful Kaizen Event

Visiting the "Gemba" in Manufacturing versus Service Environments

The Kaizen model is very adaptable and can be used in any environment. The main difference between conducting a Kaizen in a manufacturing versus a service environment is whether the team can visit an actual workplace (called the "gemba" in Lean). Clearly, manufacturing and service projects will have different kinds of gembas:

- **Manufacturing gemba:** A manufacturing Kaizen project has a clearly defined gemba, be it a single workstation, a manufacturing line, or a value stream including one or more manufacturing operations. The people, parts, equipment and information are easy to see simply by going to the gemba. The Kaizen team will spend most of the time understanding the problems by looking at the parts, people, equipment, and information. Mapping the value stream is straightforward: simply walk the parts, starting from the last step and moving upstream to the beginning of the process.
- **Service gemba:** The gemba for service projects may involve people working in different locations with information exchanged over computer networks, in documents, on conference calls and many other ways. The information flows tend to involve delays and duplicate messages. Think of your inbox for e-mails or your outbox tray on your desk. If visiting the actual workplace or gemba is impossible, you will have to go the extra step to make the work visible to the team. Develop swim-lane

---

flowcharts to map parallel and conditional information flows. Bring in samples of forms (either in hard copy or electronic versions) used during the process and attach them to flowcharts. Attach tracking forms to a work order and have staff enter relevant process data when the form hits their desks (state of the order upon receipt, problems they noticed, time it arrived, and so on).

CONCLUSION

Change happens very slowly in many organizations, where people remember the last time that change was attempted, and either ignore the new solutions or simply stand on the sideline waiting for the next priority to attract management's attention.

Kaizen is best implemented in small scale, within the scope of the project, using visual controls to make it clear to all involved what the change is about and what the results of the change are expected to be, with high priority and urgency clearly communicated by the sponsor of the project, and with a clear understanding of why the change is needed at this time. Changes that have been demonstrated to improve performance during pilot runs should be nonnegotiable—that is they are not optional and should be accepted by all the people involved.

The Kaizen format of one intense week of discovery and experimentation works well to support quick change that has high visibility, is understood by all stakeholders, and is supported by management. The support is made evident from the beginning by clearly explaining the need and the benefits of the desired changes, measuring with visible data the results of the change, training people on the new standard of work, and celebrating the results of the change. When people see how the changes benefit their work and how the results are measured and rewarded, the culture of change starts to take place. In some organizations, change is done using external resources or during overtime at premium rates. The team needs to understand that changes are expected during the work hours of the team, and the sponsor needs to provide the resources and priority to make it happen.

PART II
RAISING THE STAKES
Reducing Costs at an Enterprise Level

CHAPTER 8

THINK TRANSFORMATION, NOT JUST IMPROVEMENT

With Larry Oglesby and Damian Morgan

You may recall the story from Chapter 1 about the hose-couplings company that achieved transformative levels of performance only when it improved process speed to the point at which it could offer breakthrough levels of service to its customers. Changes of that magnitude don't come about because of one successful improvement project, or even two or three dozen. It takes concerted effort across the enterprise, coordinated around strategic priorities. Here's another example of what goes into transformative change:

> Several years ago, a consumer goods company found itself in a fierce battle to reduce costs. Across this particular industry, companies were rapidly moving facilities overseas to Mexico and China to reduce labor costs, in a desperate attempt to hang onto margins in a declining price environment. Most of the company's competitors were merely trading on labor price arbitrage, while this company was determined to transform its competitive position. Today, the company is the undisputed leader in its field and continues to quickly put distance between itself and the competition (Figure 8.1). In the end, the changes it made reduced labor by approximately 50 percent, reduced inventory by over 60 percent, and increased on time delivery by over 20 percent.

For this company, the "concerted effort" focused on three areas: (1) clarifying the vision and direction for the organization, (2) removing complexity in its manufacturing processes, and (3) innovating both products and processes. This company has transformed itself, leaving behind a slow-moving,

Figure 8.1
Transformation impact.

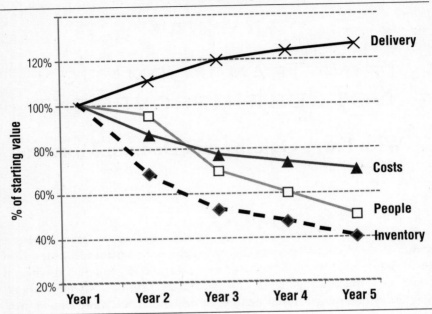

cost-burdened past to create a faster, more efficient, and more competitive future.

Another company, this one in the pharmaceuticals industry, went through a similar magnitude of change. Typically, manufacturing costs are considered to be a small part of pharmaceutical cost structures, and, therefore, that area is largely ignored. This company decided to look into its manufacturing operations and discovered an area rife with potential:

- It had a history of focusing on quality and safety, but not on productivity or costs.
- Capacity was dramatically less than potential due to issues such as scheduling decisions, maintenance, and long setup and cleaning times.
- Inventory was largely considered a cost of doing business instead of an item to be aggressively managed.
- Low-volume drugs added to complexity, and few were profitable.
- There were no governing metrics to measure plant/line/asset performance.

Through the analysis, the company discovered over $100 million in cost reduction opportunities, which would result in over a 10 percent reduction in the organization's operational cost base. It has now started down the path of capturing these opportunities, and early results are more promising than the initial assessments.

Why were these companies able to succeed while many others are still struggling? Because their leaders were thinking in terms of *transformation*, not just improvement. Transformation is the process by which companies, business units, or locations make a step-change improvement in their operating performance, which enables them to access new strategic approaches, such as repositioning themselves as a premium producer or driving market share by taking the low-cost position in the marketplace.

There are three streams of activity required for transformation:

1. Attain a proper understanding of the extent of the opportunity.
2. Consciously choose a path to capture the opportunity.
3. Build the continuous improvement execution capabilities to capture the opportunity both short and long term.

The third item in this list—building the internal capability around continuous improvement—is covered in many sources on traditional Lean Six Sigma. In fact, we describe some new alternatives for achieving that goal in Chapter 15. In this chapter, we will focus on the first two items, then describe the kind of journey required for transformation and illustrate the kinds of decisions management faces through a case study.

ATTAIN A PROPER UNDERSTANDING OF THE EXTENT OF THE OPPORTUNITY

Most companies don't truly understand the gap between their performance and high performers; as such, they undercommit to making improvements in their organization. In a recent survey we asked more than 1500 executives in over 21 countries which operational capabilities were most critical to high performance. We found significant gaps between the "masters" (those at the peak levels) and "laggards" (those with the worst performance), as shown in the Figures 8.2 and 8.3.

Looking at the numbers from our survey, it's clear that there are wide gaps in performance—50 percent overall throughput for laggards, 85 percent for masters; 35 days lead time for laggards, 3 days for masters. (Again,

Figure 8.2
Differentiating masters from laggards.

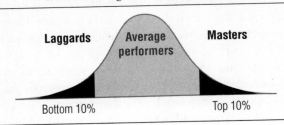

Figure 8.3
Survey results.

	Masters	Laggards
Percent overall throughput	85%	50%
Customer promise kept	98%	86%
Overall equipment effectiveness	92%	60%
Asset utilization	90%	50%
Material efficiency	98%	80%
Scrap rate	1%	10%
Manufacturing lead time	3 days	35 days
Match of production to plan	97%	83%
Delivery to schedule	98%	83%
Capital project index	90%	30%
Downtime vs. sched. run time	6.5%	19%
Workforce satisfied	80%	80%

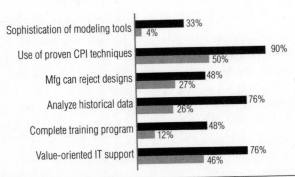

Source: High Performance through Manufacturing: Accenture Research and Insights into Manufacturing Mastery (Accenture, 2008).

it was reaching a 3-day lead time that was the breakthrough point for the company in Chapter 1.) Clearly, if companies internalized the gap being this large, they would work diligently to close it. But most companies underestimate the upside potential and ultimately underinvest to achieve excellence, leaving significant value on the table.

Even when companies do realize that a significant gap exists, and have a desire to close that gap, there are strong differences between how average performers and high performers go about addressing their cost reduction opportunities, as shown in Table 8.1.

Organizations on the forefront of getting the most out of their operational improvement efforts recognize that if left open-ended, operational targets will be negotiated *downward* to levels that are not impactful for the company as a whole. The best companies set stretch goals across the board, such as 80 percent improvement in quality, 30 percent reduction in costs, or

Table 8.1
High-Performance Approach to Cost Reduction

	Average Performer	*High Performer*
Approach to Cost Reduction	Arbitrarily cut: • Travel • Training • Advertising and marketing • Headcount • Capital projects • IS investment • Employee compensation and rewards Scale back growth initiatives and strategic investments. Sell strategic assets. Tactical mind-set.	Utilize diagnostic approach and understand implications of each initiative. Understand cost-value relationship (ROI) by: • Function • Initiative • P&L line item Use analytic evidence to make decisions. See downturns as opportunity to acquire assets (below market value). Optimize spend based on ROI. Restructure based on future growth plans and capability requirements.
Likely Impacts	Lower market share Lower employee morale Cost creep back due to lack of sustainability Lower operating margins Lower growth rates	Higher growth and market share Profitable growth Cash for value-building opportunities Employee confidence Higher share price Risk profile improvement

50 percent improvement in delivery. Setting goals like this, which many would say are unattainable, at least releases companies from the needless energy of negotiation of targets. Additionally, it pushes their thinking up to a level that requires creativity to achieve the targets. The very best require tactical-level plans to be built to show how they are going to achieve the long-stretch targets.

CONSCIOUSLYCHOOSE A PATH TO CAPTURE THE OPPORTUNITY

Once a company has decided that the opportunity available to it is important enough to aggressively pursue, the next major decision is which path to take. Our work with clients has shown that there are three basic mechanisms that companies take to close the identified gaps:

1. Continuous improvement
2. Targeted interventions
3. Transformational programs

Figure 8.4 identifies the landscape of possible changes, from the basic Lean Six Sigma programs to global operating models.

All three of these approaches can be successful in the right situation. Ultimately, the plans you create to transform your company will be populated with specific actions, but they typically need to address the following five levers to ensure sustainability in the long run:

1. Understanding value creation and destruction from the stakeholder perspective
2. Process excellence
3. Asset management and ROIC focus
4. Leadership and organizational capability
5. Performance management

Lever #1: Understanding Value Creation and Value Destruction in Your Company

You need to understand both value creation and value destruction to make wise choices about cost-cutting. For example, rationalizing a product portfolio to eliminate offerings that are destroying value is important because it

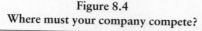

Figure 8.4
Where must your company compete?

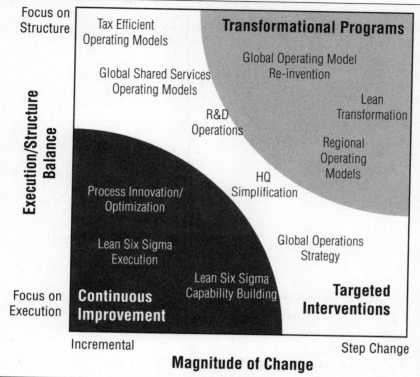

can help reduce the cost of operational complexity. But, alone, rationalization is not sustainable because companies need to introduce new products and create new market offerings to stay competitive. The balance is struck when companies have efficient and well-designed processes to help them rationalize their product portfolios and continue to innovate and introduce new products to meet customer demand.

- Value creation is ultimately linked to a better understanding of customer needs and customer behavior. Yes, customers will say they want *all* your new products and services—but do they want them enough to pay you enough to make it worthwhile?
- Value destruction means understanding which offerings in your portfolio consume more resources than can be supported by the profits you make off them. To understand value destruction, you have to look

Table 8.2
Separating Value-Creating from Value-Destroying Products/Services

Attribute	Year 0	Year 1	Year 2	Comments
Product Portfolio	3500	2079	499	Complexity reduction across the entire value stream
Product Development Projects	120	22	20	Improved R&D processes and focused development efforts
Results				
New products introduced	0	8	14	The combination of complexity reduction and better R&D processes allowed the company to be more effective in new product development and introduction

closely at your operations and how you allocate costs to know which offerings generate sufficient revenue to offset costs, and the overall impact of having variety in your portfolio (see Chapter on complexity).

An example of separating high value-creating from value-destroying products and services come from a high-tech company. The company realized that having too many products and services to support was actually destroying customer value. It led the firm to rationalize its product portfolio, eliminating the value-destroyers, then redirecting the focus on launching new products. More details on the company's efforts are listed in Table 8.2.

In this example, the high-tech manufacturer reduced its product complexity by 85 percent—while its efficient and well-designed processes enabled it to introduce new products. For example, in 2002 (Year 0), 120 product development projects yielded zero new products. By 2004 (Year 2), that process improved: 20 projects yielded 14 new products.

Lever #2: Process Excellence

Process excellence is usually defined as operating your processes to the highest standards enabled from Lean and Six Sigma practices: driving out waste in all its forms, driving down defects to unprecedented levels, minimizing variation, and implementing standard work procedures wherever consistency is demanded to maintain top levels of performance.

Our perspective on process excellence is a little broader: Achieving process excellence requires thinking about how value is delivered through the business, and viewing your organization from a process view rather than a functional view. Understanding how the business delivers value means that you understand how each of the components works together: people, equipment, and technology. Understanding the value delivery system completely provides clarity on priority and the sequence of targets on which to focus improvement efforts.

Once the landscape has been laid out and the priorities identified, the efforts of the organization can be focused on step-change improvements in the critical processes; these improvements can range from redefining a sales and operations planning process to a plant or production-line layout and redesign.

The effects of these actions can be significant, both for high-performing businesses as well as poor-performing businesses.

Lever #3: Asset Management and ROIC Focus

Understanding how assets are performing in terms of return on investment gives management a perspective on the business they may never have had before. Realistically, a return-on-assets approach, when applied to the current assets, forces management to ask different questions:

- Do we need to continue to invest in a particular asset that has low return, or should we change a process, or maybe close a facility?
- Do we need to invest in a high-performing asset that is currently critical to delivering customer value?
- Do we need to invest in infrastructure information technology or ERP systems to allow us to move to the next level of value realization?
- Is now the time to invest in people?

The answers to questions like these are typically more strategic, and they can change (for example, pulling the process excellence lever can allow a poorly performing asset to become a high-performance asset, thus changing the strategic landscape).

The other element in this lever is a clear focus on return on invested capital (ROIC). Evaluating ROIC is critical to enable the organization to prioritize what actions to take. Having the discipline to define value ROIC of actions and initiatives means that, as leaders, we can articulate why we are making these investments of resources, whether people, processes, or capital.

Figure 8.5 illustrates this perspective. The chart on the upper half shows how assets are performing; as you can see, there is a wide range of

Figure 8.5

Linking value to opportunities: This Economic Profit versus invested capital analysis shows the current utilization and effectiveness of the assets in the network, maximizing value to the shareholder.

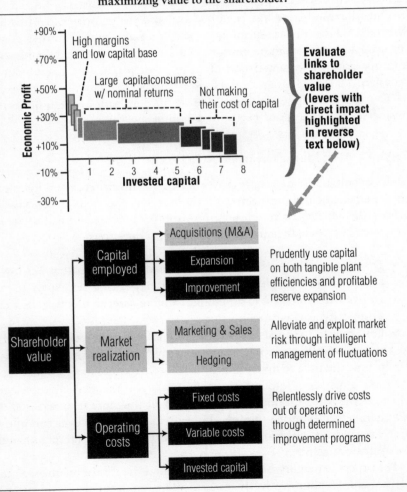

performance versus capital investment. This view allows us to ask questions about these assets in the broader context. One option is to cut poorly performing assets or plants from the network; the other option is to assess whether those assets can, through a transformation process, markedly lift performance, giving a different picture and series of options.

The lower half shows how asset performance links to value. For individuals in the midst of driving process excellence, that knowledge is critical.

Lever #4: Leadership and Organizational Capability

When we are asked to help companies transform themselves, we first have to shift the mind-set of the leadership in order to unlock greater potential. We try to help local leaders shift their way of thinking from a control-focused, cost-centered approach to an entrepreneurial, P&L-type mind-set that centers around growth and change.

In particular, we often see three leadership factors that hamper speed and flexibility:

- Decisions are made at higher levels than is really necessary because of an inability to delegate and the lack of appropriate data.
- Roles in departments are fragmented, resulting in critical operations being distributed over many people and functions. This fragmented execution results in low quality and speed.
- The corporate culture acts *against* uniformity and consistency in communication and alignment.

Lever #5: Performance Management

Performance management is the collection of management actions taken to: set appropriate goals in the organization, gather data associated with process performance, engage in dialogue around performance (and its relation to the goals), and make adjustments to the original plan to achieve the established goals. The appropriate performance management mechanisms must be in place to motivate and guide employees through the transformation and, thereafter, sustain the competitive advantage. Done correctly, performance management is the mechanism that speeds the learning of the organization and enables the delegation of improvement objectives down to the lowest position in the organization.

Figure 8.6 highlights three components of performance management. All are needed to make sure that knowledge about what drives value in the

Figure 8.6
**Components of performance management: Performance management evaluates the
capabilities of an organization by identifying significant gaps and "pain points"
when initiating change.**

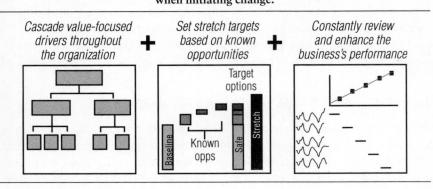

company reaches all levels; that the company uses that knowledge to aim
for higher performance than competitors; and that it constantly pushes to
achieve ever-higher levels.

You'll find more on performance management in Chapter 14.

PLAN FOR A TRANSFORMATION JOURNEY

There's a reason why transformation is often called a journey: Your company will pass through multiple stages on the way to establishing new
norms. We typically see six phases in any organization's path: awareness,
value estimation, journey development, step-change, capability development, and refinement. These are illustrated in Figure 8.7 and defined more
fully below.

Awareness: The awareness phase is often triggered by one executive's
vision of a major change possibility in the entire organization but a lack
of alignment in the leadership team. Additionally, it is sometimes used to
foreshadow to the broader organization that a change is being considered in the organization. The awareness portion of the journey is often
accompanied by a readiness assessment, consisting of wide-ranging interviews with members of the leadership team, which often leads to an
understanding of where the leadership team is aligned or misaligned.
Value estimation: This phase is completed through a thorough assessment and quantification of opportunities across either the network or

Figure 8.7
The transformation journey.

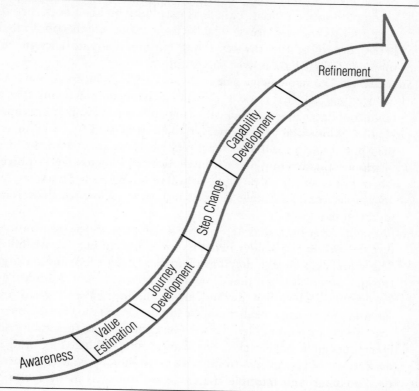

an individual facility. This phase should determine what the total improvement opportunity is, as well as what the key levers are. This should be a primary input to the journey development.

Journey development: As we described in the first part of this chapter, we believe there are several ways to start a journey. If you choose the transformation path, it is critical to express your thoughts explicitly about the capability-building, step-change, and refinement phases, and regarding what would work best for your organization. It is also important to think about the communication approach that you will use with your workforce as well.

Capability building: By capability building, we mean the process of transferring basic and programmatic knowledge to the associates in a business. This is about taking the process-oriented view of imparting knowledge. The key aspects that businesses need to figure out is how broad to build capabilities, at what pace, and what you are trying to accomplish in the rollout. Base-level capability building does need to occur across the workforce. The decision about whether to do that before, during, or after the step-change portion is a critical design factor, and all three have proven successful.

Step-change: The step-change part of the journey is about speed and confidence building. It is critical that change happen quickly and that it build confidence in local leadership, so that they believe they are capable of making large-scale changes in their business. Those who invest their best resources and drive them very hard here are rewarded with a disproportionate return on their investment. Putting too few resources where fast change isn't possible, or where no one feels personally accountable to make change happen fast, are just two of the failure modes in this space.

Refinement: After the initial step-change is complete, most organizations find themselves at a stage where they are confident but overwhelmed. The initial step-change may have left them exhausted, and most go through a period when they slow down after the large team leaves. Furthermore, when they start moving again, most have the desire and intention to change quickly but have not developed the "muscle memory" to do so successfully. This is one of the prime reasons we see companies go through cycles every five years or so where they bring in another set of consultants to improve their operations. Muscle memory for quick and effective change comes through many cycles of work, and we find that those companies that get frequent "checkups" by a much smaller outside effort are more likely to be successful over a long period of time.

Transformation Case Study

We'll use a sample case study to illustrate how the transformation phases roll out in real life, and the kinds of decisions that executives are faced with along the way.

An equipment manufacturer had a long history of incredible performance within its niche. In many ways it was the picture of high performance, with a market share of 70 percent or more for some key products, ROIC typically around 50 percent, and operating earnings around 20 percent.

In 2006, however, a new president and COO came onboard who had a strong background in orchestrating turnarounds in operations. He recognized that although the company was a strong performer when compared to the competition, it suffered in comparison to the broad range of world-class manufacturing organizations in the world. The leader realized that he had several hurdles to clear on the way to remaking the company—the first of which was to build *awareness* of the gap throughout the leadership team. This team had been together for some time and felt justifiably proud of the market leadership position that they had achieved.

In the first phase of our awareness building with this client, we were asked to provide an initial point of view on two goals the new leadership team was going to set, in addition to our first impressions of their business. The two goals were:

1. How could the company triple its inventory turns in three years?
2. How could it cut costs by 30 percent over the next five years?

The first phase of the awareness building was accomplished through a series of interviews, facility visits, and data analysis. This series led to several important conclusions:

- The fundamentals of the business position in the market were strong, and the company was considered by far the leader in product design.
- Its process performance across several parts of the business was far from world class.
- There were significant opportunities for large cost savings across the company.
- There were a few functional areas of the business that were key to its success.
- To triple the inventory turns would take a change in the go-to-market strategy, which would reposition the company in the marketplace and weaken its dominant position.

Tips for Succeeding in the Awareness Stage

- Ensure that you have alignment around the need to change, and that the dissatisfaction with the status quo is significant enough to warrant the efforts required to change.
- Confirm that the goals you are aligning against are both attainable and stretch the organization.

(continued)

(*continued*)
- Make sure you have a clear view of what the benefits are, both financially and culturally, to the organization making the change.

The next part of the journey was working through the *value estimation* for the organization. During this phase, we worked with the leadership team to analyze the company's performance across multiple dimensions. This is typically done using a combination of direct observations, analysis of internal data, and comparison to other companies (using data such as public financial filings as well as well known benchmarking data sources). Triangulating these analytical techniques yielded confidence that we could save over $500 million of costs within a five-year period by addressing the core process performance within the existing network footprint.

After the value estimation was complete, the company felt that the savings were large enough to consider putting a high degree of effort into changing, and so started moving into the *journey development* stage.

Journey development for this company was completed through a series of workshops and individual meetings with the executive teams to discuss the pros and cons of different approaches to attain the savings and shift the company's reputation in the marketplace from one based solely on product design to one acknowledged for leading process design as well.

The organization had originally intended on rolling out change through a series of Kaizen events, led by 10 Kaizen leaders. Though implementing that plan was effective, and helped to drive benefits to offset the original investment, the company discovered that sticking to that model would limit the pace of change. During the assessment and value estimation phases, the analyses showed that the physical processes had plenty of room to improve. However, intangible aspects of business operation limited the company more than the tangible items.

Another shift the team realized they needed to make was from tactical to programmatic thinking.

- When thinking *tactically*, companies typically see "point solutions" that need to be rolled out throughout the organization. These point solutions could be something simple and singular like changing policy about how much time-off all employees are allowed, or trying to set inventory goals. These solutions usually fail to deliver strong and sustainable impact. They tend to have small impact and require a lot of follow-through to make sure even their limited effect is completed and sustained. Organizations trapped in a tactical model have a difficult time driving substantial bottom-line impact because the need to follow up leads to management bandwidth limitations.

- On the other hand, developing *programmatic* solutions enables the senior leadership to provide inspiring, broad-structured change programs that will enable strong leaders down in the organization to drive change that builds into a snowball effect. This approach not only delivers the financial and operational impact needed from the business, it also provides a conduit to develop the next generation of company leaders.

As a result of these insights, the company architected a program for total business transformation that included components such as manufacturing excellence, service and sales excellence, supply chain excellence, and engineering excellence. Each initiative was designed to complete one part of the picture this company painted of a future where it would be considered world class in process performance, just as today it is considered world class in product performance.

Coming out of the diagnostic process, it was apparent to this company's leaders that small, isolated improvements typically generated from capability-building-led efforts would be insufficient to make the large changes they required. Additionally, the organization wanted to move faster than would have been possible deploying a typical capability-building-led approach. The company did not have a deep-enough "bench" of talent they could draw on to meet aggressive performance goals.

As a result, the company decided to take an alternative approach to capability building—transformational in its own right. Executive leadership would set clear direction for the organization, build initial wins via carefully selected projects to create momentum, and, simultaneously, start shifting management activities and culture of the organization.

To achieve "change, at speed," the company assembled a team in one location, and then divided it among three workstreams, each focusing on a different physical part of the business. One group worked on fabrication processes, another on assembly processes, and the third on warehousing and maintenance activities. Each workstream was co-led by a company employee and external consultant; each group also had three to six employees working full time on the workstream. Overseeing activities in all workstreams was a project management team consisting of a company manager and experienced consultant.

The *step-change* phase needs to be about aggressively making changes in the organization and quickly spreading out to touch all company employees. This phase should be timed long enough to ensure that the organization is gaining steady momentum, but not so long that the organization feels completely burned out on the process. Think sprint instead of distance run.

Key to getting all people involved is making the mid-level managers feel accountable for an aspect of the implementation. Therefore, it is important that all key midlevel managers be assigned a portion of the new cultural aspects they are responsible throughout the transformation. For instance, one manager could be responsible for performance management, one for training, and one for savings validation.

Capability development was not a standalone phase for this company. In the initial awareness and value estimation phases, capability was developed in the group of 10 managers who were given classroom training, along with one-on-one Kaizen apprenticeship, using an "I do, we do, you do" training method (see Chapter 15 for details).

In the step-change portion, the training of the team members was largely through a hands-on apprenticeship method, where they were actively co-leading a portion of the work. Capability building is deepest in this type of environment, where the instruction is one on one and the application is in a real-life situation with strong goals that must be achieved. Finally, broadscale capability building was conducted by having company managers provide training on the essential elements to all employees.

For the *refinement* phase, this company had only one outside consultant return on a periodic basis to monitor progress, hold people accountable to the plans they had committed to completing, and help them deliver value. This is a critical step that most companies undervalue. True, deep expertise takes many years to develop. Even the most talented and ambitious people will not be standalone change agents within a few months of exposure to other change agents. At best, they have the desire and will force through the changes, likely in a manner that will have both positive and negative effects. The value of a coach to talk them through the changes is critical, to help groove-in muscle memory for the first six months.

This organization is currently in the second year of its transformation journey. The initial step-change approach has been launched on three different continents, and has been praised by investment analysts as making a material impact on the company's corporate-level earnings, which was one factor in increasing the analysts' advocacy of the stock. Time will tell whether it will retain the focus and drive to continue its quest for a full transformation. If so, the company will be able to attain much more than the 10 to 15 percent in cost savings initially targeted.

LEADERSHIP CHALLENGES IN LEADING A TRANSFORMATION

The scale of change required for transformation is different from launching an improvement program, even one as broad in scale as Lean Six Sigma can be. The stakes and risks are both heightened when you're trying to make a step-change in performance levels. We've identified three areas that are particularly challenging when trying to drive that level of change:

1. Alignment at the C-level
2. Maintaining focus
3. Managing risk and reward at the leadership levels

Alignment at the C-level

While some changes can be successful even if driven from the middle out, the nature of transformation depends on having strong leaders who are all pulling toward a common vision and focusing on the vital few issues—what are commonly referred to as "North Star objectives." Without that common vision and alignment, you'll have a hard time making the tough calls, and leadership discussions can easily degrade into turf wars.

For example, your procurement department will likely resist changing how they've functioned for years, or even decades—selecting suppliers based on cost—unless the head of that department is aligned with corporate goals to reduce *overall* costs, which will require partnering with at least some key suppliers (see Chapter 11). Or what if one of your C-level leaders is evaluated based on unit cost, another on profit, and a third on customer satisfaction?

To achieve transformational change, you will have to ensure that all of your leadership understands, and even embraces, agreed-on short- and long-term priorities. You'll then have to think through the barriers that will stand in the way of achieving those goals, and identify exactly what has to change so that your leaders won't be constantly at odds with each other.

Maintaining Focus

Transformation has to be driven, not "managed." You need to have leaders out front, keeping the organization focused on efforts that are required to drive the kind of changes you've identified as necessary. While that can be easy in the short term, transformation requires a year, or perhaps two, of dedicated commitment by leadership. Just think of all the distractions that can arise in a month, let alone a year, and you will realize that maintaining focus will be difficult.

One technique for maintaining focus is to hire a coach to keep you and your site leaders accountable. Periodically having someone accompany you or your leaders to key interactions will provide reinforcement for the positive things you are doing, as well as highlight the deviations from the path when you are only, say, 5 degrees off, rather than 90 degrees off.

Managing Risk and Reward at the Leadership Levels

If the end state of transformation represented work methods and behaviors that you and your company already embraced, there wouldn't be any need for transformation in the first place. With change comes risk, and the magnitude of change associated with transformation is great.

The risk of the unknown is compounded by the fact that anyone on your leadership team—you included—got to where they are by being good at how the company currently does business. Furthermore, what kind of reward will there be for leaders after the change?

Convincing all of your leaders that it is in their best interests—not just the company's—to drive transformation is a challenge. The CEO and other top leaders will likely have to rethink how they interact with their peers and direct reports.

In our experience, where people are in their career paths has a lot to do with how willing they are to participate in and drive transformational changes. Young, aggressive managers are usually eager to prove themselves, especially if they see that the opportunity has a lot of potential upside in making the company more successful. Those late in their careers may be looking for new challenges and the opportunity to leave a strong legacy. It is up to you as a leader to find the motivational reason that will energize your highest performers to help you reach the end of your journey successfully.

CONCLUSION

Transformations are a phenomenal way to rapidly alter the cost base of your business. They establish strong initial momentum in a highly focused manner. This is an extremely reliable way to move your company to stronger process performance. At the same time, you should always remember that long-term performance is about having the muscle memory in the organization to deliver consistently. This requires an investment past the step-change portion of the transformation, to ensure that you continue to reap rewards for years to come. In addition to the changes seen in performance, resultant cultural changes and talent upgrade combine to make the organization better able to respond to any significant market and customer shifts.

SPOTLIGHT #4

TRANSFORMATION AT OWENS-ILLINOIS

Many companies seek to transform themselves through Lean Six Sigma, often responding to a crisis or a specific need. Not so with Owens-Illinois (O-I). It was already a global leader in its industry; well-respected and financially stable, with roots reaching back more than a century when it looked to Lean Six Sigma for help.

While the company had a long history of firsts in the glass industry, and invested heavily in continuous improvement in its manufacturing processes, a new CEO recognized the potential that Lean Six Sigma could bring. Al Stroucken had experienced the operational gains brought by Lean Six Sigma at his previous company, and knew it could move the organization to a new level of performance.

The company had grown extensively through acquisitions around the globe. By 2006, when Stroucken came onboard, it was an amalgam of independent business practices and cultures. Engineering and manufacturing leaders were trying to drive consistency in manufacturing processes across the globe. Best practices were prevalent throughout the company, but deploying them inconsistently meant lost opportunity in productivity and profitability. O-I needed to become more process oriented, establish a common language across all units and geographies, and enhance analytical and execution capabilities. "We're a world leader in our industry, but we've operated like many individual companies around the globe—not taking advantage of our size and scale," CEO Stroucken said at the time.

Owens-Illinois had already begun introducing a wellness culture in its offices and plants. The program encouraged change collaboration and teamwork, and asked leaders to focus forward, be open to new ideas and concepts, and incorporate other people's ideas—all of which improves improving the working environment for employees. It was a perfect foundation for Lean Six Sigma. "Many organizations underestimate the importance of culture when introducing Lean Six Sigma," says Senior Vice President and Chief Process Improvement Officer Ed Snyder.

Planning for Lean Six Sigma deployment began in early 2007, and the first training classes occurred in the summer of that year. O-I took an unusual path, by training Kaizen leaders at the same time as Black Belts. "The goal was to achieve some quick wins, while also tackling larger projects," said Snyder. "It helped quickly demonstrate the potential of Lean Six Sigma to the organization." In addition, Snyder adds, the company tackled some very complicated programs within seven or eight months after introducing Lean Six Sigma.

O-I focused on building its internal Lean Six Sigma capabilities from the start. "Lean Six Sigma builds capabilities in our people at all levels," says Stroucken. "By giving them the tools and the framework to solve complicated problems, we empower them to take on new challenges. This benefits the organization financially and organizationally," he adds. The program achieved cost neutrality in just 10 months, and O-I now has 1 percent of its employee population working full-time as Black Belt or Kaizen leaders. The company also has trained its own Master Black Belts, beginning just 18 months after the first Black Belts were trained.

O-I's Goals for Lean Six Sigma

- Enhance productivity with a contemporary toolset and a common language.
- Increase execution speed with fact-based decisions, and rapidly transfer best practices.
- Invest in and enhance employee capabilities.
- Delegate responsibility to the most effective level in the organization.
- Eliminate waste, reduce variation, and continually improve our processes.
- Enhance O-I wellness culture to be more collaborative and focused on results.

Today, five to six projects are completed at O-I *every business day,* a figure that includes Green Belt, Black Belt, and Kaizen projects.

Once the program was up and running at full steam, the company expected an annual return benefit in the range of 2 to 3 percent of cost of goods sold (COGS) per year. "When we first told this to our investors a year into the program, we expected we would need another two or three years to reach that level of maturity," says Senior Vice President and Chief Financial Officer Ed White. "But we've reached it already. It is our best defense against margin erosion."

That kind of commitment only comes when you have a strong leadership team pushing the adoption of Lean Six Sigma and, equally important, business results that convince people Lean Six Sigma can be used to address issues that are important to them. At first, says Snyder, some leaders felt Lean Six Sigma resources were being taken away from them and given to the deployment champions. O-I addressed that by creating steering committees across the organization, whose members decide which projects the Belts are assigned to—providing a direct link between priority needs and projects. Also, it uses a rigorous project selection process to make sure the company chooses opportunities with the highest potential benefit using the least amount of resources.

"When people started to see results, and felt like they had been part of creating that success, it was much easier to involve them in other projects," says Snyder.

The shift in culture has been dramatic. Employees at all levels have embraced data-based decision making and improvement projects as a way to tackle both strategic and everyday operational needs. "Our people understand that having processes and using data results in more robust decision making," says Snyder.

"Lean Six Sigma is the way we work now," he says. "It's part of our culture."

CHAPTER 9

UNLOCK THE SECRETS TO SPEED AND FLEXIBILITY

A few years ago we were asked to help improve the business performance of a global leader in consumer products by overhauling its legacy continuous process improvement program. This company had developed a home-grown Six Sigma program strategy, trained hundreds of Green Belts and Black Belts around the world, and deployed a few dozen Master Black Belts. The client wanted us to help improve project values, shorten project lead times, and infuse Lean capability into its legacy Six Sigma toolset.

In our experience, the best way to ensure high return from Lean Six Sigma projects is to conduct an operations assessment to identify hot spots and engage executive leadership in driving business priorities to every level of the organization. But this company was exclusively focused on building its internal Lean capability, so we trained dozens of Lean Masters, as requested. The company also began an aggressive rollout of Lean principles and tools across the business.

On the upside, adding Lean into this company's improvement equation did improve project values and cycle times at the process level, and cumulatively, the deployment began returning more than it cost. But despite all of the activity and investment in people and projects, only local, incremental savings and productivity gains were realized. The potential to transform was not fully exploited. In no way had enterprise speed and flexibility—the real goal of the program—been achieved.

Why? Despite countless heroic efforts on the shop floor, executive leadership was enforcing a policy aimed at "reducing the cost of capital per unit part produced." This equipment cost optimization strategy mandated the batch sizes of thousands of inventory units in order to minimize the cost of capital being allocated to each part. This was ironic because the company's investment in Lean has created production lines with greatly improved flexibility, capable of meeting customer demand with batch sizes a mere fraction of the quantity of parts being produced per schedule.

This myopic strategy was being instituted by a senior leadership team that was not aligned to Lean fundamentals and was, in fact, mandating a production schedule that went against every principle of Lean speed, flexibility, and customer-demand-driven pull. A common understanding, alignment, and focus on the North Star objective of enterprise speed would have had transformational impact on shareholder value. Instead, the company continued to offshore more and more of its production from the United States to Asia in an effort to maintain acceptable operating margins.

This company is not alone in failing to extract step-change improvement or competitive advantage despite having embraced and deployed the traditional Lean Six Sigma toolset. We may hear a new client report that they "have already done Lean Six Sigma," that they have worked on process flow, implemented 5S, reduced setup times, or invested in improving equipment uptime, yet their CFO has a difficult time seeing substantive financial improvements at the enterprise level. Why is this? As we have described throughout this book, enterprise speed and flexibility are key enablers of remarkable reductions in operating cost, and can deliver the ability to grow revenue through improved customer service, as well as improve responsiveness to the market. Yet enterprise speed and flexibility can elude even the best-crafted transformations. In this chapter we present *the other side* of transformation—the analytical side—and help you unlock the secrets of speed and flexibility.

ALIGNMENT AND ANALYTICS

The reason that most continuous improvement tends to be incremental, not transformational, is that the tools and methods are commonly applied as part of myriad, disparate projects across multiple processes, or even silos, that are neither connected nor strategically organized to drive a key business outcome—what we call North Star objectives. In fact, these decentralized efforts can lead to suboptimal solutions that may even result in costs being shifted elsewhere in the organization. Instead, there must be clear understanding of the relationships between process performance and key business metrics—not just within individual processes but across entire value streams—and how these directly influence shareholder value creation and alignment to North Star objectives.

Why is this alignment so critical to enabling enterprise speed and flexibility? There are inherent relationships between customer demand by offering, work scheduling and capacity planning, and actual process capability. These interrelationships are rarely fully understood by process improvement practitioners and management alike. The functional areas accountable for these activities are typically managed separately, without common objectives they are aligned toward and measured against.

The complexity of this situation can best be appreciated by Figure 9.1. It illustrates a typical model of Sales and Operations Planning (S&OP), which can be very effective in predicting timing and need for additional investments,

Figure 9.1
Complexity in Sales and Operations Planning

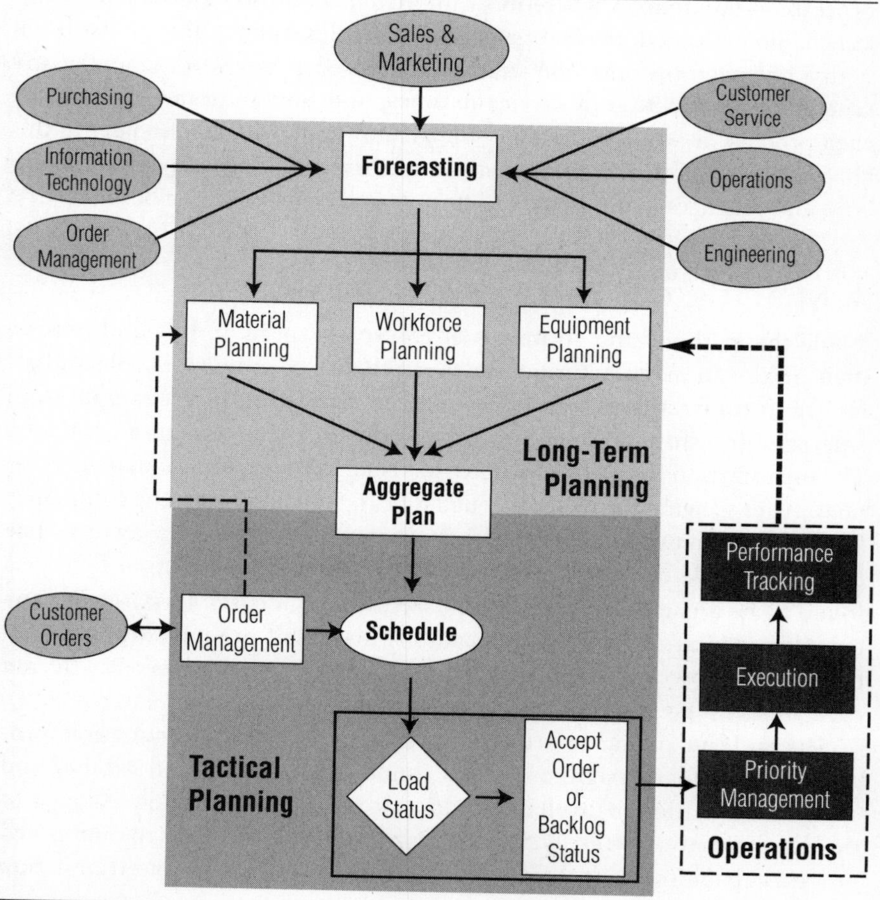

material, workforce, equipment, and facilities. S&OP links sales and marketing predictions to the planning process to support those predictions.

The pursuit of enterprise speed and flexibility not only requires an understanding of the technical interrelationships between all elements shown in
Figure 9.1, but also requires the fortitude and commitment of management
to align behaviors, protocols, rewards, and compensation across the business
toward the fundamentals of the fast and flexible enterprise. This holistic approach requires a deep understanding of Lean fundamentals at all levels of
leadership, management, and execution—an understanding far beyond the
common perception that the purpose and benefit of Lean is solely the elimination of waste.

To unlock the secrets of speed and flexibility, we must expand the scope
and focus of the transformation effort beyond production or service delivery
processes—the domain where most improvement efforts are typically contained. Simply stated, the enterprise speed and flexibility journey must begin
with a holistic transformation strategy that encompasses work planning and
scheduling, production or service delivery, and total customer demand by
each product or service offering in the portfolio. As we shall see later in this
chapter, it is only through the analysis of these combined processes, protocols, and practices that the fast and flexible Lean enterprise can be enabled.

A MODEL OF SPEED AND AGILITY

While the methods and strategies of enterprise speed and flexibility have
their origins in manufacturing, the concepts are equally applicable and effective in transactional or service environments. One such example is an
enterprise transformation at a major North American insurance company.
The organization found itself with costs rising at a steeper rate than its revenues. After viewing the issues through a Lean Six Sigma lens, the company's
leadership soon recognized the power of enterprise speed as a way to reduce
cost and enable competitive advantage. Product or transaction type was
found to be a particularly significant factor in high costs. Historically, any
complex insurance renewal transactions disrupted process flow, necessi-
tated multiple workarounds, interrupted capacity, and adversely affected
cycle times of less complex transactions as well.

Several Lean Six Sigma projects were focused on waste elimination, process flow, cellular design, and cross training, for optimum flexibility and
capacity utilization, as well as product or transaction triaging. As part of
the transformation strategy, the organization closely linked the improved
process capabilities to its work scheduling by product type and transaction

Figure 9.2
Enterprise speed and agility model: As processes are improved and made
more flexible, the planning and scheduling team allocates and sizes work batches
based on updated capability and actual demand by offering. The fewer items
in the process at any given time, the faster the process.

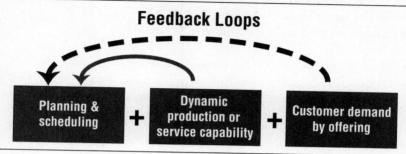

complexity. Work scheduling was optimized and became an industrialized process based on volume by transaction type, allocation of resources, and cross-trained flex capacity. This integrated strategy resulted in accelerated process speed, improved utilization, lower cost, and increased customer satisfaction.

Enterprise speed and flexibility requires a holistic, closed-loop strategy (Figure 9.2) whereby work planning and scheduling operations make decisions based on the true capability of production or service delivery channels, as well as the total customer demand by each product or service offering in the portfolio. In fact, we have seen that low performance and high cost in manufacturing companies is more often related to forecasting and scheduling issues than it is to shop-floor level production deficiencies.

The model in Figure 9.1 may appear to be both logical and straightforward. As processes are improved, shouldn't decisions regarding work planning and scheduling be made according to current capabilities? This would seem to be a simple enough task, but there are two complicating factors that make this integration of capability and planning a very tall order:

1. There are multiple elements that determine dynamic production or service capability.
2. Most production lines or service delivery channels are not dedicated to a single product or service, so the breadth of offering, product mix, and demand by product becomes quite relevant.

Let's begin by discussing product mix and demand; later in this section we'll discuss processes and what determines their flexibility.

Mix, Demand, and Flexibility

Recall from the case study in Chapter 1 about the tier-1 auto supplier that produces an array of hydraulic hoses and fittings for steering and braking systems. To simplify our illustration let's consider one product family that includes five sizes of hoses we'll label A, B, C, D, and E. For the purposes of this illustration, we'll make the following assumptions:

- There are no production lines dedicated to any single size of hose.
- Production lines can produce one type at a time, after which it must go through a changeover process that takes hours.
- The production line can produce 250 hoses per hour.

Figure 9.3

Five hose sizes on each production line: The equipment and crew required to make a batch of size-A hoses are shared resources; they must be flexible, and able to also make hoses B, C, D, and E. There is varying demand for all hoses in the product family. The production and scheduling decisions concerning any one of the hoses in the product family affect all of the others. How many of size-A hoses do we need to produce on any given run? Enough to serve demand until we can cycle through all other hoses and can make As once again.

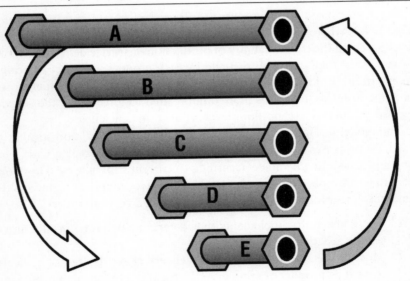

**Five sizes of hoses produced on a single line
(depicted here with the end fittings).**

Imagine that today we're going to produce long hoses, product A, for which we have a forecasted demand rate of 3000 units per month. The questions are obvious: Once we're set up, how many size-A hoses should we make on this production run? Enough to meet the full month's demand (3000 hoses)? Can we reduce the batch size and cycle time with process improvements? The answers are anything but simple.

For one thing, setting up the line for the first run or changing over from one hose type to another consumes direct labor and capacity because the production line is not running while the crew prepares to run the next hose type. Changeover incurs costs without generating profitable value, so it is natural to want to minimize setup cost per individual hose produced on any given run. The greater the quantity of any size of hose, the less the allocated setup cost per piece. If the company only produced one size-A hose after a four-hour setup, all setup costs would be allocated to that single hose—making it unreasonably expensive! Conversely, if the line produced 100,000 size-A hoses at a time, the allocated setup cost per hose would be minimal—though the company would be left with inventory it wouldn't need for years. Since the line must produce all hose sizes (Figure 9.3), the answer to how many size-A hoses to run therefore lies somewhere in between these two extremes.

ECONOMIC ORDER QUANTITY (EOQ)—THE FIRST 100 YEARS

Historically the lot size dilemma was only seen in two dimensions—the cost of changeovers (setups) compared to the cost of carrying excess inventory (see Equation 9.1). The challenge has been to strike a balance between these two costs and was addressed analytically nearly 100 years ago by Ford W. Harris in 1913. The work of Harris and its subsequent derivations manifested into an algorithm commonly known as Economic Order Quantity (EOQ). No doubt EOQ has successfully addressed the two dimensions of

Equation 9.1
Common Expression of Economic Order Quantity (EOQ)*

$$\text{Lot Size} = \sqrt{\frac{2 \times (\text{Demand Rate} \times \text{Setup Cost})}{\text{Inventory Holding Cost}}}$$

*Based on the work of Ford W. Harris as detailed in *Factory Physics*, p. 52 (Hope & Spearman 2001).

changeover costs versus inventory costs. But as we shall discuss in this section there is a third dimension that is not addressed by traditional applications of EOQ—the dimension of enterprise speed, flexibility, and responsiveness. To better understand this let's begin by examining EOQ a bit closer.

For decades EOQ was seen as a practical approach to determine the optimum quantity of each item or stock keeping unit (SKU) that should be produced. But in the last ten years EOQ has fallen under sharp criticism as a culprit in driving bloated inventories, high costs, and slow supply chain velocity. Simply stated EOQ will increase lot sizes (inventory) as interest carry costs decline. Why does this impact enterprise speed, flexibility, and responsiveness? To understand this let's return to our previous example of the hydraulic hose company.

In the hose example, EOQ would indicate an increase in the batch size of Hose A beyond current demand to minimize the cost of the changeover on each unit produced. To make certain the batch size isn't infinite, EOQ compares the cost of the changeover per hose to the interest carry cost of putting all of those size-A hoses into inventory.

On the surface this may sound logical. But again we're faced with an answer that is not as straightforward as it could be assumed. It would *not* make sense to produce a larger number of size-A hoses to minimize the adverse effects and cost of setup time as the EOQ model would dictate. Why not? First, working in large batches creates inflexible processes that blindly lock onto a particular product for extended periods of time. The process is unable by protocol to follow the Lean dictum to produce only *the minimum safe amount required to meet customer demand.*

By causing companies to produce more than is required to meet demand, if considered by itself EOQ can inhibit the ability to rapidly respond to changes in demand (creating lost sales) but also necessitates the investment in warehouses, distribution centers, material handling, and transportation, counting, obsolescence, damage, and, of course, the associated cost of capital. All the TIMWOOD wastes described in Chapter 2 raise their ugly head. And while some of these costs are taken into account by the EOQ algorithm, two critical elements are not considered by EOQ: enterprise *speed* and enterprise *flexibility*—the two attributes that, as we have seen, can be the greatest enablers of cost reduction and competitive advantage.

Further, EOQ considers only one item at a time when it calculates run length or batch size. This worked fine in 1913 when product variety was minimal and the needs for process flexibility were nearly nonexistent at any given company. But by excessively increasing the batch size of each item singularly, EOQ impedes the enterprise's capability to serve every *other* item in its portfolio. Moreover, most improvements executed on the shop floor are not taken into account by the EOQ algorithm unless it is part of a holistic sales and operations (S&OP) strategy, as shown in Figure 9.1. At many organizations this disconnect between true process capability and production planning is the single greatest impediment to enterprise speed and flexibility.

AUGMENTING EOQ WITH LEAN ANALYTICS

To understand how to meet customer demand with the least amount of inventory (WIP, or work-in-process) and enable maximum flexibility, let's return to the hydraulic hose company. Recall that it takes four hours to change the size template and make adjustments, after which the company can then produce 250 size-A hoses per hour. With a forecasted demand of 3000 A's per month, how long should we run? Would 12 hours of production suffice? To answer the question, we need to gather a bit more information.

Recall that this production must make four other products as well (sizes B through E) and satisfy their rates of monthly demand, too. To decide how many size-A hoses to make, we need to know not only how long it takes to make the quantity needed to meet a monthly demand of 3,000 units, but also how long it will be before we can return to make size-A hoses again. What if the next run will be size-C hoses (demand of 5000 per month), followed by size-E hoses (demand of 15,000 per month)? You get the idea. It should now become clear that in order to know the production rate for size-A hoses, we need to also know the time it will take to cycle through the entire product family until we can make size-A hoses again—*because the demand for size-A hoses continues even when we're not making them.*

As we're considering the impact that product demand and mix has on enterprise speed and flexibility, there's one other piece of product data we need to gather: the yield of good hoses per production run. What if 10 percent are defective? We would need to produce more of each hose type and take more time to cycle through all the variants. And what if the production capability was not stable; what if the production equipment experienced severe breakdown failures from time to time? The broader our product portfolios grow, the more complex the problem of batch sizes and production runs becomes to solve. The good news is that robust, proven analytics have been developed to do just that.

EOQ alone does not address the relationships that ultimately determine the correlation between product mix, demand, process capability, and process flexibility. To augment the potential gaps in EOQ, we've determined that the three most significant analytical concepts related to enterprise speed are: Workstation Turnover Time, Cycle Time Interval, and Little's Law. Together these equations provide the requisite unification of planning, scheduling, dynamic production or service capability, and customer demand by offering type. We'll discuss cover each of them in turn.

The Equation of Process Speed: Little's Law

One equation well known to Lean practitioners is called Little's Law, introduced in Chapter 5 and reproduced here in Equation 9.2.

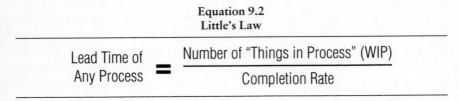

Equation 9.2
Little's Law

$$\text{Lead Time of Any Process} = \frac{\text{Number of "Things in Process" (WIP)}}{\text{Completion Rate}}$$

For example, suppose a procurement department can process 12 orders per hour and there is a backlog of 89 unprocessed orders. How long will the next order (the ninetieth) have to wait to be processed? (See Equation 9.3.)

Equation 9.3
Example of Little's Law calculation

$$7.5 \text{ hours} = \frac{90 \text{ orders in process}}{12 \text{ orders per hour}}$$

At first glance Little's Law appears elegantly simple; few can argue that the speed at which we can deliver a customer's product or service is determined by the total workload on the process and the speed at which the process completes its work.

If we accept the simple beauty of this formula, we can start to appreciate the secrets of enterprise speed and flexibility. Here are some of the concepts that Little's Law helps us understand:

- Enterprise speed (Process Lead Time; PLT) is determined not only by the rate at which processes perform but also by the amount of work being introduced to the processes.
- Introducing added work into the process does *not* speed up performance and lead time. Quite the contrary; it *increases* PLT (which means it makes your customers wait longer!).

- If the completion rate *is* constant and stable, yet the amount of work being introduced into the process (number of "things" in process) is not controlled, then the PLT cannot be predictable and may spiral out of control.
- If the completion rate *is not* constant and stable, plus the amount of work being introduced into the process ("things" in process) is not controlled, the total lead time may increase by an order of magnitude.
- If the completion rate is not as fast as the as the rate at which new work is being introduced into the process, the amount of "things" in process will increase without end and the PLT will crawl to a near halt, eventually.
- Controlling (reducing) the number of "things" in process is the simplest way to accelerate Process Lead Time (see WIP Caps in Chapter 5).
- The Continuous Improvement tools of Lean Six Sigma serve to accelerate the process completion rate.

Little's Law provides the first indication of the need to link process performance directly to work scheduling and planning—be it in manufacturing or in services. It amplifies the need for metrics, dashboards, and leading indicators of process capability, and moreover, an understanding of total demand (number of "things" in process) at any given time. It also helps us understand the impact of completion rate *instability* on Process Lead Time. Ask yourself: Does your organization continuously monitor its process capability and its completion rates? Do you know, at any given moment, the amount of work being introduced into your processes? By now you should begin to understand what governs process speed; but what affects process flexibility?

The Equations of Flexibility: Cycle Time Interval and Workstation Turnover Time

Let's revisit again the case of the Tier 1 automotive hydraulic hose and fitting supplier. The simplified example of this company featured a product family of five types of hoses in varying lengths—hoses A, B, C, D, and E, as shown in Figure 9.4.

The hose supplier had a goal of reducing order lead time, which initially was 14 days, twice as a long as any competitor. The company could have implemented process improvement tools to accelerate the completion rate, as stated in Little's Law, but this would have proven insufficient in reducing lead time by 50 percent. The challenge was that the company was historically using EOQ to determine the batch size or the number of "things" in process before changing over from one hose type to the next—meaning it struggled to balance the EOQ demands for large batch sizes against the

Figure 9.4
Example changeover pattern in hose and fitting production line.

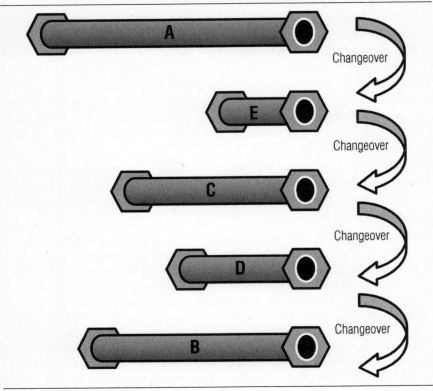

need to deliver a variety of products. There was also no question that the hose supplier needed to work on both factors in Little's Law in order to reduce lead times by 50 percent. It needed to address the completion rate (using Lean Six Sigma tools) and also the number of "things" in process, which required something more than just EOQ to plan and schedule work.

The secrets of enterprise flexibility lay before the company within the concept of *minimum safe batch sizing*. Reducing batch sizes could minimize the time the production line was locked onto producing any given hose type. The lower the quantity of any given hose type in process, the lower the TIMWOOD process wastes (Chapter 2), and the more rapidly the company could respond to changes in demand and product mix. Determining these new minimum safe batch sizes required use of two equations: Workstation Turnover Time (WTT) and Cycle Time Interval (CTI). Before getting into

Figure 9.5
Concept of Workstation Turnover Time.

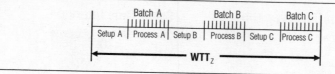

Figure 9.6
Cycle Time Interval.

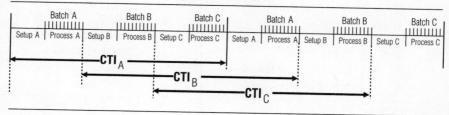

the math of these equations, look first at what they represent, as shown in Figures 9.5 and 9.6, respectively.

Workstation Turnover Time is how long it takes for the workstation to complete one full production cycle of all products scheduled for that station. Figure 9.5 graphic shows two full cycles for three products (A, B, C).

Cycle Time Interval, in contrast to WTT, is a metric that reflects the view of an individual product or service rather than the workstation. It is the time it takes from the start of one production run of the product/service to the next run of that same product/service. The graph in Figure 9.6 shows the cycle time intervals for the three products shown in Figure 9.5.

The equations for WTT and CTI are shown in Figure 9.7.

This pair of equations combines to provide the direct link between actual process capability and the product demand for each part or item in the portfolio. Taken together, they form a closed-loop system that works to accelerate enterprise speed and flexibility as well as to improve return on invested capital. Workstation Turnover Time captures the relative capability of the production process and its flexibility, while Cycle Time Interval determines the order frequency of each part or item in the portfolio, based on the rate of demand and its yield. Notice that in order to solve for the minimum safe batch size, the equations take into account the dynamic performance characteristics of the process (the production rate, setup or changeover time, and product yield), and they do so for all items in the portfolio being produced.

Figure 9.7
Flexibility equations.

Workstation Turnover Time	Cycle Time Interval
$$WTT_k = \sum_{i=1}^{N} (SU_i + P_i \times B_i)$$	$$CTI_i = \frac{(B_i \times Y_i)}{DMD_i}$$

Where:

WTT = Workstation Turnover Time
SU_i = Setup Time for Part i
P_i = Processing time per unit for Part i
B_i = Batch size for Part i
N = All part numbers produced at the workstation

Where:

DMD_i = Production rate for Part i
B_i = Batch size for Part i
Y_i = Yield for Part i
CTI_i = Cycle Time Interval for Part i (order/build frequency)

Patent-protected by Accenture, LLC.

Further, these equations help with the identification and prioritization of Lean Six Sigma projects. It becomes clear how much speed and flexibility can be improved by reducing setup times, increasing production rates, (especially through maintenance excellence), or improving product yield (elimination of defects).

This holistic approach enables enterprise flexibility by safely reducing the amount of work-in-process to the minimum level required to meet customer demand as process capability is improved. Further, these equations illustrate the impact that setup time, processing rate, and yield can have on reducing the number of "things" in process (batch size). Select most any of these tools and you can identify a factor in one of the flexibility equations or in Little's Law the Lean Six Sigma toolset applies.

Here are some of the concepts and interrelationships that these equations help us to understand:

- Enterprise flexibility is a factor of both process flexibility (as stated by Workstation Turnover Time) as well as the frequency at which each item in the product portfolio must be produced (as stated by Cycle Time Interval).
- Workstation Turnover Time (WTT) allows us to understand the impact that work-in-process (batch size) has on flexibility.
- The lower the batch size, the lower the value will be for WTT; hence, the greater the degree of flexibility.

- Setup time reduction is a primary enabler of lowering WTT and increasing flexibility. It directly affects the size of the batch required to meet demand per item in the portfolio. The lower the setup time, the lower the batch size can be reduced. Smaller batches equal increased flexibility, as shown in the Cycle Time Interval (CTI) equation.
- Equipment or operator processing rate also affects WTT: the higher the processing rate (per minute, hour, or day), the lower the batch can be reduced. Processing rates can be greatly improved by maintenance excellence—reducing the frequency of equipment failures and mean time to repair them.
- Cycle Time Interval (CTI) helps explain the frequency at which items in the offering portfolio must be produced.
- The frequency of required production (CTI) is determined not only by demand but also the batch size required and product yield.
- The lower the CTI value, the greater the enterprise flexibility.
- If WTT is high because of poor process operating conditions (low or unstable processing rates, long setup times), then batch sizes must be increased to meet demand.
- Increased batch sizes adversely impact CTI—increasing the interval and lowering the frequency at which all other items in the portfolio can be produced—extending the duration during which we must wait to be able to produce any given item again greatly degrades enterprise flexibility.

THE EQUATIONS IN ACTION

Here is a case study to illustrate the benefits of implementing these equations in product planning and scheduling as part of a holistic Lean Six Sigma transformation: A few years ago we were supporting an enterprise deployment of Lean Six Sigma at a multibillion dollar continuous process industry manufacturer of household building products. When developing their value agenda for project selection, the team found that one plant had particularly high costs: slow enterprise speed, the fewest number of inventory turns among all plants, large amounts of finished goods inventory, and high costs of scrap and obsolescence. The plant was not able to meet changing customer demand for the increased numbers of products in the portfolio and had excessive lost sales. Quite the antithesis of fast, agile, and flexible.

Part of the assessment included analyzing the company's production planning process. We found that all schedules and batch sizes were determined using EOQ alone. This particular plant needed to be able to produce

2850 linear feet of product per hour. On average, the plant would run most part numbers for 14 hours nonstop before shutting down, doing a setup or changeover, and then running the next part number in the schedule. As we have seen in many transformation initiatives, reliance on EOQ alone to size batches can tend to increase them, unnecessarily, which degrades both Workstation Turnover Time and Cycle Time Interval—the true determinants of enterprise flexibility. This plant was no exception.

An operations assessment included gathering the data for calculating WTT and CTI. Even though the plant was experiencing an array of process-related problems, and was a ripe environment for Lean Six Sigma, applying the equations demonstrated that running batches for longer than 8 hours had diminishing returns. In other words, the plant could reduce the run length (or batch size) per part from 14 hours down to 8 hours and still produce 2850 linear feet of product per hour (see Figure 9.8)—all without having to make any shop-floor improvements.

Reliance on economic order quantity alone was causing the scheduling team to increase the run length (batch size) between product changeovers

Figure 9.8
Run length versus product changeovers.

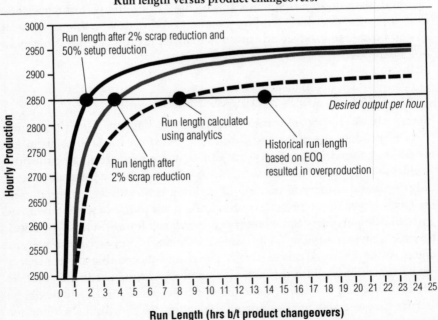

by 42.8 percent! Refer to the equations for WTT and CTI: What is the affect on enterprise flexibility if we reduce the batch by 42.8 percent?

The company found that product yields could also be improved by implementing Lean Six Sigma's quality tools to reduce variability. Readers familiar with high-volume, continuous-process industries know that small process improvements can yield huge financial benefits. We identified opportunities to reduce defects and enabled a 2 percent improvement in product yield. With improved yields, we recalculated CTI, which is determined in part by yield. The 2 percent improvement in quality not only reduced direct operating costs but, as the analytics showed, allowed a further reduction of run length (batch size) from 8 hours between item changeovers down to 4 hours run length (see Figure 9.7)—reducing run length by an additional 50 percent.

Focusing on setup reduction lowered the changeover time from 5.2 hours to 2.6 hours. If you refer back to the WTT equation, you will note the impact that reducing setup time has on improving process flexibility (reducing workstation turnover time). Using the equation, we proved that this 50 percent improvement in setup time would produce yet another 50 percent reduction in product run length (batch size).

Again look at Figure 9.7 to see how these combined efforts enabled a total reduction in run length (batch size) from the original 14 hours between changeovers down to only 2 hours. An improvement in enterprise flexibility of 85 percent!

In addition to reducing the cost of poor quality, the client was able to reduce finished goods inventory by $4.7 million, freeing up needed capital—not to mention gaining the flexibility to rapidly respond to market demands and grow revenues by avoiding lost sales.

In this client case, run lengths were reduced gradually, and safety stocks were recalculated to account for any variation in production rate, as well as variation in demand and seasonality. The key takeaway from this case is that without the implementation of the two equations of enterprise flexibility, WTT and CTI, the client would have reaped incremental improvement in cost at the process level but not at the enterprise level. The client would have indeed saved 2.6 hours of direct labor in setup time and the reduced the costs of poor quality by improving yield. Without linking these process improvements to production planning and scheduling via WTT and CTI, the client would have gone on using EOQ alone, run lengths would have been excessive, and the opportunity of enterprise flexibility would have been lost.

CONCLUSION

Enterprise speed and flexibility can enable step-change reductions in cost, as well as provide opportunities to grow revenue by means of rapid response to changes in demand and product mix. Most organizations focus improvements at the process level, without linking the improved dynamic process capability to work scheduling and planning. Many organizations implement economic order quantity alone to determine their production schedules in an attempt to balance setup costs with inventory carrying costs. But as product portfolios expand and cost strategies dictate lower inventories EOQ may fall short in that it only considers one part or item at a time—without comprehension of the adverse affects it has on enterprise flexibility and market responsiveness by increasing batch sizes. Lean analytics have been developed to address this issue, but these equations present but one aspect of the analytics and approach required to support a Lean Six Sigma transformation. There are multiple considerations and efforts involved, such as demand and supply planning, sales and operations planning (S&OP), pull system implementation, safety stock strategies, materials sourcing, maintenance excellence, and others.

Still, the equations offer an understanding of why the tools of process improvement by themselves will not enable enterprise speed and flexibility—especially if work planning and scheduling is not based on the actual, dynamic, capabilities of the business. Deploying the tools only at the process level will fail to deliver their full potential; they need to be implemented as part of a transformation journey. This journey toward enterprise transformation requires understanding, commitment, fortitude, and the engagement of leadership to align the organization to a vital few key North Star goals and stay the course.

CHAPTER 10

REDUCE THE COST
OF COMPLEXITY

With Danny Lin and Jon Hunter

A global retailer had been aggressively expanding its market presence through larger stores and more product types, moving away from the staple products that was core to the legacy business.

There had finally come a point when the retailer realized it was hitting a limit on its functional capabilities. The increased product variety moving through the replenishment process had created inconsistent demand/forecasting utilization, leading to profit seepage and lower overall process efficiency. The company was also burdened by higher costs to serve customers. Combined, these issues created a burning platform around the need to reduce overall costs and assess total process performance.

The retailer's first attempts at trying to improve productivity and cost savings had been carried out at a functional level, and when those efforts led to unimpressive results, it realized it needed to take a completely different approach.

The second time around, it began by building an end-to-end cross-functional view of the replenishment process, mapping out the links from forecasting and planning to bringing the products to the shelf's edge. The company performed an in-depth targeted analysis of base and hidden costs tied to executing the current processes, looking at how the greater complexity in product lines was affecting the supply chain. The cost of this complexity came from the intricate handoffs and interactions between the merchandising, supply chain, and store operations functions, in the form of lost sales, excess inventory, high degrees of damage, employee theft, and the significant but unmeasurable lost employee productivity from trying to navigate the maze of product options.

By adopting this end-to-end view, the retailer realized that its functional focus was driving waste and inefficiencies. Further, its lack of performance metrics that measured *overall* value stream performance, end to end, had created blind spots about what the increased complexity was costing them, and thus limited the ability to respond to issues.

These realizations opened the door for major changes in how the retailer managed its replenishment system. It standardized and simplified in-store replenishment, developed a more accurate demand signal system, reduced inventory levels, and made costs more transparent through the value stream. Overall, the analysis uncovered opportunities representing a staggering 4 percent cost-out—a major improvement for an industry used to 1 to 2 percent gross margin performance.

This retailer's experience with complexity and the hidden costs it imposes on an organization is becoming more and more common. Whether through organic growth or acquisition, numerous companies have reached a point where their portfolios of products or services are bloated, their internal processes resemble a nightmarish web, and they are carrying significant capital costs and personnel needed to support all of that complexity.

Worst of all, many companies have no clear idea of what their complexity is costing them. The complicated web of products, processes, and capital resources that companies weave hides the very costs it creates! In good times, the high water level of profitability hides the jagged rocks of complexity. But in times of financial turmoil—whether through environmental change, competitive forces, or overexpansion—the costs of complexity quickly overtake the organization. Issues long hidden in the balance sheet spring to life and infect the organization's earnings.

Ironically, the solution to business complexity is relatively simple. Having worked with numerous organizations, we have seen a variety of challenges solved simply by taking a step back from the "crime scene" and evaluating what is killing the business and what is sustaining it. The revelations from this holistic point of view are staggering and sometime revolutionary. In the remainder of this chapter, we will examine the issue of complexity in more depth and then walk through a set of simple techniques for evaluating how complexity both hurts and helps your organization in its goals of delivering enterprise value to your shareholders and market-relevant products or services to your customers.

THE HIDDEN COST OF ADDED OFFERINGS ON PROCESSES

An agribusiness company had long prided itself on being responsive to customer demands, offering many feature options to its customers. Delivering these features cost the company dearly; one division, for example, needed 120 additives. When the company decided to look at the complexity it was carrying, it realized that the actual performance of its agriproducts did not rely on the features that had been requested by (and were now marketed to) customers. It had locked itself into very expensive production processes that could never return as much value as they consumed because of hidden costs, such as all the warehousing of numerous products with different combination of options, increased inventory, higher supplier costs, and so on (see Figure 10.1).

The speed of innovation has been both a blessing and a curse. While a differentiated portfolio of products and services is effective in winning new customers and driving new growth, portfolio complexity can mire productivity and actually destroy shareholder value. Blind growth without a deep understanding of the asset base required to produce additional products and services can create hidden costs as the offerings intersect with processes across

Figure 10.1
Hidden costs of complexity.

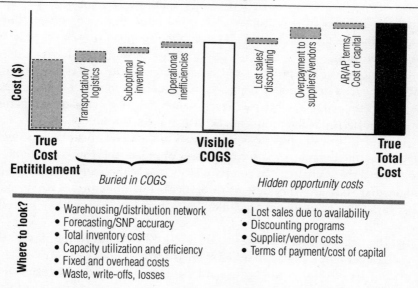

the different functions in the organization. Many managers fail to fully understand these impacts because the complexity creeps in slowly over time.

For example, in today's world, a telecom company needs to create a wide array of packages to entice customers. However, the breadth of this assortment can lead to significant levels of complexity, as the technical challenges of pairing different systems together leads to complexity in all functions of the business. Operations must allow connectivity between vastly different systems or create complicated deployment strategies; finance must be able to track the pricing and discounts for a burgeoning array of service combinations; the legal department must support different regulatory commitments; customer service must create complex scripts to support the customers in the field . . . and on and on. Such complexity magnifies if the telecom service users cross state lines or country boundaries, and becomes a nightmare to unravel when the decision is made to sunset a particular service.

Understanding True Costs

When described in black-and-white as in the preceding examples, it seems like the impact and costs of complexity should be obvious. But they aren't. Why not? The short answer is that the cost of an overly assorted portfolio of offerings is often masked by inappropriate cost allocation techniques. Managers often make the mistake of assuming that offerings consume the utilization of an asset equally (such as plants, equipment, people, systems, and so on), when in fact the opposite is true. Offerings have very different levels of asset utilization.

In typical cost allocation, fixed costs are generally represented by the G&A expenses or overhead captured in the bottom line. But costs are not closely examined at the offering level, which creates an inaccurate picture of the *true* costs of each product or service in the portfolio.

Consider, for example, two toaster lines in the same portfolio, one sized for bagels and another sized for four slices of bread (this four-slice model is considered the standard). To compare true costs of these two products, you might first start at the middle of the process (manufacturing) to evaluate cost variation. Typical issues include:

- The bagel toaster shell has to be molded by another vendor, and the cost per unit is higher than the standard size.
- The bagel toaster molds are harder to maintain, and breakage causes delays, which leads to expediting costs to accommodate the schedules.

- The bagel toaster may see much lower volumes than the standard, so the carrying cost for production of the lower-volume bagel unit is higher because you have two to three times as much inventory.

Further, manufacturing isn't the only place you might find differences in costs that are hidden from typical accounting practices:

Upstream Costs of Complexity

- Marketing may tell you that products that don't fit easily into retailers' thinking may be charged a premium for shelf space.
- Low-volume products (like the bagel toasters) often aren't included in sales programs.
- Low-volume products are notorious for having high variation in demand, making it hard to forecast sales.
- The may be additional quality assurance (QA) testing costs. In this case, toast reacts one way to heat and bagels a little differently. There might also be considerations around how consumers might use the product other than for the designed use. What would happen if someone stuck a bagel pizza in a bagel toaster? That would require a separate testing model.

Downstream Costs of Complexity

- Consider the variation in packaging, cubing, shipping volumes, and delivery channels. High-volume products move very differently than the lower-volume bagel toaster. You don't pack and ship the same way or through the same channels. High-volume products are often moved by the pallet load; lower-volume products might be grouped with other products.
- Retailers take the products in different ways and have expectations about how they are arranged for display. For example, a club store (e.g., Sam's or Costco) will want a certain volume and pallet size. With the lower-volume product—arranged in nonstandard ways to accommodate smaller and more variable numbers—retailers may not even be willing to take on the product because of higher handling costs on their end.

None of these costs may be huge by themselves, but start piling on cost after cost, and before you know it there is a true cost difference between the base product and this low-volume "differentiated" product in the portfolio.

Costs allocated in accordance with a simple spread approach for like-type products or services hides the real cost impact of product variation.

ASSESSING COMPLEXITY IN YOUR BUSINESS: A HOLISTIC VIEW

Complexity results from the systemic impact of too many processes, services, customers, parts, and variants on your costs, growth, and ability to execute. Addressing any one single element (that is, customers or offerings) can lead to suboptimal results; step-change requires an integrated, holistic approach. If piecemeal approaches won't work, the question becomes how to develop a holistic view that offers the kind of information you will need to make holistic decisions about complexity in your business.

Before You Begin: Anchor on the Customer

Before starting the assessment, you need to develop a strong understanding of the customer(s) benefiting from the processes. Remember, complexity is unwanted only if customers do not value it highly enough to pay you sufficiently for what it costs to deliver. (In this context, the customer doesn't have to be external to the organization. If the value stream under evaluation is an internally facing support function, such as training or finance reporting, the "customer" is the business itself. That would color how you frame the processes, define the products and services, and compile the organizational functions that should be reviewed.)

As you walk through your process during the assessment, imagine you are the product or service being worked on. Where would you get pulled in multiple directions simultaneously? Where would your time be wasted, or worse? Where would you be sitting around waiting? You gain an insightful point of view when you start to turn the customer eye on every element of your process, not just the ones that directly touch customers. Sometimes it isn't the storefront that causes the most damage, but rather the missed instructions during the packing process, or the poor decisions about design before the product is even built, that hurts the customer the most.

To evaluate complexity in your business and come up with an agenda for tackling it, we recommend a four-phase approach, shown in Figure 10.2.

The process should be led by a small group of complexity experts who know which questions to ask, what data to look for, how to recognize

Figure 10.2
Overview of the complexity analysis process.

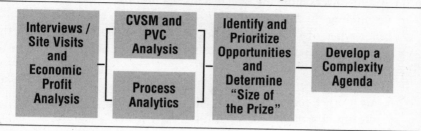

complexity in all its manifestations, and how to help decision makers set an agenda for tackling complexity.

The secret to complexity analysis lies not so much in the generic description of these steps but in knowing which questions to ask, which red flags to look for in daily operations, and how to bring all the information together into a coherent picture so that executives can see their business and its opportunities in new lights.

Going through these steps in detail is beyond the scope of this chapter, so, instead, we'll cover a few highlights, then walk through a case study to show how all of these pieces come together to provide strategic insights that executives would have trouble getting in any other way.

HIGHLIGHTS OF THE COMPLEXITY ANALYSIS PROCESS

As we've said, complexity is good at hiding in your organization. Looking at traditional management data or reports won't help you much. Similarly, talking only to high-level executives will give you a skewed or incomplete view of the impact of complexity: Though it is their decisions that create complexity in an organization, they usually have little or no exposure at the process level, where the impact of that complexity is felt directly.

That's why the assessment process we recommend includes:

- Interviewing people at all levels—starting with those who are experts in your process (by virtue of working with the core value stream processes day in and day out) and including various levels of management so you can see how *they* view their part of the business and relationship to other parts.

- Following up the interviews with site visits so you can see for yourself exactly how complexity affects daily operations.
- Grounding the effort with an *Economic Profit* (EP) *analysis*. Unlike other types of financial analysis, EP looks at the relative value that products and services are contributing to (or taking away from) the business.
- Establishing benchmarks by comparing ROIC and return on assets against other companies in the same industry and other companies of a like business model, size, or product/service type.
- Reallocating costs to individual product or service *families* and then to individual product or services so that you gain a better understanding of the true costs (as explained by the earlier bagel versus standard toaster example). This will allow for additional analysis on the areas of the portfolio that are disproportionately burdening the operation.
- Calculating PCE (Process Cycle Efficiency) on the value stream(s) or processes that are part of your analysis. (PCE was described in Chapter 5.)
- Performing both a Prime Value Chain analysis and Complexity Value Stream analysis (see below).
- Using all of the information above to identify opportunities, grouped by impact or functional sets.
- Identifying the drivers that impact the metric(s) being targeted (such as cost).
- Evaluating risk, feasibility, and benefits, and constructing a benefit/effort matrix for all opportunities—the matrix can help shape a potential roadmap for addressing complexity (see Figure 10.3).

The two analyses in this process you are probably least familiar with are the Prime Value Chain and Complexity Value Stream. Before getting into the case study, we wanted to give you some idea of what those tools are and what how they help.

Prime Value Chain Analysis: Finding the Hidden Cost of Value Streams That Traverse the Business

Key insights into what complexity is doing to your organization comes from looking at the flow of work from the customer or value-chain perspective. We call this a *Prime Value Chain* (PVC) analysis. PVC analysis assesses whether your processes, organization, and structure are aligned to deliver your strategy.

Figure 10.3

Mapping a complexity roadmap: A typical complexity agenda would include plans for using Lean Six Sigma to tackle some quick wins (upper left), then proceeding (arrow A) to the low-feasibility/low-impact opportunities (lower left), to be considered if they help set up success in higher-impact effort. Following arrow B, attention then turns to strategic priorities (upper right), which are typically issues that only management can address. The high-effort/low-impact projects (arrow C) would be a last consideration, done only if you have the time and budget.

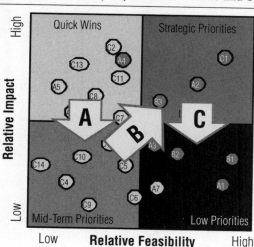

The endeavor to understand how value streams traverse a business is essential to reinforcing the core objectives of organization. By drawing out a Prime Value Chain and the related interactions between organizational functions, you can:

- Create a holistic view, often leading to new insights:
  — Considers the ecosystem of participants.
  — Identifies issues and constraints that impact process or business performance.
  — Shows broken or misaligned linkages.
- Identify broader, more strategic issues often missed with other approaches.
- Identify highest-value areas and issues on which to focus improvement efforts.
- Identify key leverage points in which to "overinvest."

Figure 10.4
Step 1 in PVC construction.

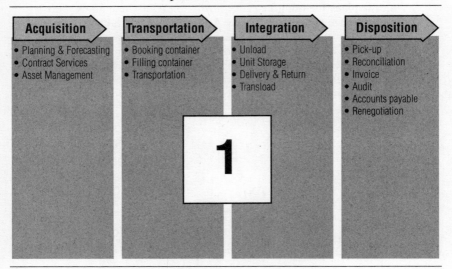

Following is a summary of the steps for performing a PVC analysis.

1. *Define core value-chain functions:* Listed at the top of the diagram in large chevrons are the highest-level functions of the business that together deliver value to the customer (Figure 10.4). These functions set the boundaries of the Prime Value Chain. There should be no more than three to five functions, with little overlap between them. The divisions should be mutually exclusive, collectively exhaustive (MECE), to the extent possible.
2. *Define supporting departments:* This step involves identifying the departments that support the high-level functions established in step 1. They are usually depicted as smaller chevrons right below the core functions listed at the top (Figure 10.5). Aim for two to three support functions in each main division. MECE once again applies.

PVC Construction Tip

The boxes in the PVC sections are not meant to represent particular organizations or business units, but rather processes and systems/tools. So you won't find anything labeled "marketing department" on a PVC, but you will find boxes such as "promoting the product" and "defining customer needs."

Figure 10.5
Step 2 in PVC construction.

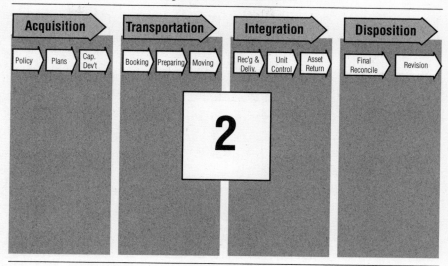

3. *Populate the PVC with functioning units:* Construct "bins" defining functioning units (for example, systems, organizational units, internal/external stakeholders, and so on) that represent major investments in the business. The relative size of the boxes that represent these units can be weighted by budget size, importance, relevance to the value chain, and so on (Figure 10.6).

4. *Draw the interactions:* Finally, use arrows to depict the interactions between functioning units (Figure 10.7). The arrows cans indicate the flow of information, resources, or simply strong relationships or process drivers. You would likely be able to completely fill your PVC with arrows, so it's important to focus only on the high-level, significant relationships.

As you are completing the diagram, be alert for potential problems areas, such as:

- Poor utilization of assets
- Breaks in the process or information flow from one functional area or activity to another
- Redundancies (for example, one organization reaching out to multiple orgs that do the same things)
- A lot of work flowing into one organization; that might represent a bottleneck

Figure 10.6
Step 3 in PVC construction.

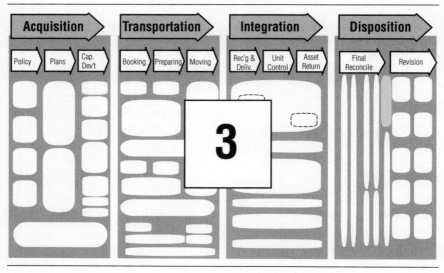

Figure 10.7
Step 4 in PVC construction.

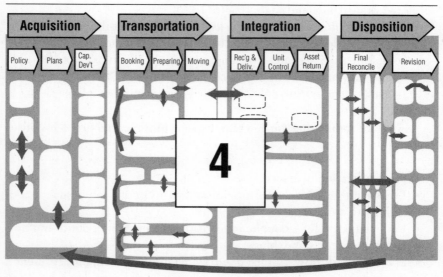

Impact of PVC Maps

The overall impact of the PVC point of view is a holistic understanding of the key activities and capabilities required to execute against the organizations current or planned strategic objectives. The PVC view allows you to focus on the value streams that, when looked at across the enterprise, are not aligned or performing in a manner consistent with the objectives.

For example, if an organization has aligned its resources so that there is low support on the front end and a high level of resourcing on the back end (that is, order processing), you would expect to find a value stream that needs to support *high volumes of post buy-decision activity* (such as order processing, payment, invoicing, and so on) and standard/minimal customer requirements on the front end. However, that resource alignment would not make sense if the portfolio of products was complex and it was hard to push clients to make a buy decision; or even worse, the portfolio had evolved over time and there was a diverse mix of demand.

Complexity Value Stream Maps

Through Prime Value Chain analysis, you will have a better understanding of the functional challenges that exist. One key takeaway from the PVC should be identifying which particular value streams are responsible for the most enterprise value destruction. That said, you cannot fully understand all of the interactions between functions and the cost- and growth-impact of the variety in processes based solely on a PVC diagram. For that kind of information, a technique call *Complexity Value Stream Mapping* (CVSM) comes in handy.

Like regular value stream maps, a CVSM is focused on the flow of work through your business. But instead of focusing on just one value stream, you look at the interactions *across multiple value streams*.

Constructing a Complexity Value Stream Map is very similar to traditional mapping (some of the steps are the same) but CVSMs allow for greater visibility into the complexities your organization. (See the comparison in Figure 10.8.) They help you determine the complexity you should get rid of and the complexity you should keep.

Overview of CVSM Steps

Building a CVSM begins as you would any process-mapping exercises. Once you have the basic process steps depicted, the next task is to

Figure 10.8
Comparing CVSMs with typical process maps.

From As-Is / To-Be Process Maps...	... To Complexity Value Stream Maps
Traditional Approach	**Complexity Approach**
As-Is processes are mapped with standardization in mind and are blind to process complexity	Complexity is captured throughout the analysis, inlcuding key hand-offs systems impacts, and NVA activities
"To-Be" solutions are based on logical structuring of work	Recommendations focused on reducing complexity and variability that is destroying enterprise value
Results are documented and standardized, but there are no measures of success	Data-rich analysis establishes measurable results and provides a means to determine success
Targeting of analysis usually based on anecdotal information	Targeting of analysis based on true economic profitability and enterprise value

determine the level of complexity you are going to explore. For instance, if you believe there is a greater degree of complexity as you cross geographical boundaries, then you should examine the process through that lens. Once you've established which perspective you are going to be viewing from, start navigating the value stream from that perspective. So if you've used geography as your lens, "walk" the value stream and document how the process changes for one region; then go back and repeat for each other region. Make sure to highlight the path of each region in a different color so as to capture where the process takes a different route.

Now, identify where the greatest concentrations of variability exist and highlight them with color coding or special symbols. One example is shown in Figure 10.9. In real life, different-colored self-stick notes were used to indicate different types of information, as described by the labels on the figure.

Figure 10.9
Photo of an actual CVSM in progress.

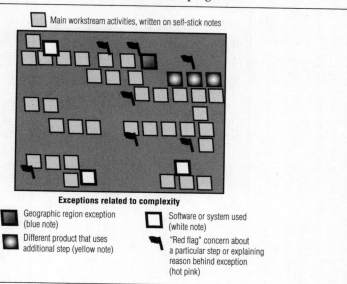

For each cluster, determine whether the issue is system related, process related, or people related. Questions you should be asking are:

- Is a system limitation (that is, legacy system, data handoff between systems, and so on) the reason one group diverted from the standard process?
- Does the process have to be this complicated to establish a differentiated product or service? Can it be simpler?
- Are the right people involved and properly trained? Are they resistant to a new technology or policy?

By asking these questions at each stage, the reasons for complexity become more apparent. The final product looks something like Figure 10.10.

As you go through this analysis, you will be able to narrow the number of functions represented down the left side to focus on the functional groups key to the process, information, and decision-making flow. For example, you would want to keep human resources as a represented group if a key issue is retention and training. Representing human resources probably would not be important, conversely, if the issue at hand was assessing supply chain performance.

Figure 10.10

Example CVSM: In this type of chart, colors are used to help to quickly highlight areas of interest or concern. Shaded boxes (red on the real thing) are the equivalent of red flags. The intention of the map is twofold: (1) to highlight the areas that have caused the most problems; and (2) to allow the team to evaluate the places that, when viewed individually, may not seem significant, but when looked at thematically, comprise a substantial issue hindering performance.

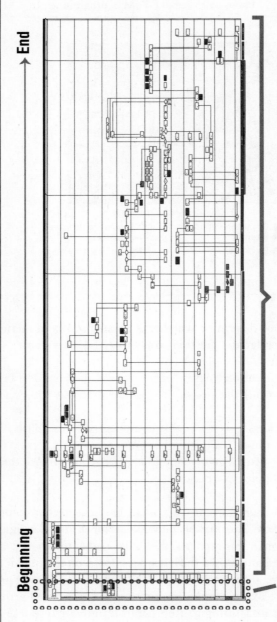

Beginning ——————→ **End**

Key stakeholders
Each functional group should be represented by a "swim lane" on the chart.

Value Stream Activities
Each major step in the value stream must be represented by boxes in the map and placed in the swim lane of the stakeholder who "owns" it. Lines connecting the steps show the interactions across functions. Using different colors can help in identifying process variation.

Creating a Complexity Agenda: A Case Study

One recent experience that clearly demonstrates how the pieces of complexity analysis come together to help executives set an agenda for reducing complexity and its costs comes from a consumer foods company. In going through the steps outlined in this section, the company discovered five strategic levers that management could tackle to reduce complexity.

Lever #1: Rationalize the portfolio. The portfolio of food products was bloated; the company had not effectively managed SKU proliferation. The Economic Profit and cost allocation analysis components demonstrated that management had an inadequate understanding of true cost of introducing new products.

Lever #2: Reevaluate production scheduling and capacity constraints. The company had severe capacity limitations. The fixed assets (manufacturing plants, primarily) were designed to produce high-volume products. But the portfolio expansion had added a lot of lower-volume products demanded by the market. Producing the low-volume products took up production capacity, so the company ended up having to use a third-party producer to keep up production levels on the high-volume products.

The company had decided to absorb the third-party costs because, according to standard accounting practices, the low-volume products looked like they were generating much higher margins. However, once it reallocated costs based on a better understanding of the impact of the low-volume products, that margin shrunk substantially. The margin of the low-volume products was still higher than the standard high-volume products, but the choice about which to produce was no longer a slam dunk.

Lever #3: Change how they manage back-end inventory (returns). Because this company produces food items, it had a dogmatic approach to managing returns, expending a lot of time and effort to recapture and reprocess unsold inventory (yet because of poor scheduling and communication, the reprocessed product was seldom sold). The hypersensitivity was understandable—the company did *not* want its products sold under its label on the secondary market, after the expiration dates.

Here again, though, once the company understood the true costs of trying to handle these returns, a much better option presented itself: just destroy the unsold product.

Lever #4: Change quality assurance practices. This company had been in business for a long time, and though its production processes had evolved, its QA practices had not. Because the risks having a faulty

(continued)

(continued)

product intended for human consumption were so great, the company had never reexamined its QA procedures.

However, through the complexity analysis, and particularly the site visits, company management began to truly appreciate the impact of the frequent and major interruptions to the manufacturing processes because of QA procedures. They saw, for example, that products with bad labels was pulled off the line and sat there, waiting to go through the standard QA procedures even through there was a not an issue with the its quality. More broadly, they saw the cumulative impact of QA procedures all along the value chain, and how it threw off planning and forecasting. In all, QA accounted for 36 percent of the total cycle time.

Lever #5: Revise the planning and forecasting model. In completing the Complexity Value Stream Map, the team began in the middle of the process and then branched out toward the beginning and end points inside the company. (Actually, the ideal is to trace the work until it completes a loop, so you can see how what happens at the end affects what happens at the beginning.) As indicated previously, part of the "aha" here was how both returns and QA practices affected planning and forecasting.

Summary of the Situation

Managers at this food company were faced with a number of high costs built into the way it conducted business, exacerbated by the complexity it carried:

- Too many products (which increased costs at every step in production and planning).
- Time-consuming, high-cost practices, which, although prompted by good intentions (avoiding very real risks, primarily), were destroying more value than they created (handling of returns, QA practices).

In addition to the strategic levers, the complexity team identified 75 tactical opportunities (problems that could be solved with the array of Lean Six Sigma methods), which they displayed on a benefit/effort matrix, like the one shown previously. Ultimately, the complexity agenda for this company therefore included a mix of Lean Six Sigma projects to address the high-priority tactical projects, plus strategic projects focused on the capacity constraint and SKU proliferation issues. In the first year, the company cut 20 percent of its SKUs, and the next time around made even tougher cuts because management got smarter at understanding how to better evaluate true margins that accounted for complexity costs.

COMPLEXITY REDUCTION AS THE GATEWAY TO TRANSFORMATION

A global, billion-dollar manufacturer and servicer of specialized equipment was alarmed because, although sales were high, profit margin was being eaten away by the high cost of doing business. Because inventory had risen $60 million in its prior fiscal year, management was focused strongly on improving their working capital by reducing inventory. In fact, an initial diagnostic revealed $77 million in working capital improvements through three levers:

- Increase in manufacturing throughput through setup time reductions, improved production planning, and preventative plant maintenance
- Improvements in order to cash processes, including standardized A/R procedures and development of a packaged throughput improvement solution
- Reduction of excess and obsolete inventory and mitigation of future inventory buildup through strong checkbook processes, once effective forecasting was in place

When the company launched an initiative to figure out how it could move these levers and capture the $77 million prize, it discovered a number of operational barriers to improvement, all linked to complexity.

For example, though the company had a limited number of products in its portfolio, the repair service operations it ran had been expanding in recent years. While not necessarily a bad thing in and of itself, Economic Profit calculations showed that many of the new types of repair work being taken on could not generate sufficient profit to justify the expense. Furthermore, taking on this additional work often meant the repair operations provided slower service to the purchasers of the company's own equipment (and increased inventory levels across the value chain as the repair operations attempted in a backhand way to minimize its cycle time).

Also, there was no coordination across the service operations, either, which meant no possibilities for economies of scales. Every repair center had to be prepared to service every kind of equipment, which also led to increased inventory levels across the company.

In looking at the interactions *between* value streams—a Complexity Value Stream exercise—the company discovered that the lack of a true enterprise view had created a "death spiral" of negative interactions, each of which increased inventory and hindered its ability to serve its current customers—let alone grow the company. For example: Poor maintenance increased bottlenecks, which increased the variation between forecasts and actual production levels, and affected what was shipped to customers, and when, which in turn led to problems with invoice reconciliation.

Before it could really capture the capital benefits from inventory reduction, the company had to address these underlying complexity problems. For example, it concentrated different kinds of repair work in different facilities, which cut lead time from 100 days to 10 days. In essence, it kept the complexity in its service portfolio, but made it less expensive (and much faster) to deliver. The company also worked on improving connections between its different value streams, which is a critical enabler to the forecasting improvements it needed to make.

Gains from tackling the complexity agenda and beginning the broader transformation have already topped $30 million, and the company is continuing its journey to capture the rest of the $77 million prize.

CONCLUSION

Of all the forms of waste discussed in this book, complexity is one of the most insidious. Overproliferation of products, services, features, and processes eats away at your profit margin in ways that are hard to detect if you stick to traditional accounting practices. To truly know whether the variety you are offering to customers is paying for itself (and then some), you have to look closely at how that variety impacts the processes you use to design, produce, deliver, sell, and service it. Trimming off any variety that customers do not value highly enough is one of the most effective steps you can take to trim costs across your entire organization.

CHAPTER 11

LOOK OUTSIDE YOUR FOUR WALLS TO LOWER COSTS INSIDE

Developing an Extended Enterprise Mentality Can Help You Capitalize on Cost Reduction Opportunities with Suppliers and Distributors

With Jeff Howard, Chris Kennedy, and John Smith

There comes a point in every Lean Six Sigma deployment when leaders realize that the best way to drive more cost reduction *inside* the value chain is to look outside that chain. Or, rather, to extend their view of that value chain both upstream and downstream.

What does it means to extend the view of your value chain? Here's an example:

A year after launching a very aggressive Lean Six Sigma program, the CEO of a global heavy equipment manufacturer was impressed that the initial $30 million investment had already paid for itself. The CEO then began to wonder what kind of opportunities he might be missing by focusing only internally. So he expanded the program both upstream and downstream, developing partnerships with both suppliers and dealers. The company paid to help train staff inside suppliers, identified projects both within the suppliers and joint projects

197

that crossed organizational boundaries, and began developing partnerships with dealers (the companies that sold to the final customer). The benefits were immediate, and included those listed here.

Upstream Improvements

These are changes within suppliers that directly affected performance and/or costs to the manufacturer.

- Significantly reduced scrap, both at suppliers and in the company's own manufacturing operations.
- Reduced scrap by half at one supplier by establishing a common measurement systems.
- Helped a key supplier apply advanced improvement techniques to resolve a long-standing performance issues, which reduced both the supplier's operations and the manufacturing operations.
- Achieved improved material runability from one supplier, which greatly improved manufacturing operations and reduced scrap.
- Reduced lead time by 60 percent by eliminating non-value-add activities *between* the company and some suppliers.
- Reduced supplier inventory costs by implementing replenishment pull systems, analytical batch sizing, and strategic buffers.
- Reduced operational costs.
- Reduced billing errors, which lowered overall costs due to rework.
- Decreased time, errors, and rework that had stemmed from engineering changes to vendor-supplied parts and components.
- Reduced supplier bidding and improved accuracy by 70 percent.

Downstream Improvements

These are dealer improvements that also benefited the manufacturer.

- Reduced shipping charges associated with returned/unused parts.
- Reduced delivery costs and improved parts availability and repair centers.
- Reduced maintenance costs.
- Reduced frequency and amount of repair costs when equipment returned after rental period ended.
- Reduced carrying charges by $100,000 annually (associated with unbilled work balances and errors).
- Increased warranty acceptance rate and revenue generation by 20 percent.

- Improved inventory accuracy from 30 to 95 percent, with $2 million growth in sales/rental revenues.

In addition, the customer-focused (downstream) activities led to product growth, improved customer satisfaction, and a better understanding of customer requirements.

The experience of this global manufacturer is typical. Most organizations implementing Lean Six Sigma are able to very quickly take costs out of their day-to-day operations. But it soon becomes clear that no matter how much they improve their own operations, significant components of cost are determined beyond their four walls. In fact, the performance of a company with world-class process excellence can be overshadowed by the performance of its suppliers and dealers/distributors. The overall result will be dissatisfied customers, high cost, and lackluster growth.

To achieve the next level of improvement, Lean Six Sigma companies begin to look at the flow of work both before and after their operations. In many ways this is a natural outgrowth: After you've begun to clean your own house, you will want to make sure that the suppliers and immediate customers (perhaps dealers or retailers) you work with to create value for an ultimate customer will also need to be a partner in improving their costs.

We label this move to consider operational excellence in terms of what comes before and after your internal operations as an *Extended Enterprise* (EE).

In this chapter, we'll discuss what's involved in adopting an Extended Enterprise view, the benefits it can bring, and how to put the concept into practice.

What Is an Extended Enterprise?

The fundamental premise behind the notion of an Extended Enterprise is changing from a *functional view*, where departments and individuals have narrowly defined responsibilities related to specific functions, to a *process view*, which focuses on the work needed to deliver customer value.

A functional perspective helps realize some financial performance and scalability, but often can cause:

- Excess overhead and investment
- Long cycle times
- Poor customer satisfaction

A process view starts with an understanding of customers and their needs and then strengthens links between the work that deliver what customers value, and reduces or eliminates work that does not add value This gives the organization a view *across* functional boundaries. In addition to improving work within a function, a process focus develops centered on defining and managing interfaces and resolving problems/gaps.

You probably have heard the terms "value chain" and "supply chain" applied to this process view. We prefer the term Extended Enterprise because it has some important connotations missing from value or supply chain:

- It reflects a mentality that considers the "outside" steps in your value chain as part of your organization. This fosters a more collaborative approach, a tendency to work more closely as partners than as adversaries.
- It recognizes the variable nature of the relationships: Some firms in the Extended Enterprise may operate independently (for example, open-market exchanges) or cooperatively (for example, agreements, partnerships, and contracts). Some linkages may be commodity based (purchases made on price alone), and therefore vary as to who the players are; others may be more permanent (and therefore warrant a more partnershiplike relationship).
- It emphasizes the need to view the entire system as a whole.

No matter what term you use for extending your process view beyond the walls in your organization, you will need to make some fundamental shifts in how work gets done:

- Develop production/R&D/delivery strategies based on *actual customer demand* and holistic demand and capacity planning.
- Change to a pull-based supply chain (one step in the chain sends input for the *next* step in the chain *only* when a signal indicates that next step is ready).
- Work to improve information flow and quality at the points of interaction.
- Identify, deploy, and align all points of the process around common objectives and metrics.
- Restricting the traditional competitive "drive down costs" relationship with suppliers to a few commodities; developing a collaborative partnership with all key suppliers.
- Moving from a reactive to a proactive mentality. For example, an aluminum can manufacturer would normally just watch prices from competing suppliers and purchase on price. That is a reactive way of

Figure 11.1
Linking beginning to end in an Extended Enterprise.

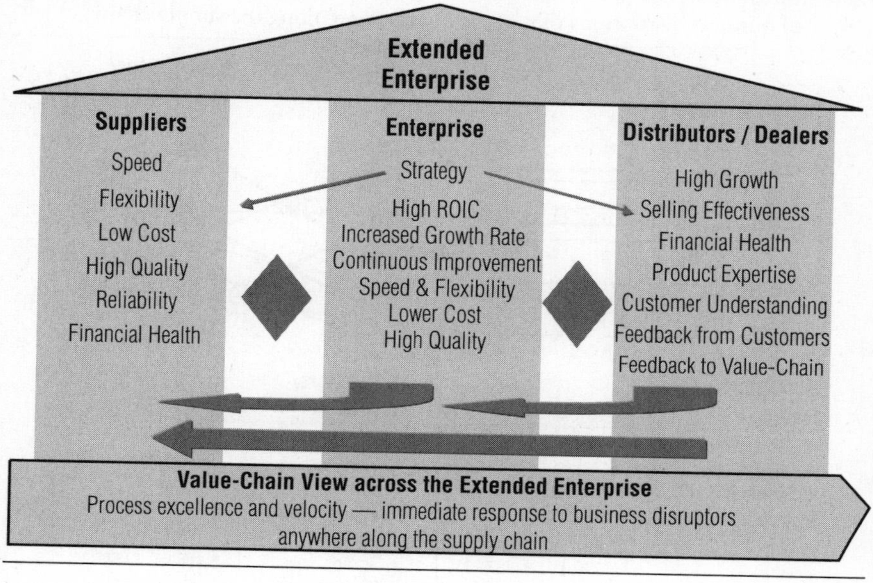

looking at supplier relationships. Under the new mind-set, the can manufacturer would look at its suppliers and say, "How can we work together to reduce overall costs?"

The focus of your efforts will vary depending on whether you are focused on the supplier end or distributor/dealer end, as shown in Figure 11.1.

The benefits of making these changes are manyfold, as summarized in Figure 11.2. Areas of benefit include:

- Shortened lead times
- Increased agility, enabling responsiveness to customer needs
- Improved quality; less rework and fewer returns
- Clear common approach to solving intercompany business problems
- Achieving major financial gains
- Improved value (economic profit/ROIC) across the Extended Enterprise
- Decreased working capital employed across the value chain
- Optimum flexibility and responsiveness to business disruptors
- Improved communication and trust among all EE partners because you're using a common approach, speaking a common language

Figure 11.2
Benefits of an "extended" view: A high-performing Extended Enterprise ensures the
right product or service gets to the customer as fast as possible every time, regardless
of business disruptions that occur at any point along the supply chain.

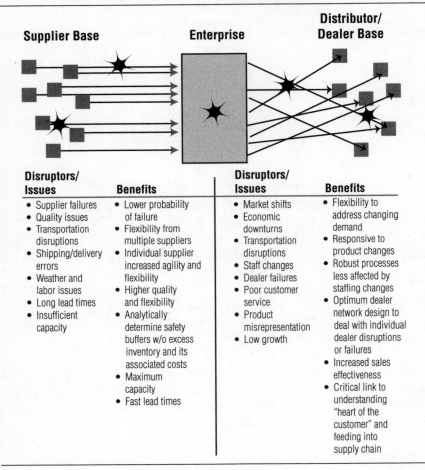

Disruptors/ Issues	Benefits	Disruptors/ Issues	Benefits
• Supplier failures • Quality issues • Transportation disruptions • Shipping/delivery errors • Weather and labor issues • Long lead times • Insufficient capacity	• Lower probability of failure • Flexibility from multiple suppliers • Individual supplier increased agility and flexibility • Higher quality and flexibility • Analytically determine safety buffers w/o excess inventory and its associated costs • Maximum capacity • Fast lead times	• Market shifts • Economic downturns • Transportation disruptions • Staff changes • Dealer failures • Poor customer service • Product misrepresentation • Low growth	• Flexibility to address changing demand • Responsive to product changes • Robust processes less affected by staffing changes • Optimum dealer network design to deal with individual dealer disruptions or failures • Increased sales effectiveness • Critical link to understanding "heart of the customer" and feeding into supply chain

Not only is there a compelling argument as to why to start building an
Extended Enterprise, there are also compelling arguments regarding what
will happen if you don't. Companies that continue with an adversarial or
competitive approach with all of their suppliers are often:

• At the complete mercy of suppliers and dealers or distributors in terms of
speed, quality, cost, capacity, and knowledge of what the end-user needs

- Subject to higher costs overall
- Stuck with an inflexible supply chain
- In a riskier position during slow economic times
- Likelier to miss out on new technologies and innovations
- Ultimately at risk of suffering a loss of market share

Start Measuring What Matters to Customers

A prerequisite for creating an Extended Enterprise is defining measurements that reflect performance across functional boundaries, especially in terms of how well you are serving your customers. Typical metrics are shown in Figure 11.3.

Figure 11.3
Examples of metrics that matter.

	Performance Attribute	Performance Attribute Definition	Level 1 Metrics
Customer-facing Metrics	Supply chain delivery reliability	The performance of the supply chain in delivering: correct product, place, time, condition and packaging, quantity, documentation, customer.	Delivery performance Fill rates Perfect order fultillment
	Supply chain responsiveness	The velocity at which a supply chain provides products to the customer.	Order fulfillment lead times
	Supply chain flexibility	The agility of a supply chain in responding to marketplace changes to gain or maintain competitive advantage.	Supply chain response time Production flexibility
Internal-facing Metrics	Supply chain costs	The costs associated with operating the supply chain.	Costs of goods sold Total supply chain management costs Value-added productivity Warranty/returns processing costs
	Supply chain asset management efficiency	The effectiveness in managing assets to support demand satisfaction. This includes the management of all assets: fixed and working capital.	Cash-to-cash cycle time Inventory days of supply Asset turns

WORKING ON THE SUPPLIER END OF THE EXTENDED ENTERPRISE

More than a decade ago, a company had manufactured a particular piece of sophisticated equipment for the government. But then demand for that equipment fell off and the company shifted from producing new equipment to maintaining the existing equipment. Then, suddenly, the old equipment was back in demand. What could the company do? The knowledge and systems for producing it had long since dissipated in a supply chain with hundreds of players.

Trying to use brute force to make all the pieces fit together wouldn't work, so this company decided to apply its Lean Six Sigma expertise across the extended enterprise. Being able to ramp up quickly and smoothly would be a strong differentiator that would allow the company to keep the government business.

As you know, historically, companies have developed a semiadversarial relationship with suppliers, where they made demands to "drive costs out." That may be okay if you're dealing with a commodity, but how well do you think that approach would work for this specialized equipment manufacturer?

Rather than just saying to suppliers, "Here are the requirements, and we'd like you to use Lean Six Sigma," the company took a more involved approach, looking for opportunities for coinvestment in improvement and shared resources for their critical suppliers. The benefits of this can't be overstated. The increased open communications, mutual understanding of each other's issues, direct experience of how each impacts the other, development of a common approach and language, and a clearer line of sight through to the other links of the extended enterprise all contribute significantly to a higher-performing extended enterprise, one in which all companies benefit.

Even if your company isn't as reliant on supplier cooperation as the specialized manufacturer, the notion of beginning your extended enterprise journey by looking upstream still applies. After all, working with suppliers puts *you* in the customer seat, and will give you more leverage (at least with some suppliers).

Types of Supplier Relationships

The type of relationship you have with suppliers will naturally influence the type of work you should include in an Extended Enterprise plan and how much benefit you can expect. Generally speaking, we divide the level of maturity into four levels, as summarized in Table 11.1.

Table 11.1
Types of Supplier Relationships

Type	Focus of Work	Pros/Cons/Expected Benefits from Projects
Basic	Spot buy, one-off optimization opportunities, simple price requests	Shortest time to implement changes (may take only 2 to 3 weeks)
		Lowest potential benefit—leverages previously known or easily identified (and typically local) opportunities
		Benefit: <25% of total potential
Speed	Price alignment, leveraging volume (selecting fewer suppliers based on a defined criteria, request for quotation, auction)	Good to tackle at an initial stage of Lean Six Sigma deployment—taking the low-hanging fruit
	Utilizes known or obvious players in the industry (the "best" choice for the supplier is relatively obvious)	Longer than basic procurement; potentially larger benefit (may take 1 to 2 months)
		Benefit: 25–<50%
Strategic	Formal methodology used to analyze opportunities and work joint projects (7-step process; Total Cost of Ownership-based measurements)	Analysis and project completion can typically take 2 to 6 months, but large improvement potentials, particularly in relation to the basic and speed sourcing activities (upwards of 75%)
	Request for proposal; implementation planning and savings	
	Leverages recognized partners as well as focusing on developing potential players in the industry	
	Focus on potential players as also being strong candidates for further development of their potential via Lean Six Sigma methodologies	
Deep	Business redesign and supply chain integration	Decrease level of inventory within a supply chain
	Accomplished through integrated planning function to allow pull system's implementation to connect company-to-company inventory levels	Increase the velocity (number of turnover) of a supply chain
		Can reduce warehouse space needs
		May take more than 6 months to achieve

Which Suppliers? How Many to Approach?

Developing successful supplier relationships takes time and attention. So our top piece of advice is to not take on too much at first. The global equipment manufacturer, for example, had hundreds of suppliers, but started its Extended Enterprise work with just the top nine, based on dollar-spend for each.

If you have a lot of suppliers, look first at those with whom you want a strategic sourcing or deep sourcing relationship. Within those categories, prioritize the potential candidates based on factors such as how much business you do with them ("spend analytics") and indications of their interest. (Obviously, the more business you do with a supplier, the more influence you will have on the firm.)

However, there are situations where you may want to work with either basic or speed sources as well, such as when there is a high defect rate among products, materials, or information, where your choices of suppliers is limited. Factors to consider include:

- Expected growth in the business you do with each supplier.
- Performance issues (cost and quality)—which of your biggest problems with cost, delivery, or quality have some aspect that you cannot address without collaborating with suppliers?
- Relationship building—how interested your leadership and the supplier's leadership are in working collaboratively to improve performance across the value stream.

Helping Suppliers Develop Lean Six Sigma Capability

Once you have identified specific suppliers to work with, the next step is to make contact with those companies. Who makes contact and at what level of the supplier company will vary by situation. Sometimes, executive teams reach out first; other times, it may be more appropriate to have a leader of a Lean Six Sigma or Quality Improvement team make the initial contact.

You will also have to decide what kind of involvement to have with the suppliers. Usually, this includes some combination of:

Joint improvement projects: Collaborative projects between you (as the customer) and your suppliers are ways to achieve common goals—higher sales revenue, increase customer satisfaction, lower costs, and/or faster, more accurate deliveries. Initial projects are typically:

- Selected around the areas of cost reductions and quality improvements.
- Lean in nature (that is, focused on waste reduction).
- Worked using the Kaizen format.

Once you have made progress removing waste via Kaizens, the projects will become more complex and require more than Six Sigma problem-solving tools and a traditional project team structure. Regardless of the type of project (Lean versus Six Sigma), DMAIC is used to add the required structure and higher probability of success.

Joint participation adds some challenges to the team facilitation (since team members likely work at different locations), but the gains are greater. These challenges can be overcome by planning and using video technology.

Exchange visits by leadership and/or work team: Having managers or executives of your company visit the supplier, and vice versa, is a good way to establish rapport across organizational boundaries and give both management teams a better understanding of the challenges and realities of each other's workplace. (The level of management will depend on the type of issue being addressed.) Alternatively, or in addition to management visits, you may want to have people who work on your end of the value stream do a site visit to the counterpart operations at the suppliers.

Collaboration around the supplier's Lean Six Sigma education: The benefits of having you and your suppliers speak the same language around continuous improvement are immeasurable. Helping suppliers develop their own internal expertise in both Lean and Six Sigma tools and concepts will have direct benefits to your company, in terms of greater reliability and quality levels. The nature of collaboration will vary widely depending on your resources and a supplier's level of interest. Companies will sometimes share training curricula with suppliers; those that can afford the resources may offer to loan Black Belts to the suppliers (to work as trainers and project leaders or coaches). Other companies will open up slots in their internal training courses to supplier employees.

The company described at the beginning of this chapter—a large, multinational company with a lot of internal Lean Six Sigma resources—did all of the above. It gave training curriculum/materials to the suppliers and taught them how to use the improvement tools. Though it did not happen often, the manufacturer would occasionally lend out trained resources to help coach or even lead improvement teams at the supplier sites (this happened when the supplier was new to Lean Six Sigma and it was critical that a trained coach drive rapid progress on a priority issue). The company exchanged visits to the supplier sites, based around agreed-on quality issues and/or high-volume output. The supplier management team was always invited to audit the training classes, which they did. Attendance by the supplier management improved the relationship between the two companies and increased the suppliers' awareness of the tools/methodology and commitment to ongoing improvement. Also, during the training events, the equipment company's leadership would work with the supplier management team to better understand their concerns and issues. They also would lend resources to the supplier to coach or lead an improvement team.

Of course, few companies have the size or resources of this manufacturer. But gains are still possible. For example, another company worked with its supplier to reduce accidents at the supplier location. The accidents, which had led to 44 workman compensation claims in the previous year, were driving up product costs, which were passed to the enterprise. A cross-functional team (both locations) worked on this project for two months using Lean Six Sigma tools and sharing safety best practices. The results: The supplier saved $396,000 annually, which allowed it to reduce product costs to company. It also reduced its OSHA recordable injury rate and increased its supplier reputation as a safe place to work.

WHAT TO DO WHEN YOU'RE THE SUPPLIER: EXTENDING YOUR ENTERPRISE DOWNSTREAM

Depending on how much influence you have over your downstream dealers, distributors, retailers, or other customers, working with your Extended Enterprise downstream may be much different from working upstream. Some companies have lot more power when they are in the position of a customer than when they are the supplier. Others have a lot of influence over their dealers. Sometimes it's mixed: you may have influence over some but not all customers.

Why go to the trouble of trying to expand Lean Six Sigma efforts downstream if you're in a weaker position? The company described at the opening of this chapter has a powerful answer to that question: working downstream with its dealers gave it a much stronger, faster link to its end customers. When a customer complained to a dealer about something that wasn't working, the dealer immediately passed the message back to the company, and often a Black Belt would be assigned to investigate the issue and resolve any problems with defects or poor product design.

(As an aside, defect problems were usually traced back to the company's suppliers. So having strong value stream connections in both directions meant end-user needs and problems could quickly be communicated to the very beginning of the process.)

There are other more tangible results of working downstream. Here are two examples:

1. *Improved inventory accuracy, from 30 to 95 percent, with $2 million growth in sales/rental revenues:* A tool and equipment manufacturer worked with the dealers who would rent its products to the public to increase inventory accuracy, which had became a major issue. A cross-functional team applied Lean Six Sigma problem-solving methods, and within four months the issue was greatly improved—generating increased revenue for both the dealer and the manufacturer.

2. *Reduced roots causes of uncollected cash sales ($150,000 revenue impact):* A dealer for another company was facing a serious cash issue due to uncollected revenue. A joint project team looked into the issue using Lean Six Sigma and resolved it within a month.

The best argument you can make to persuade your customers to get involved in Lean Six Sigma is by explaining the benefits your company has seen and the benefits that will directly affect your customers. Typical examples include:

- Helping dealers/retailers better anticipate and deal with market shifts.
- Ensuring their base survives economic downturns.
- Helping these organizations deal with staff/personnel issues/changes.
- Helping them improve service and customer satisfaction.
- Improving product representation and understanding (which leads to increased sales).
- Helping them improve growth and revenue performance.
- Increasing shareholder value by helping dealers focus on critical customer requirements for process improvements.
- Developing process improvement experts within their organizations to execute projects in all areas, not just as part of their relationship with you.

In general terms, the benefits you can see from downstream partnerships include:

- *Generating more passion around your products inside the dealer/distributor:* Many times, customers purchase the services or products because of caring relationships. Those relationships have to be maintained every day. Working with your dealers directs a focus on the most important aspect of the business, and that is of course the end customer. This is where the focus should be: delighting your existing customers. Due to the expanding competition, relationships are becoming more and more critical to the organization's success.
- *Developing a common language across your value stream:* Doing so will help you communicate more easily up and down your value chain.
- *Gaining much deeper customer insights (both the dealer/distributor, as a customer, and its customers):* For example, one company we worked with sold high-performance, high-quality home products through retailers. However, in the course of working with the retailer (its direct customer), the company learned that this product was about to be dropped due to strong customer migration to a competing product. The reason: high price. The level of performance exceeded customer needs so customers were shifting toward a lower-performance and lower-priced product. The company was out of touch with the needs of the ultimate customer. This insight motivated the company to make some product changes, sell more product, *and* increase profit, due to the lower manufacturing and raw material costs of the modified product.
- *Gaining greater insight into competitors:* Often, distributors/dealers work with many companies (your competitors). This is a great way to learn about them and your customers' perception of them.

Options for Working with Your Customers

In some ways, a lack of influence simplifies things greatly. For the majority of companies we've seen, there isn't any lengthy method for deciding which players at this end of the value chain they should be working with. Their options are much more limited: Either they work with their biggest customers (applying the 80/20 rule) or they work wherever they can find willing partners. If you have a lot of power over your dealers or distributors, then you should develop a screening process, much as we described for the supplier end of the value stream, identifying criteria for picking which suppliers to work with.

The nature of the work will depend largely on your resources—both in terms of how many partnerships you can reasonably handle and what kind of Lean Six Sigma support you can offer—and how much influence you have (or, if you lack influence, their interest level in Lean Six Sigma). For example:

- If yours is a large company with a lot of control/influence over your distributors of dealers—and with money or resources to spare—you can offer training courses in Lean Six Sigma inside your customer companies. (That's what the global company described at the start of this chapter did. In fact, they hired an outside consultant to deliver the training.)
- If your company is smaller, but still has influence or a willing partner, you might invite your customer to send a few staff members to your internal training courses. And/or you could share your training materials and course curricula with them so they could sponsor their own training.
- In either case, consider offering a project identification workshop inside your customer company. Engaging its leadership that way can help them appreciate the benefits to be gained, and motivate them to be more willing to allocate staff time to becoming educated in Lean Six Sigma and working projects.

CONCLUSION

Chapter 8 described the five tenets of operational excellence. The Extended Enterprise concept ties all five of these tenets together:

1. *Customer-perceived value:* As demonstrated by the equipment manufacturer's experience, extending the view of your enterprise upstream and downstream improves both your ability to get information about what customers value and to act on that knowledge.
2. *Asset management and ROIC focus:* This tenet reflects the need to maximize asset effectiveness by receiving what you want, when you need it. Having your suppliers working toward the same Lean and Six Sigma goals that your company is—forecasts based on demand, pull systems, eliminating waste—is one of the best mechanisms for improving asset utilization and, thus, ROIC.
3. *Process excellence:* As your company begins to apply Lean Six Sigma internally, you will eventually reach a point where performance is

limited either by what comes before your internal processes (what your suppliers are doing) or imperfect knowledge of what comes after (how your immediate and final customers perceive your products or services and what they want or need from you). You need to identify the Prime Value Chain for your organization and extend your focus on process excellence to the parts of the chain that are beyond your direct control.

4. *Leadership and organizational capabilities:* Just as your internal process excellence is limited by what happens in the parts of the value stream outside your organization, the ability of your leaders to drive improvement throughout the Extended Enterprise is limited by the amount of Lean Six Sigma leadership and organizational capability in your suppliers and customers. The more that leaders throughout the Extended Enterprise are aligned around values and goals, the faster and most smoothly you'll be able to affect change.

5. *Rigorous performance management:* Good partnerships with vendors and customers don't happen by chance. They take the same attention to priorities, methods, education, and metrics that is necessary to establish internally, to make sure your Lean Six Sigma investment is giving you the maximum payoff.

All of these tenets can be taken to an even higher level when you expand your vision beyond the borders of your company and think instead in terms of the entire value stream that serves your immediate and end customers.

PART III
SPEEDING UP DEPLOYMENT RETURNS

Strategies for Getting More, Faster, from a Lean Six Sigma Deployment

CHAPTER 12

CREATE A PIPELINE OF COST IMPROVEMENT PROJECTS

The Secret to Protecting the Heart of Your Business

With Claudio Noriega, Pam Altizer, and Sean Simoes

When a senior executive in a division of a large Fortune 500 office/consumer products company was asked how they had been selecting Lean Six Sigma projects for the past three years, he said it was "by committee," but couldn't provide any specifics. In fact, the division staff wasn't sure how it was done. People picked pet projects (not considering potential return) and were very risk-averse. "We measure our deployment based on the number of events/projects, not on dollar values," admitted the executive. When pushed further, it seemed that the focus on *quantity* of projects, instead of quality, came out of the company's need to find a project for all of its Green Belts.

The situation had once been marginally better. The executive went on to say, "Originally, financial needs drove the project selection. Since projects are championed at the site level, and since the plant manager controls the Black Belt resources, we let them choose which projects to work on."

Projects took anywhere from four to nine months to complete in this company. And management did launch another project each time one was completed, to keep the pipeline filled; but the metrics they tracked were very narrow. "The pros of focusing only on the site metrics meant we were attacking significant profitability issues," said the executive. "But we lost

215

sight of payback on other items." Overall, leadership was disappointed in the results.

This company ran into problems because there was no cross plant alignment, no discipline around selecting projects (no benefit and effort screening or criteria), and no replication across plants to optimize project resources and ideas.

Contrast that company with a leading pharmaceutical firm that had decided to launch a Lean Six Sigma program across North America. The pharmaceutical company's initial goal was to identify projects it could assign to the first wave of 20 Black Belts being trained. But on our advice, they participated in conducting short, focused assessments at eight sites, looking at factors such as strategic objectives, process performance and alignment, and ROIC sensitivity across functional areas such as manufacturing, quality, sales and marketing, supply chain, and regulatory affairs.

These assessments each took only one to three weeks, and very quickly the company had identified and validated more than 100 project opportunities—enough to stock a pipeline for multiple waves of Black Belt candidates—valued at over $100 million. The estimated value and the prioritization of these projects was arrived at via *data-based analysis of actual performance*, not just opinion, which helped the program generate substantial value for the company from the get-go.

Project selection done well can make the difference between a deployment that lifts the entire company and one that flounders into irrelevance. In Chapter 16, you'll read about a company where fixing its project selection process was critical to generating $50 million in type 1 and type 2 benefits (described later in this chapter) within two years.

If you are just starting out, or so far have been disappointed in the results from your Lean Six Sigma deployment, you need to develop a process that helps you identify business priorities that you can effect with Lean Six Sigma. You will need to answer questions such as:

- What are the opportunities available now?
- Which of these should you work on first?
- What will it take to successfully complete those projects?

Once you have been through a first round of project selection, there are also ongoing questions to ask, such as:

- How do we continue to identify and prioritize project ideas, and create a pipeline that is always filled with the *best* opportunities?

- What do we do with projects that may have looked promising originally but no longer represent the best investment of our time and energy?

Developing mechanisms to answer these questions is management's responsibility, as it is their job to make sure the company is expending its resources on projects that are contributing directly to business priorities (or that they are confident *will* contribute, given available information). That involves deciding not only what to work on, but also which projects to *stop* working on.

Many factors contribute to effective project selection and portfolio management: understanding the overall business strategy and operating plans, engaging the broader organization, gathering business data and information, and understanding the tools and approaches for identifying opportunities and prioritizing projects. We will touch on these factors in this chapter as we define leading practices for establishing and sustaining a robust project selection and portfolio management process.

DEVELOPING RIGOR IN PROJECT IDENTIFICATION AND SELECTION

The experience of the second company described at the beginning of this chapter demonstrates that *project selection cannot be isolated from organizational assessment*. The only way you can identify Lean Six Sigma projects that will contribute significant value to your company is to understand your *organizational* needs, not just look for problems you think could be addressed with Lean Six Sigma.

A simple way to depict activities that will raise the odds of picking the best ideas is to use the four-step project identification and selection process shown in Figure 12.1. The process includes everything from identifying, translating, and screening the opportunities to qualifying the projects to prioritizing the top 20 to 25 percent projects and, finally, to developing an improvement roadmap.

In this section, we'll walk through each of these steps.

Step 1: Conduct a Rapid Assessment and Validation

Our definition of "best" opportunities means the projects most likely to move the business toward an important goal. So the first step in the project

Figure 12.1
Project selection process.

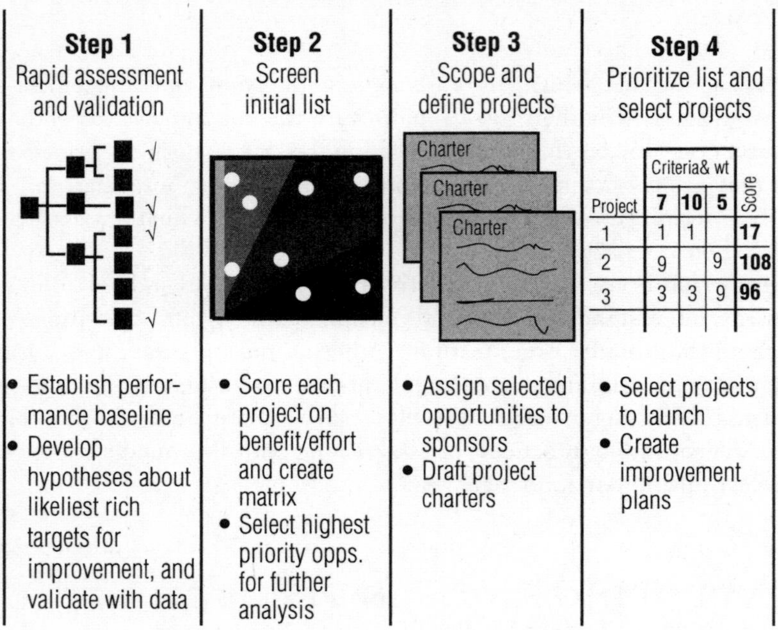
Step 1
Rapid assessment and validation
• Establish performance baseline
• Develop hypotheses about likeliest rich targets for improvement, and validate with data
Step 2
Screen initial list
• Score each project on benefit/effort and create matrix
• Select highest priority opps. for further analysis
Step 3
Scope and define projects
Charter
Charter
Charter
• Assign selected opportunities to sponsors
• Draft project charters
Step 4
Prioritize list and select projects
Criteria& wt
Project
7 10 5
Score
1 1 1 17
2 9 9 108
3 3 3 9 96
• Select projects to launch
• Create improvement plans

identification process is to identify which levers you can move to produce the biggest impact on your business priorities.

The way we prefer to reach that goal is to start by doing a rapid assessment of the organization, which typically takes about two to six weeks per site. During the assessment, you first establish a baseline around issues such as:

- Strategic objectives and focus of operational improvements (cost, capacity, inventory, quality, delivery).
- Financials (buckets of cost/inventory, raw materials, etc.).
- Product mix and economic profit by product line/offering group.
- Planning, scheduling, and forecasting policies, procedures, and systems.
- Return on equipment and resources: utilization, work management, labor profiles, overtime, downtime/overall equipment effectiveness (OEE), space utilization.

- Production or service delivery performance evaluation, including cycle time, capacity, throughput, process capability, and stability.
- Primary workflow (using value stream mapping, as described in Chapter 4, or Complexity Value Stream Mapping, covered in Chapter 10).
- What leaders believe the organization's or their unit's main priorities are, and the biggest barriers to improved performance (information usually gained from targeted interviews).

This work should be done by a team of people who collectively have extensive Lean Six Sigma experience and knowledge of your industry. Ideally, the team should include both people from inside the organization being assessed and external people (either from another business unit or outside the company entirely). This mix helps lend an outside perspective on your issues and opportunities, while helping gain buy-in from the people inside the organization who will ultimately be tasked with sponsoring or implementing projects. For example, only someone with knowledge of your industry would know that your one-week order-to-delivery is three days beyond the industry average; and it would require someone with Lean Six Sigma experience to know what will be necessary to take advantage of that opportunity and what kind of gain you can expect in return.

The first job of the assessment team is, therefore, to establish the baseline. The second job is to use their combined knowledge to develop hypotheses about what levers exist, then collect and analyze data to validate each potential opportunity.

The purpose of formulating the hypotheses is to focus the investigation; this task is key to the "rapid" label we give to this kind of assessment. We advise assessment teams to capture their logic on hypotheses "trees," estimate the value of opportunities and how much specific initiatives will contribute, and then adjust the trees as they use data to validate hypotheses (see Figure 12.2). This level of rigor makes the team much more efficient and effective during this assessment step. For example, does it seem as if your biggest opportunities will be in asset management, setup reduction, or defect prevention in the order-taking process? And based on the baseline just established, what do you estimate that these opportunities are worth?

The insights derived from this holistic assessment approach can truly make the difference between incremental cost improvement versus generating 5 to 10 percent or greater improvements in economic profit. Why is this so? The assessment leads to an understanding of *where and how* value in the organization is being created or destroyed, first by looking at profitability by the offerings, and then at the efficiency and effectiveness with which that

Figure 12.2
Excerpt of postvalidation hypothesis tree: This figure shows a portion of a hypothesis tree centered on how to significantly improve overall equipment effectiveness (OEE). It also shows the original estimates and update figures based on data collection and deeper process analysis.

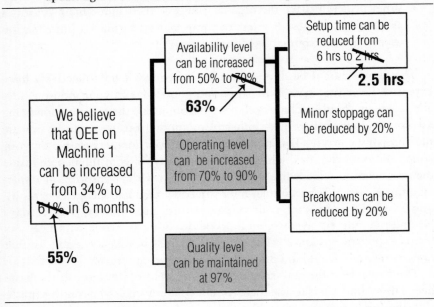

value is delivered by the company's resources, capital, and systems. For example, the assessment would help identify which Lean Six Sigma improvement projects will enable the greatest value creation. When it comes to creating value for the organization, products and processes are inseparable. At the shop-floor level, you may find that the longest setup times may not be the first ones you want to improve; or you may decide not to address them at all, if in fact the setup procedures are for products that contribute a negative percent economic profit to the firm.

The validation work is needed to make sure that your leadership team is making decisions based on reliable estimates of the worth of different types of efforts. Wherever possible, existing operational and financial data is used to validate hypotheses. However, if data to validate a particular hypothesis does not exist, the team may, for example, observe a process for a few hours and then use their expertise to make larger inferences about the overall process performance.

The purpose of the assessment is to establish a baseline understanding of hypotheses that have received preliminary validation: You end up with a list of opportunities, validated and quantified based on rigorous analysis. Many of the insights generated are new, or quantified for the first time. At the pharmaceutical company referenced earlier, for example, the assessment revealed that one plant could double its output by making very feasible improvements in setup time, downtime, and line speed, which ultimately resulted in several Lean Six Sigma projects.

Along the same lines, at a heavy manufacturing company, the assessment revealed that highly skilled employees were spending almost 70 percent of their time on tasks such as walking to obtain parts, waiting on something, or searching for parts or information. At another company, the assessment revealed that poor planning processes were generating very significant air shipping costs, which were not recoverable from customers. In each of these examples, the assessment generated new insights (or a fresh way of looking at known issues), which led to quantified opportunities and, ultimately, a set of Lean Six Sigma projects and other actionable initiatives.

Step 2: Screen Initial List

The outcome of the assessment is often a long list of potential projects (recall the pharmaceutical company from the chapter opening that ended up with more than 100 opportunities). In this initial screening, you want to narrow down the list to something that is more manageable.

One of the fastest and easiest ways to screen ideas is by performing a benefit/effort analysis, and plotting the results on a matrix like that shown in Figure 12.3.

A matrix like this can be used to evaluate anywhere from a handful to 30, 40, or even 100 improvement opportunities. In general, you would pursue the ideas in the following sequence:

1. *Low-effort/low-impact opportunities:* Look at this area (shown in very light gray) just to see if any could be quick hits that solve a nagging problem. If not, it may not be worth expending any effort since the payback would be small.
2. *Low-effort/high-impact opportunities:* This area (in medium gray) is where you get the biggest bang for your buck and on which you should focus your Kaizen and initial LSS projects.
3. *Medium- to high-effort opportunities, with high impact:* Impact is the more important criteria, so look next at these opportunities (in dark

Figure 12.3
Benefit/effort matrix.

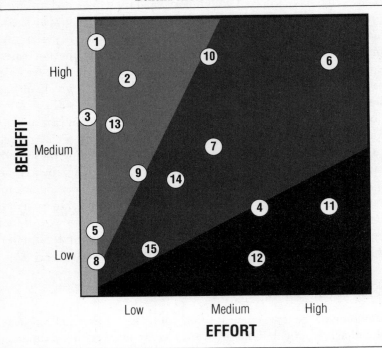

gray). Many are either more strategic or complex, which will require either a case team approach or a better trained LSS project leader, such as a Black Belt.

4. *High-effort, low-impact opportunities:* The only reason to bother with projects in this category (shown in black) would be because they are required for legal compliance of some sort, or lay the groundwork for a subsequent project.

Creating a Benefits/Efforts Matrix   To plot opportunities on a benefits/effort matrix, you must first *decide on the benefit criteria.* When a company is initially focused on selecting cost reduction projects, benefit is usually defined as realized hard savings, and projects are divided into levels:

Low benefit = less than 100,000 USD or euro
Medium benefit = between 100,000 and 250,000 USD or euro
High benefit = greater than 250,000 USD or euro

Of course, the thresholds depend on the size of the business unit or function being assessed and the maturity of the business with continuous process improvement. Companies new to continuous improvement will find it easier to find higher-valued hard savings projects; companies with a history of continuous improvement, which have already gone after most of the "low-hanging fruit," will find it more difficult.

Maturing into a Mix of Benefits

Once you have gotten past the initial focus on cost reduction, you will want to create a greater mix of project types, including cost avoidance, customer satisfaction, and compliance projects. At that point, revisit your screening benefit criteria.

The next step in the screening process, *defining the effort criteria*, is usually a bit easier. Most companies use straight project time. For example, given the same team resources, how long would it take the team to execute the project?

Low effort = less than 3 months
Medium effort = between 3 and 6 months
High effort = greater than 6 months

Of course, there could be many other considerations in setting up the benefit/effort matrix, depending on the organization's goals and maturity, so the key takeaway is to be flexible in establishing the initial screening criteria. Remember that the matrix is a screening tool and that the goal of the team in step 2 is to be directionally correct in prioritizing the opportunities. Typically, teams begin project charters for the opportunities at this stage to help document information such as expected timeline and resources required, which can help in the final prioritization decisions.

Completing the Screening   The idea is to screen *all* of the opportunities and convert only those opportunities likely to become projects. That said, there are a few other considerations when evaluating opportunities. For example, the longer-term value of a project with replication opportunities is greater than it is for a single project with limited replication opportunities. Projects that can be easily replicated represent a chance to have high-impact/low-effort opportunities in the future. For the purposes of completing the screening the first time through, a team will plot each opportunity's "benefit/effort score" as if it were a stand-alone project, and then discuss the other factors when deciding which opportunities to move forward with.

Clearly, this step is far from a science, and so requires an intelligent, sometimes subjective discussion with the business leaders and other stakeholders in the room to determine which opportunities best align to the annual business plan and will have the most long-term impact on the business.

Another tip as you work through this step is to consider Little's Law when selecting ideas to advance to the next step. All companies struggle with too much to do. As discussed in Chapter 5, having too much work in any process slows *everything* down. Little's Law teaches us that if we carefully control the number of active projects at any one time, we can maintain a reasonable cycle time to completion.

Those ideas that pass through this screen means they will move on to step 4, where you will be drafting project charters—usually a three- to five-hour time investment per charter. When too many opportunities make it through the screen, you'll end up wasting a lot of time in step 4 writing up charters for projects that ultimately end up on the shelf.

What to Do with Ideas That Don't Pass the Screen?

Do *not* discard an idea just because it doesn't seem worthwhile at this point. Frequently, effective project selection is based as much on the quantity of ideas as it is on the quality—and, remember, bad ideas can become good ideas if circumstances change, or another idea comes along later that enables you to convert a bad idea to a good idea. All the ideas you have at this stage should remain in the opportunity queue and be considered for chartering in future opportunity-review sessions.

Step 3: Scope and Define Projects

After the initial screening, you need more information about each opportunity so you can make a better comparison about which ones to pursue first. We've found that the best way to do that is to write project charters for each of the best candidates. The charter is a living document, begun during the project selection process, then refined as more is learned about the project opportunity (and even after a project has been launched). It is important to do charters at this stage because, up to this point, the only basis of comparison has been the pain associated with each opportunity and the perceived benefits of improving the process. Though valuable, that comparison is subjective, based on knowledge and experience of what is happening within the business. By developing a charter, you populate a structured document with specific information that will help you better evaluate the impact and effort of the project, because you will have to be more specific about scope, goals, resources required, and timeline. Each element of the charter will be used to determine how to numerically score each benefit and effort criterion in step 4.

Step 4: Prioritize List and Select Projects

You will be coming in to step 4 with draft charters for all the project opportunities that made it through the screening step. You can now use different sections of the project charter to better evaluate these opportunities. We recommend that you develop a set of benefit and effort criteria, then score the charters for each criterion on a scale of 1, 3, 6, or 9. For scoring purposes, note that the Business Impact, Project Plan, and Team Selection sections of the charter generally end up being most important.

Companies known for building solid project portfolios have worked hard to remove politics and personal agendas from the project prioritization process. Of course, each company and its various stakeholders may have different objectives in identifying improvement projects. It is always something of a balancing act to build a project portfolio; but regardless of the mix of strategic (transformational/cross company) and tactical (incremental/within a business) projects, the senior executives for a company must agree on the project selection approach and the objective criteria to support it.

Adding Team Resource Considerations to the Mix Most companies are under the impression that finding and assigning project leaders is the limiting factor in resourcing and managing projects. What we've found, however, is that the constraint is not finding project leaders *but identifying the right subject-matter experts and team members*. It is important to balance your portfolio of projects not only by types of project but also by business area. Too often, a company will launch several projects in one area only to discover later on that key members are already involved on several other projects and so are unable to adequately support priority improvement efforts while managing their day-to-day activities. To prevent resource overload, it is important to consider the availability of the team members during final project prioritization (step 4) and improve resource visibility by identifying resources by name and time commitment on project charters. (Most companies nowadays load this information in a project and resource management database to make it easy to keep track of which people are being deployed to which projects and for how long.)

Developing a Project Roadmap and Change Agenda   After the prioritization process is completed, we recommend creating an implementation roadmap that clearly outlines the projects, the high-level project plan, expected benefits, and scheduled completion date. It should also clearly articulate who is responsible and accountable for successfully completing the project. This document, which we often refer to as a roadmap, should become part of the improvement plan that the company works toward on a day-to-day basis.

Like a charter, a portfolio of projects and roadmap is a living document that should be updated regularly as situations and circumstances change. Priorities shift, so we would also recommend that a more thorough review of the business and the issues it is facing be conducted on a regular basis. The frequency will depend on the organization and the environment in which it operates.

FROM FIRST-TIME TO ALL THE TIME: SHIFTING FROM A ONE-TIME EVENT TO AN ONGOING SYSTEM OF PIPELINE MANAGEMENT

There is often a lot of excitement generated the first time a company goes through the project selection process—people see the many possibilities for driving meaningful change in the organization. The challenge lies in capturing that energy so that you can maintain a pipeline of projects, one that is always filled with the best opportunities available. Here are four key guidelines to meeting that objective:

1. *Think both top-down and bottom-up:* Too often, six months to a year after launching a major continuous improvement initiative, companies tell us they are planning a second project identification and selection workshop to repopulate their project portfolios. Project selection is an ongoing, dynamic process. The point is: Don't wait to identify ideas.

After the initial project identification, you need to establish systems that ensure you are continually cascading strategic priorities top-down *and* regularly collecting ideas bottom-up, from the front line through every level of the organization. Such systems generally include some aspect of Hoshin planning (a mechanism for doing the top-down cascading of priorities), plus elements such as making data-driven problem solving a standard part of daily and weekly staff meetings, quarterly sales meetings, annual business planning sessions, and customer visits and calls. You will also need to decide which group will review the ideas, how often, and by what methods.

2. *Develop benefit and financial guidelines for benefit determination:* The primary reason companies undertake continuous improvement initiatives and adopt a project portfolio management process is to create value for the organization and its customers. To quantify this value, a company must engage its finance team before starting the project selection process, and work with them to establish approved financial guidelines. Often, companies will identify a senior member of the finance team to sponsor development of the financial guidelines, which are broken down into several subcategories, in this way:
   - Define how to *calculate benefits* for each project:
     — What are the appropriate *benefit categories*?
     — What are the *calculation guidelines* within the different categories?
     — How will avoidances be handled?
     — What are some examples?
     — Will benefit calculations be net of costs?
     — What is the realization period for project benefits?
     — How will we develop a presentation and guide that will solidify understanding and increase financial literacy?
   - Create a *financial review process* to track and report benefits, answering these questions:
     — By whom, to whom, when? How will they be trained, calibrated?
     — Which reporting templates will be used? Which software/ system?
     — Do we need a validate phase, six months after the control phrase?
   - Design an *auditing process* to ensure calibration and completion.

A company will want to balance the types of projects it works on and the areas of the business where it executes these projects. Some of the projects in the portfolio will directly impact either the income statement, balance sheet, or both, while other projects will improve performance and customer or shareholder satisfaction, but won't directly tie to revenue, cost/budget, or capital.

3. *Formalize Little's Law:* How many active projects should you have at one time? The answer to this question depends in part on the answer to the resource question, and in part takes us back once again to Little's Law. As we noted already, companies will always have more opportunities than resources and time; and the longer a project takes, the less likely it is that the team will close out the project and realize the business benefit. (In the language of Lean Six Sigma, we say that "project velocity is directly correlated to project closure.")

4. *Create a pull system:* Once you have a target for the optimal number of active projects to be working on at any one time, apply the Lean principle of pull systems and create a mechanism whereby as soon as one project is completed the system is triggered to "release" the next project into the pipeline. Having a pull system that limits the number of active projects (based on your Little's Law calculations) saves time and money. An example of this is shown in Figure 12.5. The organization keeps the *opportunity and project buffers* well stocked so that projects can be launched when the system shows that other projects are about to be completed. The project buffer contains the prioritized chartered projects from step 4, so if you use some discipline around selecting and prioritizing projects, the opportunity buffer and the project buffers should be continuously up to date. Applying the same discipline to project execution is important to help monitor project cycle time and completion, which will trigger the rest of the pull system.

Typical Benefit Categories

Type 1 savings: Hard savings for budget-line item. Examples include:
- Reduction in labor cost (salary and fringe benefits)
- Nonlabor cost reductions (for example, travel, training, supplies)

Figure 12.4
Example of benefit capture.

	Type 1	Type 2	Type 3
+ Revenue	Increase in revenue; 90% confidence in results and cause-and-effect		Increase in revenue and 70% confidence in results and cause-and-effect
+ Cost	Permanent cost reduction	Re-assignment of costs, resources freed up, or future cost avoidance	
+ Assets	Permanent asset reduction	Re-assignment of assets, resources freed up or future asset avoidance	
– Project costs	All project costs, both ongoing and one-time		

Total Net Benefit of Project
+ Other benefits, such as Intangible projects or projects where benefits begin 12 months after completion
+ External benefit such as customer or business partner improvement in their processes

- Space reductions, enabling termination of leases
- Scrap or material reductions
- Contract cost reductions

Type 2 savings: Freeing up resources to work other strategic initiatives (in essence, driving efficiency and effectiveness). Examples include:

- Partial man-year savings across multiple programs can be redirected to other critical work.

(continued)

(*continued*)
- Space requirements for an activity are reduced, but we are unable to vacate the building.
- Allows reallocation of government space and potential reduction in leased or temporary buildings.

Type 3 savings: These are difficult to quantify, but include areas such as quality-of-life improvements, mission readiness improvements, customer satisfaction, and personnel safety improvements.

Obviously, in a cost reduction project, the most important benefit will be type 1 savings, but you should capture all the expected benefits. One example is shown in Figure 12.4.

CONCLUSION: MAINTAINING A DYNAMIC PIPELINE

As in any other business processes, it is relatively easy to set up a pull process to ensure projects are available when resources close one project and are ready to start the next. To effectively manage a pull process, a company must have visibility, enabling it to forecast project status, resource availability, and projects in queue—all topics covered in this chapter. And don't forget Little's Law: We've seen many Lean Six Sigma deployments falter because the company tried to tackle too much with too few resources. By managing the pipeline and reducing project cycle time, you will ensure good project closure rates and early recognition of dollar benefits, as summarized in Figure 12.6.

When you know you have limited resources but still start several projects, and end up assigning two projects to each Black Belt, what ensues is a situation where none of the projects gets completed on time; worse, you do not achieve the projected financial benefits. You will also end up with low team morale and difficulty in getting people to sign up for subsequent teams. The pull approach starts fewer projects at one time and focuses resources on completing those projects on time, so you can accrue project results earlier. A new project is started only when another project is completed, which helps you keep the number of active projects under control.

Figure 12.5
Pull system for managing the number of active projects.

"Project Production Line"

Pull system based on Little's Law

- Project launches are constrained by the projected availability of *all* required resources
- Capacity (diameter of the pipe) is sized by the available people and capital

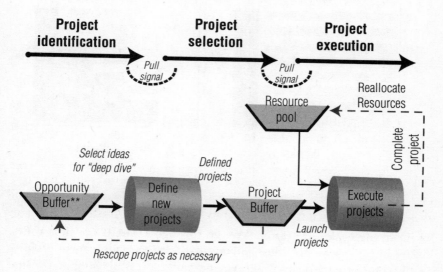

**Original opportunity identification plus...
- Regular review of strategic focus
- Update info on customer CTQs
- Brainstormed ideas
- Reevaluation of financial drivers
- Process classfication

Other reasons that this scenario is more effective:

- You have the flexibility to reprioritize projects to suit business needs.
- You can better match scarce resources to projects (for example, if IT resources and SMEs are critical enablers of projects, they're spread too thin, as shown on the left side of Figure 12.6).

Figure 12.6
The pull approach to driving financial benefits faster.

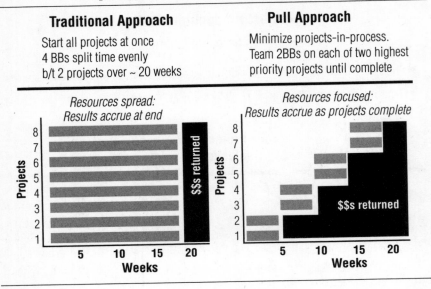

- Learning cycles are faster. You go through DMAIC multiple times, which allows you to adjust and improve with each subsequent project.
- By completing projects faster, you develop successful teams and ensure organizational buy-in.

SPOTLIGHT #5

LINK PROJECTS TO VALUE DRIVERS

As described in the previous chapter, a lot of considerations go into selecting projects. One of the most important factors, especially when you are relying on Lean Six Sigma projects to improve your cost position, is to have a deep understanding of what drives value for your company. That includes determining just how much measurable gain you can expect in business metrics from productivity gains within a given work area, function, or process.

In this spotlight, we'll walk through three types of financial analyses you can use to identify goals for potential Lean Six Sigma projects.

OPTION 1: VALUE DRIVER TREES

Throughout this book we have been emphasizing the concept of value—what customers value, what will improve shareholder value. To understand what will create or drive value for your company, you need to have a clear strategy and recent and reliable information on what customers need (as covered in Chapter 3); and you need to know how well your processes are operating (see Chapters 4 and 5) and which factors have the biggest effect on the financial metrics of your company (see Figure SP5.1).

A tool called a *value driver tree* (Figure SP5.2) is a good way to use financial information to feed into your project identification and selection processes.

The purpose of creating a value driver tree is to *understand where the money lives* and understand if you can get to that money via:

- Closing competitive gaps, if you lag behind your industry; increasing the gap, if you are in the lead.

233

Figure SP5.1
Linking strategy to value: Looking at the levers that create value for the organization provides a starting point for identifying project opportunities.

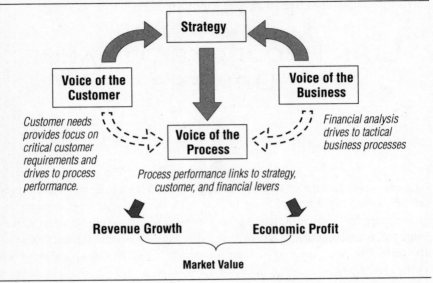

- Closing gaps around customer needs/markets.
- Recapturing previous levels of performance, if you have slipped; understanding what it will take to achieve a step-level change of improvement, if performance has been steady.
- Establishing internal benchmarks—are some functions or units greatly outperforming or underperforming others?

To create a value driver tree, start with whatever financial statements your company already generates:

- Income statement
- Balance sheet
- Cash flow statement

We recommend starting at the lowest level possible, because it is easier to consolidate financial line items than it is to dissect summary data if you lack the supporting detail.

As you go through the information, you want to understand:

Figure SP5.2
Value driver tree: A tree diagram helps you sort out which factors contribute the most (positively or negatively) to Economic Profit. Competitive gaps, negative trends, and underperforming processes or areas are typically good targets for Lean Six Sigma projects.

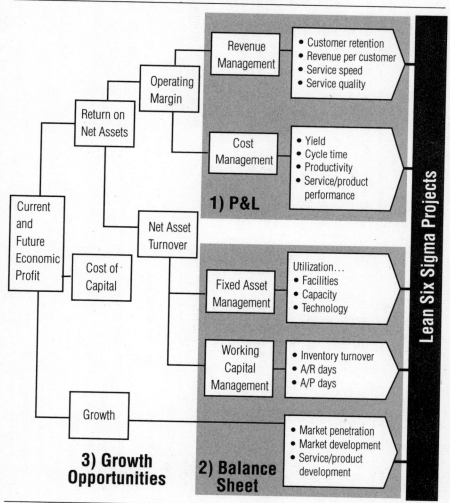

1. Where do we have competitive gaps from a cost perspective?
2. Where do we have internal benchmark gaps from a cost perspective?
3. Where are our processes underperforming, resulting in either increased costs or impacts to our customers?

Table SP5.1

SP Potential Areas to Explore in Fiscal Areas

Revenue	COGS	SG&A	PPE	Working Capital
Strengthen value proposition.	Improve yield.	Reduce time to market.	Increase mean time between failure (MTBF).	Reduce work-in-process (WIP) inventories.
Improve service.	Reduce parts purchase price.	Prioritize projects.	Decrease mean time to repair (MTTR).	Reduce finished goods (FG) inventories.
Improve product mix.	Reduce material cost.	Clarify requirements.	Increase capacity.	Reduce raw material (RM) inventories.
Improve customer mix.	Improve material utilization.	Increase accountability.	Evaluate capital allocation.	Reduce rework.
Improve features/ quality.	Standardize materials.	Increase project management skills.	Consolidate operations.	Improve planning and scheduling.
Improve warranty.	Reduce overtime.	Decrease engineering changes.	Outsource operations/noncore competencies.	Improve forecast accuracy.
Improve sales effectiveness.	Reduce turnover.	Reduce transactions.	Evaluate lease versus own.	Improve planning for product phase in/outs.
Strengthen brand.	Automate.	Increase effectiveness.		Standardize products/ components.
Improve distribution channels.	Consolidate.	Redistribute territories.		Implement consignment.
Add customers/ products.	Reduce setup.	Outsource admin functions.		Reduce obsolete material.
Rationalize products.	Improve productivity.	Consolidate (shared services).		Shorten terms.
Develop innovative products.	Improve design efficiency.	Improve productivity.		Improve collections.
	Increase span of control.			Reduce transactions.
	Outsource.			Improve technology.
	Improve processes.			

4. Which financial drivers have been ignored in past improvement efforts?
5. Which drivers have been identified as strategic focus areas?

Typical areas and types of issues you want to explore in each are summarized in Table SP5.1.

OPTION 2: FINANCIAL ANALYSIS DECISION TREE

One variation on the value driver tree format is called a *financial analysis decision tree*. It follows the flow of a value driver tree and asks "why" until a level is reached to identify potential projects. The key is to push the question set down through the P&L and balance sheet drivers, and then use this as input to a deeper analysis to identify potential projects. A financial analysis decision tree (Figure SP5.3) is a more focused tool than the value driver tree, and helps generate more fruitful discussions around achieving strategic planning line items.

Figure SP5.4 shows a financial driver tree analysis of project opportunities.

OPTION 3: ECONOMIC PROFIT

Companies are often familiar with reporting benefits tied to revenue and cost. However, many companies today are taking it a step further and adopting Economic Profit (EP) as the final financial reporting metric. Economic Value or Profit relates to the return on an investment after deducting the cost of capital. This has three contexts for continuous improvement:

- *Identifying where to look for opportunities:* By understanding what drives value, a business is more likely to identify where to find high-value projects.
- *Selecting opportunities:* Increasing productivity through process improvement enhances the return on investment (ROIC), whether it is a piece of equipment or a group of people. Therefore, projects that create the greatest improvement in Economic Profit (increase in ROIC × the amount of invested capital) should, all other things being equal, be given priority. This is supported by how companies often develop their project prioritization criteria.

Figure SP5.3
Financial analysis decision tree.

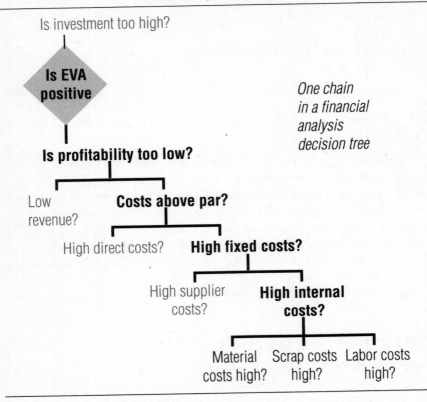

- *Allocating resources:* Increasing the return on the organization's investment in continuous improvement. All initiatives need to justify their existence and deliver value for the organization. By working on the highest-value projects, the impact of the initiative is greater, and this builds support within the organization and leadership, which then enables even more rapid and widespread improvements in performance.

The Economic Profit calculation is new to many organizations, but leadership and finance teams appreciate the additional focus on capital and understand how EP extends their traditional operating income calculation to include the impact on capital and taxes. Figure SP5.5 shows the Economic Profit calculation.

Figure SP5.4
Project ideas driven by financial analysis.

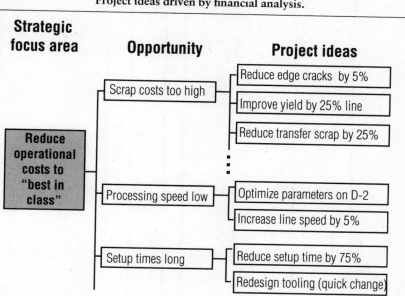

OPTION 4: EP SENSITIVITY ANALYSES

One type of question that constantly presents itself to managers planning improvement efforts is: "How much improvement do we have to see in the process metric to get the financial impact we need?" Or, on the flipside, "How much financial impact will we see if we change this lever 1 percent?"

An EP sensitivity analysis helps you answer those questions by identifying which levers on the P&L and balance sheet most affect EP. The key is to first understand the levers, then generate potential project ideas to impact the biggest levers.

To perform an EP sensitivity analysis, first create a table of P&L and balance sheet items and calculate how a 1 percent change in each line item affects EP (see Figure SP5.6).

If you graph the results, you can see the impact of each lever. An example chart is shown in Figure SP5.7.

You can also look at how reductions in cost will affect EP. The smaller the profit margin of your business, the more sensitive it becomes to

Figure SP5.5
Economic Profit calculation.

Type I

	\$				Month					
	1	2	3	>>>	10	11	12	Total
Allocated Admin	$ 10.0	$ 10.0	$ 10.0	>>>	$ 10.0	$ 10.0	$ 10.0	$ 120.0
Allocated Admin	$ (1.7)	$ (1.7)	$ (1.7)	>>>	$ (1.7)	$ (1.7)	$ (1.7)	$ (20.0)
Operating Income	$ 8.3	$ 8.3	$ 8.3	>>>	$ 8.3	$ 8.3	$ 8.3	$ 100.0
Tax (39.6%)	$ (3.3)	$ (3.3)	$ (3.3)	>>>	$ (3.3)	$ (3.3)	$ (3.3)	$ (39.0)
Capital Incr / (Decr)	$ (100.0)	$ (100.0)	$ (100.0)	>>>	$ (100.0)	$ (100.0)	$ (100.0)	$ (100.0)
Cost of Capital (7.8%)	$ (0.7)	$ (0.7)	$ (0.7)	>>>	$ (0.7)	$ (0.7)	$ (0.7)	$ (7.8)
Economic Profit	$ 4.4	$ 4.4	$ 4.4	>>>	$ 4.4	$ 4.4	$ 4.4	$ 53.2

Type II

					Month				
	1	2	3	>>>	10	11	12	Total
Allocated Admin	$ 6.5	$ 6.5	$ 6.5	>>>	$ 6.5	$ 6.5	$ 6.5	$ 78.0
Operating Income	$ 6.5	$ 6.5	$ 6.5	>>>	$ 6.5	$ 6.5	$ 6.5	$ 78.0
Tax (39.6%)	$ (2.5)	$ (2.5)	$ (2.5)	>>>	$ (2.5)	$ (2.5)	$ (2.5)	$ (30.4)
Capital Incr / (Decr)	$ -	$ -	$ -	>>>	$ -	$ -	$ -	$ -
Cost of Capital (7.8%)	$ -	$ -	$ -	>>>	$ -	$ -	$ -	$ -
Economic Profit	$ 4.0	$ 4.0	$ 4.0	>>>	$ 4.0	$ 4.0	$ 4.0	$ 47.6

Figure SP5.6
Compiling data for EP sensitivity analysis.

Excerpt		1% Price	1% Material	1% Volume
Revenue	150,000	(151,500)	150,000	(151,500)
Cost of Sales				
40% Direct Material	60,349	60,349	(59,745)	(60,952)
6% Direct Labor	8,613	8,613	8,613	(8,699)
4% Variable Mfg Expense	5,933	5,933	5,933	(5,992)
10% Fixed Period Expense	14,646	14,646	14,646	14,646
	89,541	89,541	88,937	90,290
0% SG&A	-	-	-	-
0% R&D Expense	-	-	-	-
Restructuring & Other	-	-	-	-
	-	-	-	-
Operating Income	60,459	61,959	61,063	61,210
Tax @35%	21,161	21,686	21,372	21,424
Operating Profit After Tax (OPAT)	39,299	40,274	39,691	39,787
Inventory	23,377	23,377	23,377	23,377
Net PP&E	48,983	48,983	48,983	48,983
Invested Capital	72,360	72,360	72,360	72,360
Capital Charge@10%	7,236	7,236	7,236	7,236
Economic Profit	32,063	33,038	32,455	32,551
Impact		**975.0**	**392.3**	**488.2**

incremental cost increases. In other words, a firm with a 3 percent profit margin has a 97 percent cost base measured against revenue. If costs go up 1 percent, that means that margin will be contracted by 0.97 percent, which is pretty ugly. A very small increase in costs (1 percent isn't much, right?) results in slashing profitability by a third! Likewise, if you can get just a little more productive, that 1 percent improvement in cost results in a 33 percent increase in profits just by sharpening your pencil a bit. Similarly, a firm with a fat margin of 50 percent will be far less shaken by a 1 percent increase in costs.

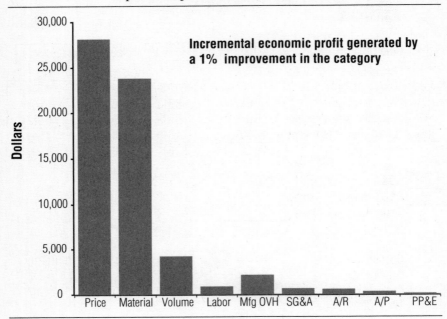

Figure SP5.7
EP sensitivity (incremental EP generated by
1 percent improvement in different areas).

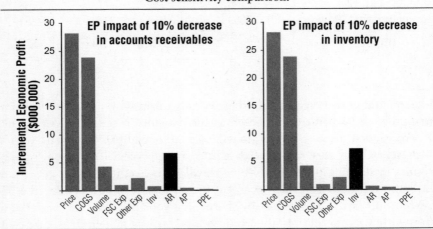

Figure SP5.8
Cost sensitivity comparison.

Too often, managers get focused on their departmental or purchasing budgets and forget what they mean in terms of the big picture. Perhaps a good cost management measurement system needs to include context, to make the measurement more relevant, understandable, and meaningful.

Analyze cost drivers to see which ones are sensitive to volume, pricing, and environmental factors (for example, interest rate changes, regulatory changes), and then develop measures to reflect their responses to those drivers. Included in that would be the need to actually manage those costs appropriately for their drivers. An example is shown in Figure SP5.8. Always love it when finance yells at ops for their high depreciation numbers, or the overtime needed when volume was up.

VALUE DRIVER EXAMPLE

A medium-sized merchandiser and distributor of office products, furniture, and cleaning supplies had selected Lean Six Sigma as an improvement methodology to reduce costs within its operations. The COO wanted to make sure the projects aligned to the economics of the business, so an economic value driver tree was used to understand which value levers should be focused on to identify project opportunities. Working with the financial staff, a definition of what would be considered an economic benefit was agreed to among the leadership. Then a value driver tree for the business was created using the past year's financial statements and operations reports.

The value driver tree (Figure SP5.9) was a key input into the project identification and selection workshops. The static view was used as a baseline, to engage the cross-functional leaders, and then a sensitivity analysis was performed to highlight the economic value impact, based on a 10 percent improvement in any specific area. The sensitivity approach allowed the participants to assess the relative ease or difficulty of impacting a value lever and its corresponding impact on the economic benefit delivered.

Working from the targets identified in the value driver tree, in the first project identification workshop, the company identified 30 projects estimated to generate in excess of $13 million in economic profit. The projects covered all areas of impact within a value driver tree. Figure SP5.10 shows the cost reduction projects this company chartered:

The company continued to reevaluate opportunities based on its new understanding of what drives value, and is now on target to generate about $30 million in benefits over the first three years of the program.

Figure SP5.9
Example value driver tree calculations.

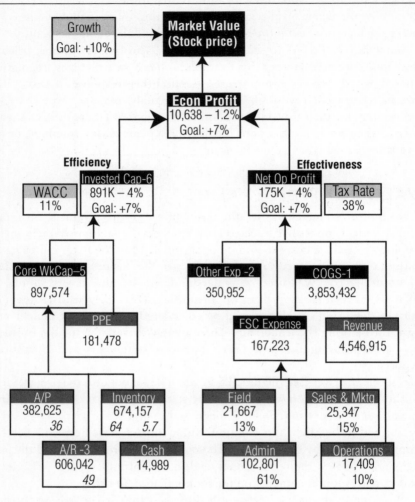

$60.6MM for non-recurring margin adjustments

Figure SP5.10
Cost projects linked to value driver tree.

Project Name/Description	Cost
New supplier product contracting	$ 2,361
Cash app efficiency	$ 484
Dealer net price catalogue	$ 300
Freight cost to serve	$ 250
Business reporting	$ 220
Financial month-end close	$ 220
Furniture quotation	$ 180
Advertising services	$ 180
Customer deductions	$ 180
Vendor debit memos	$ 50
AP vendor terms	$ 25
New product launch	$ 22

CHAPTER 13

SMOOTH THE PATH THROUGH CHANGE

With Pam Altizer, Eric Carter, and Mitali Sharma

A North American-based $18 billion-plus publicly traded company had established a traditional corporate structure, but with very autonomous business units. The C-level was reluctant to drive top-down initiatives, preferring to leave major initiatives up to the business units. By and large, the company was successful, so no one in the C-suite felt any particular need for change.

At one business unit, however, a midlevel visionary felt strongly that the company would need to use Lean Six Sigma (LSS) if it hoped to achieve an aggressive growth target in five years. Lacking support from the corporate office, this VP decided to pilot LSS in his area and use it as a launching pad from which to achieve short-term cost objectives and hit future growth targets.

Since the VP owned the deployment in his area, he had control over the outcomes. But once he made plans for replicating throughout the rest of the organization, he had to choose wisely which area would be next, because going forward he would have limited direct influence. A common approach would be to deploy next to the area with the greatest financial opportunity or, conversely, to the area experiencing the greatest "pain" in the organization. While not a bad approach, the VP knew that strong leadership would be the key to success, so he looked for areas led by other early adopters and risk takers. He targeted leaders who had successfully led change in the organization before, who were willing to embrace a new way of doing things, and who were open to new ideas and approaches. These were the leaders and business areas ripe for implementing change.

After piloting the deployment in various areas of the business, the VP studied what had gone well and what could have gone better. He prepared a communication—more of a PR campaign—to demonstrate the value of the deployment and explain why the results could have been even better than they were. He elaborated how the organization as a whole learned from the experience, and framed the results of the pilot within the context of the organization's pro formas (its P&L statements) to help the leaders understand the impact of the pilot. He graphically mapped how the Lean Six Sigma projects, both individually and as an aggregate project list, impacted the business unit leader's value chain. This was very effective for enabling the business units to see the big picture and how many "small" Lean Six Sigma projects could cumulatively make a big impact.

Whether you are implementing change across the enterprise or within a specific business unit, it is worth taking the time to "check the temperature" of the organization, to identify the change leaders who understand the value of assessing and managing the change.

Change management is a huge subject well beyond the scope of any one chapter. What we want to focus on here are four aspects of change management that are especially critical if your company is launching major cost reduction efforts tied to Lean Six Sigma:

1. Conducting a change readiness assessment at various times during the journey.
2. Understanding the difference between leading and managing change.
3. Upgrading your communication plan.
4. Establishing process ownership and cost accountability, especially during transitions.

CHANGE READINESS ASSESSMENTS

Managing change is important at every step of the journey but you first must understand where the organization's mental headset is before you can develop a plan to manage it. A focus on cost savings or cost reduction activities is sure to invoke some anxiety in the organization. Therefore, irrespective of the magnitude of the change your organization is facing, it's important to understand how *ready* people are for change, how *able* they are to perform work in a new way, and how *willing* they are to do so.

At the organizational scale, the best way to find out that information is to conduct a readiness assessment *before* the bulk of the activity gets

Figure 13.1
Four dimensions of change readiness assessments.

Process
Are the processes READY for change?

Culture
Is the organization
WILLING to
make the change?

Improvement Engine

Infrastructure
Is the organization's
infrastructure designed
to ENABLE the change?

People
Are we ABLE to make the change?

underway. The outcome of such an assessment will dictate how you will lead and manage the change. In this section, we will discuss the topics of an assessment and then cover how to conduct one.

To assess the organization's readiness for change, we want to examine four dimensions: Process, Culture, Infrastructure, and People (see Figure 13.1).

Process: Based on the whether there are long-term or short-term improvements to be implemented, it's important to assess whether the organization is ready for change and whether the staff understands what it means to work in a process environment. Are employees working in process activities and tasks? Are they being measured by process metrics? Are process owners in place and functional lines deemphasized? Most importantly, does staff understand the cost targets that must be hit to achieve organizational goals?

Culture: Based on the business environment of your organization, the level of communication, and the activities that have taken place regarding the cost reduction initiative, the assessment must test the organization's willingness to change. At this early juncture, we must test whether employees feel that leadership understands the issues and is engaged appropriately at all levels. Has the proper amount of communication occurred? Does the organization understand the situation and challenges? If there is a lack of willingness to change, the assessment must uncover barriers and possible root causes. From the answers, the organization's business case or burning platform can be developed or enhanced, to ensure that the organization desires to change and demonstrates its willingness to do so.

Infrastructure: In order for the organization to effectively implement process improvements to reduce costs, leadership must develop the proper infrastructure to enable the organization to make the change. Every organization has several initiatives occurring at the same time, and these must be well aligned, otherwise there will be conflicting objectives. The assessment can uncover how much alignment is needed to clarify the objectives. At various levels of the organization, are process sponsors and process owners engaged to lead the improvements? Specific areas that require additional support can be uncovered. Most importantly, has the accountability to measure the performance been designed and communicated appropriately, to ensure success?

People: To achieve the change needed, people must be assigned the proper roles and responsibilities, as well as trained for their new jobs. The assessment should measure whether people feel that they are prepared. If a gap exists, it will help the deployment planning team to understand where additional clarification is needed. Once people are given the right level of training to do their new jobs, they will feel more capable of participating as valuable team members. Finally, the organization may need to provide help to develop team effectiveness and leadership skills, to ensure success during all of the phases of the effort.

LEADING VERSUS MANAGING THE CHANGE

After the assessment has been conducted, the next step is to use the findings to develop detailed plans, interventions, events, communications, and so on, that will enable employees to be ready, willing, and able to carry out the change. There are, in fact, two distinct roles for executives: *leading* the change and *managing* the change:

- *Leading change* means being the source of energy, commitment, and vision. It involves catching the attention of the organization and inspiring both intellectual and emotional commitment to the fact that change is needed and that change *is* going to happen. Failing to produce at least some anxiety around the status quo will lead employees to assume that what the company is currently doing is acceptable, when, in fact, it is the status quo that got the organization into the cost situation it is in. Leaders should have a commanding knowledge of the strategic need to change, shape the vision of the future, and create the sense of urgency. They also should be able to explain the reasons why, for example, some processes must implement new Lean Six Sigma methods to achieve the cost-saving targets. Instilling the confidence that people will keep their jobs but that they may be working differently will restore the faith and belief they need to accept the change. Assuring people that they will be trained in new methods to do their jobs will give them hope that the organization can make the change to achieve its goals.

- *Managing change* means being both architect and building contractor: designing detailed plans and then putting those plans into action. Very specific actions and communications contribute to instilling the belief that the organization can, in fact, be successful to achieve the cost targets it has set.

Importance of Leadership Roles at Different Stages of Change

Leaders and managers plan together, but execute different tasks, sometimes at different times. Some will be asked to play the role of psychologists, and just listen; others will be asked to be communicators, to build faith and talk about the implementation details. Which tasks they should assume will depend on what stage of change the organization is in. The typical change curve shows four major stages: Awareness, Understanding, Buy-in, and Commitment (see Figure 13.2).

With a cost reduction initiative, taking employees from understanding to buy-in is a challenge, given the uncertainty of the cost reduction activity. Two guidelines will help with this effort:

1. *Leaders of change should focus on awareness and understanding:* A company we'll talk about in the next section ran into trouble because people did not understand what the new Master Black Belt (MBB) positions were, let alone how becoming an MBB would help them. On a broader scale, that same phenomenon sabotages many change initiatives before they even get underway. That's why leaders have to be visible and vocal very early on, explaining what is happening and why, and creating a vision of the future. As mentioned previously, using an assessment survey can identify the areas where employees are hesitant about committing to change, or bring attention to the areas where more information is needed.

Figure 13.2
Change curve.

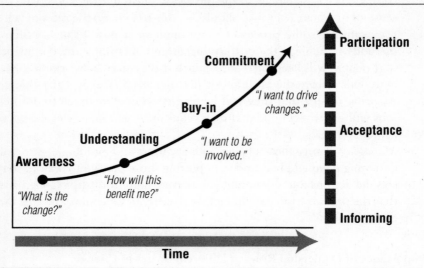

2. *Managers of change should focus on buy-in and commitment:* Once employees understand what is involved, the leadership's job shifts to enacting steps that will produce the needed change. Those include the detailed work of developing communication plans, which we discuss later in this chapter. Managing change also involves identifying people who demonstrate that they want to be involved, then recruiting them to participate in the work of planning and taking action. In addition, it is important to publicize the success of projects by announcing early wins, so that any skeptics are made aware of what has occurred and who was involved. Demonstrating results is the best way to build belief.

Drive Engagement at All Levels

Lasting change is neither solely a top-driven nor a grass-roots effort; it needs sustained efforts from all levels. This can be difficult to achieve, and requires addressing issues of motivation and control.

Part of the goal of both leading and managing change, therefore, has to be finding messages and mechanisms that will *increase the personal investment of each employee at every level in sustaining change.* (This will also make them more open to learning about and embracing Lean Six Sigma.)

If your cost reduction efforts have included job cuts, there is the danger of producing a "survivor mentality" among those who are "left behind" after all other cost-reduction actions have been taken. Some employees will likely feel overworked and under tremendous job and cost pressures; others will become disengaged and just go through the motions in their jobs; still others may want to contribute but feel there is no place in the evolving organization for their passion, creativity, and ingenuity.

Any level of disengagement will result in subpar implementation and thus directly impact the potential cost savings. Additionally, if key employees are not engaged, they will negatively influence others; or they may leave, causing further disruptions.

Therefore, you will need to use process owners, functional leaders, and other stakeholders to engage every level of the organization in the effort to drive results for the long term. In particular, seek out and use people who have a lot of influence—formal or informal, no matter what their official job title—to lead high-profile, short, quick-win projects. Some may be project sponsors of key improvement areas; others may be project leaders or team members. Whatever their roles, look for those who understand the need for change and can influence and convince others to believe that what management is doing is good for everyone. They will be the first to espouse the use of new methods to achieve cost reductions and enlist the help of others.

Over time, the architects of change must build in methods to ensure that people are moving up the change curve. This includes shifting who delivers what message. As the implementation plan continues to migrate, the focus of the communications must shift from senior executives to their direct reports and, eventually, to middle managers, whose involvement will be key to sustaining the momentum to achieve long-term gains and lasting cost reductions. It's important to ensure that key influencers are given some special attention so that they are recruited and then can recruit others. Monitor how well people are advancing up the change curve by assigning unofficial change agents to keep a thumb on the pulse of change and alert management to any changes of heart in the workforce. Allow change agents to talk about new jobs, new roles, and how the organization will be different. Create the environment in which people can believe that the cost improvements to be implemented will ensure growth for the future.

UPGRADING YOUR COMMUNICATION PLAN

About six months into a new Lean Six Sigma deployment, a senior executive told us he was frustrated. One-quarter of the people they had put into

the Master Black Belt position had quit, and the shortage of internal competence around Lean Six Sigma training and project coaching was stifling
progress toward cost reduction goals.

Truth is, we weren't surprised by the results because we had seen how the
executive handled the internal recruitment process when the MBBs were selected. Despite advice to the contrary, he kept the details about the positions
close to his chest. Employees were left to guess what the MBB responsibilities would entail, whether there was a clear career path for MBBs, and so
on. Consequently, many of the people who would have thrived in the MBB
position—and drive great results for the company—didn't even apply.

This company fell into just one of the pitfalls surrounding communication: failure to provide information to the people who need it to make the
right decision for themselves. This executive was well intentioned—he
thought that keeping the MBB job descriptions nebulous would convey to
staff that they would have some power to shape the jobs themselves. Unfortunately, that strategy backfired. What he got instead was a lot of be-
hind-the-scenes grapevine chatter, employees voicing fears about stepping
into entirely new job positions without knowing what to expect.

As this company discovered, good communication is critical to success.
That's true whether you're leading a single project in your department or a
global deployment. It can be especially true if your cost-cutting efforts will
involve job reassignments or cuts. Even if eliminating jobs is not part of
your cost-cutting plan, your organization will still experience some level of
stress due to the focus on cost reduction and the anticipation of change—be
it a small change affecting a single process achieved through continuous improvement, or a large-scale enterprise wide change achieved through transformational efforts. Anywhere along that scale, employees will want to
know how the changes driven by cost reductions will ultimately affect them.

The basics of designing an effective communication plan are well known.
Odds are you've run across descriptions that go something like this:

- Communications will be most effective if they're context-specific
  (shaped for the audience and their needs, and considering the forum
  for the communication, the business needs).
- Messages need to be stated clearly and crisply.
- Communications must be delivered frequently.

Rather than rehash these details, we want to focus here on two secrets
that will help you make better choices when shaping your communication
plan:

1. Consider "feedback feasibility" when determining which methods to use.
2. Address both logic and emotion.

Secret #1: Consider Feedback Feasibility When Determining Which Methods to Use

Imagine three scenarios:

1. A CEO is announcing new cost-cutting targets to the entire company.
2. A department manager wants to publicize the results of completed projects.
3. A project sponsor is handing off a project charter to a team.

In each of these scenarios, some form of communication is necessary. One characteristic that distinguishes which method will work best is the advantage of creating two-way communication—meaning whether the communicator gets and responds to feedback. Looking at these three scenarios in reverse order, for example:

- The project sponsor will be best served if the project team has a chance to respond to the charter by asking questions about the cost targets or boundaries, for example. Without that opportunity, the team may unknowingly go off in an unintended direction.
- The department manager doesn't need to be concerned about feedback, so posting results on a bulletin board would accomplish the goal of publicizing successes and recognizing team members.
- The CEO probably discussed the cost targets with executive leadership one-on-one or in small teams so that he or she could get detailed comments from each person. When announcing the final targets to the entire company, that level of feedback is neither necessary nor practical—though a video conference or live meeting would be preferable to simply sending out an e-mail.

If you provide an opportunity for feedback, you will: (1) let the speaker/communicator know how well their message was communicated; (2) help improve the communications plan and communications.

One of the coauthors of this chapter, Eric Carter, coined the term "feedback feasibility" to capture this theme. In the context of a communications plan, feedback feasibility refers to how easy it will be for the "audience" to communicate back to the "speaker." May they ask questions, voice

Figure 13.3
Feedback feasibility.

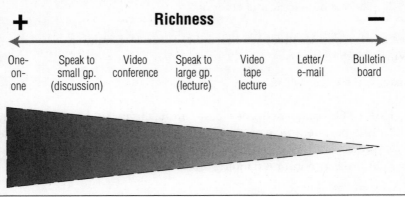

Diagram © 2009, Eric Carter. Used with permission.

concerns, provide comments, and so on? Feedback feasibility also refers to the opportunity for the communicator to *listen* and *respond* to the feedback.

Obviously, different communication media vary widely in the opportunity they provide for feedback. The greater the opportunity for feedback, the greater the richness of the communication (see Figure 13.3).

From the standpoint of deploying change in the organization, communications should have the highest feedback feasibility earlier in the change initiative, then decrease as the initiative moves through the different phases of change. Initiating two-way communications, especially early on, is a powerful way to learn from the past and improve what happens in the next stage.

Tip: Capturing Feedback

There are many methods to capture feedback. These can be as structured as a survey or as informal as verbally asking the group for their comments, questions, or concerns throughout or at the end of the communication. When gathering feedback, listen to what the members of the group are saying. If they are taking the time to complete a survey, make sure they know that someone is reading their responses. It will give further credibility to the communication—and the change initiative—by closing the feedback loop in a timely manner. Last, do not make an empty promise to take action based on feedback. Empty promises will lead to diminished credibility in communications, and ultimately, the change initiative itself.

Secret #2: Address Both Logic and Emotion

A global equipment manufacturer was going through a merger and trying to become much more service-centric and cost-efficient. The leadership did a great job communicating the *logic* of why things needed to happen—"this merger will help us expand market share"—but did not reach employees emotionally at all. Resistance was high.

We sat down with the CEO and helped him craft a visioning statement, then helped the company revise its communication plan with the provision that the CEO would speak more often and in more informal settings about the vision of the future. Few employees will speak up or feel any emotional attachment to what's being said when they are participating in a videoconference or jammed into a room with several hundred coworkers. In contrast, few can remain uninvolved if they are among, say, only 10, 15, or 20 people in a room and can look the CEO in the eye as he explains why the changes are happening, and, more importantly, what it means for them personally.

For this company, that kind of personal engagement between the CEO and employees turned the tide. Attitudes did not reverse overnight, but hearing leaders talk about how this was the "right thing to do for the future" and deliver inspirational messages about the change led to a gradual shift in the tone of everyday conversation, away from antagonism (Why is this being done that way?) to positive cooperation ("Here's a problem and I think we can tackle it.").

It's not at all unusual for companies to favor one side of the brain—either logic or emotion. Most often, like this manufacturer, they are good at logic and not so good at emotion, but we've seen reverse cases as well. Another company we worked with, for example, was very good at visioning and explaining to people what the change would mean, but very poor at spelling out the business reasons driving the change in the first place.

Any change that is significant will produce a sense of urgency that, in turn, creates its own agenda as employees scramble to figure out if and how they will fit in after the change. Leaders need to step back from the urgency—take a deep breath, to calm themselves—something that is not always easy to do. It helps to take the time to figure out where the stakeholders reside and then build an "emotional chart" of the organization—where are the doers, the thinkers, the excitable people, the calming influences? Who needs to know what, from the emotional side? It may be the head of operations, the head of manufacturing; or a primary influencer on the emotional side may be the CFO or the head of HR, or even a long-time employee who has seniority and respect, but not an impressive job title in the emotional map. You're looking for people who can be the glue that will hold the organization together during transitions.

When dealing with change initiatives, addressing the emotional side of the argument usually involves both the "what's in it for me?" (WIIFM) aspect and the "what's at risk for me?" (WARFM) factor. To do that, identify what people care about most: how they are compensated, job security, career growth, career stability. Making it clear how those issues will be handled—especially to key influencers—can go a long way toward shifting employee behavior. For example, one of our clients was undergoing a cultural shift driven by the need to be more forward-thinking in its strategy. Staff who were not cutting-edge were let go, replaced by people with more technology skills and knowledge. As a result, there was a major rift in style and thinking between the remaining "old guard" staff and the newcomers. The solution for this company was to look at its key performers and figure out what the transition offered them in terms of job growth opportunities, increased responsibility, and so on, *and* what they were putting at risk by not participating. The company made those messages clear, then delegated the ongoing management of the change to those key performers.

These kinds of approaches don't eliminate the challenge of going through change, but they do make the change process easier. For this company, once

---

Communication to the Extended Enterprise

While we have focused this chapter on the "internal organization," we urge you to apply the same communication and involvement guidelines throughout your Extended Enterprise. Your suppliers, distributors, and customers usually are a part of, or are affected by, major changes in your organization. For the suppliers and distributors that help with the cost solutions you implement, understanding their concerns, establishing two-way communication plans, and ensuring feedback feasibility are just as important to the Extended Enterprise as it is to the internal organization. Helping suppliers and distributors establish process improvements and asking them to be accountable for their plans and actions are paramount to the success of the processes that they supply and interact with.

At the other end of your value stream, it's important for your company to communicate to your customers about any changes, particularly any that will affect how they do business with you and that will lead to improvements they will experience and see (such as improved delivery or service). The communication plan and forms of communication to the customer should be part of the overall change plan.

people were aligned, they had an easier time adjusting responsibilities and accountabilities, providing consistent messages to the organization, and getting buy-in at different levels.

PROCESS OWNERSHIP AND COST ACCOUNTABILITY

One thing that differentiates an improvement initiative focused on cost reduction is the very real possibility that work will be done very differently *after* the change, as compared to *before*. Major chunks of work—the waste or non-value-add activities discussed in Part I—will, hopefully, disappear. At the very least, job roles and responsibilities may be very different afterward, and if your company is linking improvement to job cuts, there may be a major reshuffling of job duties and responsibilities.

It is a time of great confusion. Sometimes key responsibilities aren't assigned at all. Other times, you'll find two or more people who think they are responsible for the same work. Duplication of effort is a symptom of organizational inefficiencies, which ultimately results in a higher cost of delivery.

Most companies seem to have a handle on defining roles and responsibilities at the start of a change initiative. Some are forward-thinking enough to spell out how those ownerships and accountabilities will change in the final stage. But very few pay attention to what happens in between—the transitional stages when jobs may be shifting temporarily. It is during the transitional periods that we've seen many change initiatives fall into chaos.

To help your organization implement actions through all stages of the change journey focused on cost reduction, you need to address two factors:

- *Process ownership*, not just functional ownership. A change in how work is done means changing the processes you use to accomplish that work. At every stage of change, there needs to be someone in charge of each key process—the person who makes the call if something isn't working right with a process.
- *Cost accountability*: If your change is driven by a need to significantly cut costs, you must have clear accountability of cost management during each phase of change, to enable consistent focus.

As your company develops its change management plans, think ahead to envision what will happen both during and after the transitions. A company we worked with, for example, was merging departments from different locations. By its own internal measures, the transition in departments that did a good job of identifying "who makes the call" during every stage went more than twice as smoothly than the transition in departments that did a poor job of clarifying shifting responsibilities. (Their measures included the number of complaints, number of interpersonal issues, and so on.)

How to Manage Accountabilities during Change

1. Identify the changes you're likely to see in the current process.
2. Define the future state.
3. Clearly articulate (as much as is feasible) the transition phase.
4. Develop a "critical process" focus, rather than a functional focus.
   - Clarify end-to-end responsibilities in the process to reinforce hand-offs between functional areas.
   - Ensure overall ownership of key processes within the organization, so that during the transition phase there is someone accountable to drive the change and manage the associated costs.
   - Clearly specify the transition plan, with emphasis on new or broadened roles.

CONCLUSION: RESTORING FAITH, HOPE, AND BELIEF

In times of stress, a strong change management plan can help you restore faith, hope, and belief that the initiative is critical to growth and/or survival. Leading and managing change focused on cost reduction requires a diverse set of skills: The leadership team needs to be part architect, part psychologist, and part cheerleader. These times can be seen as difficult and scary, especially when employees do not know how they will be impacted by the change. Getting through the change with flying colors takes leaders who can plan and manage the change process while being honest and open, actively listening and communicating frequently with information that is on-target and useful to each person hearing it.

CHAPTER 14

ESTABLISHING A CENTER
OF EXCELLENCE

With Stephen Elliott, Pam Altizer, and Matthew Peterson

A global packaging manufacturer with more than 20,000 employees and about 100 plants and operating sites had grown significantly over two decades as the result of acquisitions. The company wanted to transition from its original holding company model (where each acquired business retained its individual processes and culture) to an operating company model (with more consistency worldwide) because key customers were consolidating and increasing their expectations of packaging suppliers.

As the same time, the CEO set goals of reducing costs by 2 percent of revenue on an annual basis and improving operational flexibility. Fast results were critical due to a downward trend in operating profit margins. The company selected Lean Six Sigma as the mechanism for driving down costs, and, because a rapid rollout was critical to achieve breakeven within one year, it chose to drive LSS implementation through a Center of Excellence (CoE):

- A small (three full-time employees) central office, the CoE focused on program design, methodology selection, building infrastructure, and performance measurement and reporting.
- The staff reported to the CEO.
- Representatives from different geographic regions (12 employees) had matrixed reporting relationship to the CoE and business units, with the goals of identifying personnel to become LSS leaders, selecting high-impact projects, and aligning with business units objectives

261

Eventually, the CoE coordinated the work of more than 300 LSS leaders dispersed throughout the company

Within 10 months of taking these steps, the packaging supplier saw significant returns, with an annual savings rate approaching $200 million.

The deployment model this company used is similar in some respects to the standard Lean Six Sigma deployment model used for much of the past two decades: There are still champions and Black Belts and Master Belts inside each business unit, but having centralized coordinating and support functions through the Center of Excellence gave it the jump-start and ongoing energy and commitment it needed to drive results quickly throughout the organization.

A Center of Excellence can also be used to rejuvenate stalled initiatives. For example, a chemicals company ran into problems soon after launching a Lean program. The company had trained a number of employees (though inconsistently) and launched a few small projects (chosen mostly on the basis of convenience)—and that was it. The program stalled.

After a thorough assessment, the company redesigned and then relaunched a full Lean Six Sigma program driven through a Center of Excellence, which had responsibility for maximizing results and managing risk. Within nine months, the LSS program became cash positive and was viewed by senior leaders as integral to delivering on their strategy and business objectives.

Both of these companies found that having a CoE:

- Focused the organization on important projects.
- Aligned cost reduction projects with the business strategy.
- Established a structure, roles, skills, and common language that supported the evolution of cost reduction efforts.
- Provided critical training, coaching, and guidance to business units.
- Enabled active monitoring and managing of ongoing performance.

As a result, both reaped many benefits. Establishing the CoE:

- Accelerated all key program decisions and established commonality across their organizations.
- Exposed significant opportunities for replication of projects and solutions across multiple plant sites, which sped up results and reduced implementation costs.
- Allowed them to more effectively align strategy and LSS program priorities.
- Drove engagement further, faster.

Creating a Lean Six Sigma Center of Excellence requires a high degree of alignment and commitment within your organization. This chapter discusses what a Center of Excellence is and what it does, options for structuring the CoE, and steps to take that can help ensure success.

What Is a CoE and What Does It Do?

Centers of Excellence are typically small teams of 5 to 10 employees consisting of the CoE director, a business analyst, and process improvement experts—all full-time roles. Together, these staff members provide support to the business unit champions, project sponsors and the project leaders.

How Big Should Your CoE Be?

The CoE needs to be sufficiently staffed to help during the launch and the initial rollout, and to sustain the gains of the organization over time. As with all organizations, the purpose and roles can migrate and change as the organization's needs change. The ratio of process experts (housed in the CoE) to project leaders (housed in the business units) is typically 1 to 8 in the beginning of a deployment, then drops down to 1 to 15 at maturity. This will ensure that the process experts also have time to lead complex process projects and help coach when needed.

What a CoE Does

A CoE typically has five primary objectives:

1. Set focus on LSS cost reduction within the organization.
2. Generate faster returns on the invested resources (via improved project selection).
3. Establish a critical mass of capabilities and resources.
4. Develop organizational capability for sustained cost reduction.
5. Optimize the LSS deployment across the organization.

In addition, because of its strong cross linkages, a CoE enables you to better leverage advances and lessons learned, no matter where they occur in the business. The CoE will play a lead role in:

- Identifying avenues of collaboration when different business unites are faced with similar problems.

- Ensuring that business units are not duplicating effort (working on the same issues/projects).
- Alerting one business unit about relevant improvement ideas successfully implemented in another business unit.
- Establishing standard process metrics across the enterprise.
- Linking up process improvement expertise resident in on area with needs in others areas of the company.

The CoE will be the central source for information about LSS methodology, providing the organization with:

- *Curriculum:* Paper and/or electronic class materials that cover introduction, basic, and advanced skill levels (often referred to in LSS as White, Green and Black Belt classes). Usually, these are purchased materials that may be customized as the organization program matures.
- *Access to experts:* The experts typically teach Lean Six Sigma classes; coach team leaders and team sponsors on all aspects of project work and management; lead challenging projects that span organizational boundaries; and can also serve as team members (though that is rare).
- *Project repository:* An electronic database or file of all projects initiated and their current status. These records become a critical source of information to refine project selection skills, identify successful projects that can be repeated, and capture data needed to track results. (Small organizations that perform 50 to 100 projects over a few years may find an Access Database or Excel file sufficient. Global organizations may find it necessary to use tools such as PowerSteering or Instansis to track hundreds of projects each year.)
- *Forum for LSS champions:* Each business unit should have its own LSS champion, who is considered a member of the CoE but who reports to the business unit leader. The CoE has a role to play in bringing the champions together so they can share lessons, ask for guidance, bridge gaps, and so on. The role of the Champion Forum will vary depending on how the CoE itself is structured (see page 278), ranging from helping equalize resources across the business units to ensuring standardization of practices and approaches to prioritizing initiatives either across the entire enterprise or within business units.

Two key CoE activities that we want to discuss in more depth revolve around performance management and project replication, because both dramatically increase the kinds of benefits you can reap, yet are missing in many Lean Six Sigma deployments today.

FOCUS #1: PERFORMANCE MANAGEMENT

Performance management means having a mechanism that closes the loop between *estimates* of project savings and *actual* results achieved. Without that closed loop, a company cannot know when corrective action is needed, appropriately allocate resources, and learn lessons from each project that can be used to improve the next projects. The value of that capability is clear: well-planned and executed LSS cost reduction programs generate earnings quickly—often reducing costs on a corporatewide basis by 2 to 5 percent of revenue. Implementing performance management makes the benefits more visible to the entire organization, which increases buy-in, which in turn improves the probability of success and raises the potential for dramatic results.

The CoE should take the lead in managing LSS performance by having the organization agree on how project benefits will be captured and defined (see the "types of savings" discussion in Chapter 12). CoE staff should also act as advisors to project teams to make sure they understand and implement those definitions.

Of prime importance is the CoE's role in reporting *aggregated* project results and program performance. It is that cross-project view that allows senior leadership to better understand how the deployment is going overall, where it has been successful and where it hasn't, and what roadblocks are standing in the way of even better performance.

Typically, the aggregation compares information across business units or divisions, geographic location, project type (Black Belt, Green Belt, or Kaizen), and project area (for example, manufacturing, finance, human resources, sales, marketing, customer service). Also typically, the compiled data is presented in a dashboard, as we'll discuss next.

Developing Metric Dashboards and Control Plans

Identifying what it is you want to measure is one part of successful performance management. You also need to capture that information in a way that is easily digestible; know what it is you're looking for in the patterns (or lack thereof) in the metrics; and identify how you will respond, depending on what the metrics show you.

Step 1: Identify the Critical Xs and Ys   Most Lean Six Sigma practitioners are familiar with the equation:

$$Y = f(X)$$

This is read as "Y is a function of X." All that means is that to deliver a particular output (Y), you have to understand the inputs (Xs) that drive that output.

If your primary purpose in using Lean Six Sigma is to reduce costs, that is your critical Y. In Figure 14.1, that is referred to as the Deployment Goal. As a CoE we want to identify and control the Xs that will lead to cost reduction. Successful cost reduction programs are a function of Acceptance, Number of Projects, and Value per Project. More detailed Xs and associated metrics are identified on the bottom side of the chart.

Step 2: Develop Metrics for a Dashboard   A CoE track three kinds of results:

1. Project results
2. Indicators of how well the CoE is doing its job
3. Indicators of overall LSS program success

Deployment metrics often include how long projects take to finish, cycle time of the DMAIC phases, percent of projects canceled, number of people trained, number actively working on projects, and so on. These are important indicators of project performance, and trends can indicate the need for corrective action in project selection, resource loading, and prioritization of LSS projects.

Metrics specifically related to the Center of Excellence tend to focus on measures easily collected that indicate degree of rollout, awareness, and adoption.

Table 14.1 summarizes some of the most commonly used metrics to support performance management of an LSS program.

A good program will monitor a mix of all three types, as summarized in Table 14.2.

Once you have identified the metrics, the CoE should then create a standard reporting package for monthly updating (Figure 14.2). It should be graphic and convey trends and static information.

Step 3: Take Action Based on the Metrics (Closed-Loop Management)
Focusing on controlling the Xs—the key inputs that have the biggest effect on the desired outcome—is a critical capability for the Center of Excellence.

Figure 14.1
Finding the critical Xs for deployment monitoring.

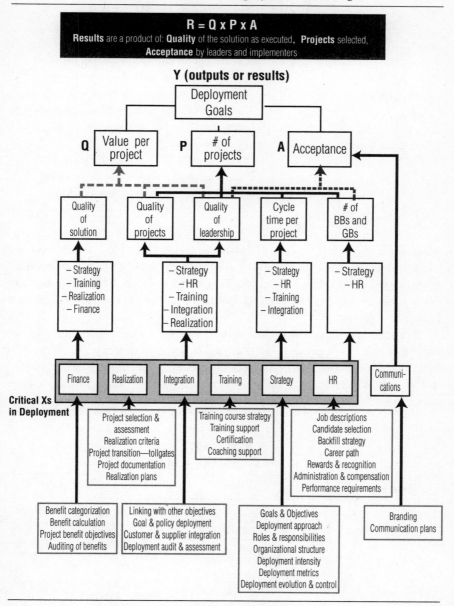

Table 14.1
Metrics for Managing a Lean Six Sigma Deployment

Performance Measure Focus	Example Metrics
Project	Type 1 hard savings achieved
	Cycle times for DMAIC phases per plan
	Percent of savings realized versus estimate
Center of Excellence (CoE)	Ratio of projects in process to project leaders
	Projects waiting to be assigned inventory level
	Percent of locations participating
LSS Program Success	Aggregated savings
	Cycle-time trends for project completion
	Percent of project leaders that are full-time
	Percent of organization leaders who have sponsored projects

Management typically wants to know the result (Y): "How much have we saved?" However, it often takes six months for complex projects to be identified, scoped, staffed and completed. (By using Kaizens, Chapter 7, you can often shorten that payback period, but there will always be delays between launch and results.)

Of course, the most important metrics are the average estimated and actual savings of each project. If the amounts begin to decrease, steps need to be taken to adjust the project selection process or to modify expectations. We've found that average project savings tend to remain consistent over several years. Early projects might find easier savings ("low-hanging fruit"),

Table 14.2
Mix of Metric Types

Program	CoE	LSS Deployment
Average estimated cost savings per project	Number of completed projects	Total cost savings (all savings to date plus savings broken out by period)
	Number of full-time project leaders	Average actual cost savings per project
	Number of projects in process	Percent actual savings realized versus estimated
	Heat map of organization engagement	Cycle time of completed projects
	Inventory of ready-to-launch projects	

Figure 14.2
Example dashboard charts.

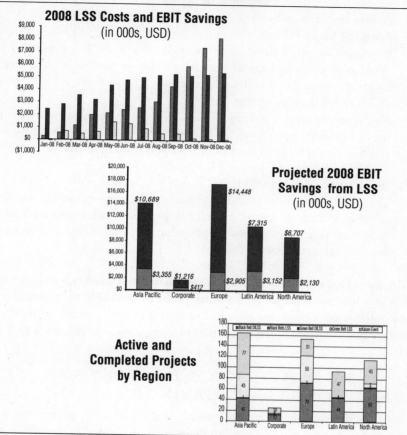

but as the LSS skill sets become more proficient, project leaders are able to drive similar benefits from more challenging projects.

If you monitor only the outcome metrics, you won't know about successes and failures until long after its too late to do anything about them. So your company needs to focus on which input metrics you will monitor and what you will do about them. For example:

- A *heat map* of organization engagement can be an early-warning indicator, where "red" departments are in need of more connection with the CoE to better engage the organization unit and ensure there will be meaningful results.

- *Number of full-time project leaders*: How many projects your organization can complete will be a direct function of how many full-time project leaders you have.
- Per Little's Law (Chapter 5), you don't want to have too many projects in process or you'll slow down results for everyone. If the monthly ratio of projects in process divided by number of project leaders gets to be greater than 2.0, you are in danger of increasing project cycle times and slowing the cost savings rate.
- *Health of the project pipeline*. The CoE needs to design a balanced system of project generation and completion. Having an inventory of ready-to-launch projects of about 50 percent of the full-time project leader headcount is a reasonable target.
- Project cycle time should be measured by DMAIC phase and in total. Long cycle times tend to indicate too large of a project scope, resource constraints, or too many projects in process. A first step to address long cycle times is to review scope and understand issues with proceeding through gate reviews.

In summary, the CoE should think of the metrics, dashboards, and controls as a system. The metrics are interrelated: The dashboards should provide information that can be acted upon, and the control activities to manage the X inputs are the levers that can be changed or influenced.

Focus #2: Replication: Copy and Paste Your Cost Savings

A key advantage to implementing a CoE is a significantly greater capacity for replicating past projects and applying lessons learned from one area to another in the organization. Through the CoE, organizations avoid reinventing the proverbial wheel for each improvement project.

By replication, we mean deliberately capitalizing on previous successes, growing institutional knowledge of project execution in the process. Replication speeds up the improvement learning cycle, enabling the enterprise to collect the benefits of better practices, sooner rather than later.

Replication is a relatively easy concept to grasp. In practice, replicating LSS project successes can take several forms:

- *Proliferate solutions:* A solution has already been validated at one particular location, allowing the organization to copy the solution to other appropriate target locations.

- *Meet compliance requirements:* To comply with regulations, organizations may leverage an existing solution that meets compliance, and institutionalize this across the enterprise.
- *Copy tactical better practices:* A better method for an operation step may be observed at one or more locations, generating an opportunity to copy the new method to other appropriate locations.
- *Copy process-level better practices:* An organization may find that gains from improving one process may be applied to another. This carries more risk than tactical-level changes, given the greater scope.
- *Institutionalize standard practices:* There may be a need to reduce variation of a particular practice across the enterprise. In this case, the organization can institutionalize one particular practice to be the standard across the entire enterprise.
- *Copy tactical better practices from industry:* The organization may observe the opportunity to utilize an industry standard operation step or activity, copying the better operation step from industry to one or more locations.
- *Copy industry standard processes:* The organization may observe (for example, through the use of industry subject-matter advisors) the opportunity to incorporate an industry standard process. In this case, the organization can copy the better process to one or more locations.

The CoE should publicize newfound solutions to an organizationwide problem, contributing to a culture of continuous improvement. Individually, project teams can copy an existing solution, beginning with actually leveraging previous project charters and analytical frameworks, to leverage institutional knowledge.

Another important aspect of replication is identifying the opportunities: processes that are identical, or nearly so, in different parts of the organization; common technologies; and concepts that can be transferred from one situation to something that seems very different on the surface. Just how much is transferable takes some experience and expertise—hence, another role for the CoE. A well-functioning CoE will assist business leaders in actively seeking out areas where better practices can be applied across the organization. Likewise, the CoE is an important vehicle for identifying areas where process variance is generating hidden costs to the organization, and for which institutional standardization can drive real benefit.

One model for guiding a CoE's role in fostering replication is the SAFE model, captured in Figure 14.3.

Figure 14.3
The SAFE model for project replication.

SAFE Replication

Select and verify: *Ensure validity of "good practice"*
- Select next replication opportunity
- Differentiation between "good practices" and "good intentions"
- Identify type of replication and risk
- Draft initial goals for replication
- Identify all target (local) locations

Adopt: *Gain local acceptance for replication*
- Engage & negotiate with local subject matter experts
- Document and communication good practice
- Adjust for local requirements
- Establish local replication goals
- Establigh high-level replication plan

Fix: *Execute change and monitor progress*
- Visit a working implementation
- Rapid Improvement Event or quick win
- Develop local action plans
- Pilot, implement changes
- Monitor & report progress
- Validate benefits

Energize: *Replication is in place and proven*
- Go Fast—move on to the next location
- Gain the benefits
- Update local SOPs and control plans
- Document results including benefits
- Celebrate success!

In all cases, the key to successful—and sustained—replication is to loudly communicate improvement successes. It's impossible to replicate an unknown success. To this end, the CoE should be the primary conduit for communication of these successes across the organization, and must enable the organization to leverage a growing and accessible body of improvement work.

HOW CAN A CoE FIT INTO AN ORGANIZATION?

As an organizational entity, the Center of Excellence reports to a steering committee, CEO, or appointed senior leader responsible for the process improvement initiative. The CoE director works with each of the business unit (BU) leaders and business unit champions to ensure that the proper projects are identified, prioritized, and selected, given specific cost targets. These projects are then assigned to a project sponsor, chartered and staffed by BU resources. The CoE director assists the BU champions by providing process improvement expertise and capability development to the project leaders and team members, as needed. These relationships are captured in Figure 14.4.

Figure 14.4
The Lean Six Sigma infrastructure within a business unit follows the standard model common in Lean Six Sigma deployments, with a BU champion who has full-time project leaders. The project teams are commissioned by a project sponsor who owns the project and its results. In addition, there should be channels of communication between the business unit staff and CoE staff.

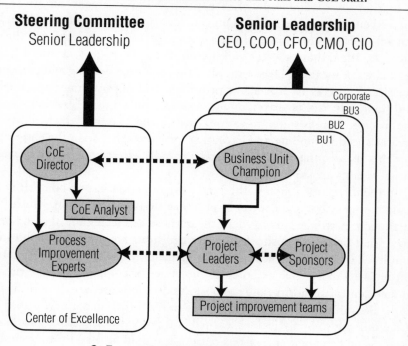

Steering Committee
Senior Leadership

Senior Leadership
CEO, COO, CFO, CMO, CIO

CoE Director

CoE Analyst

Process Improvement Experts

Center of Excellence

Corporate
BU3
BU2
BU1

Business Unit Champion

Project Leaders

Project Sponsors

Project improvement teams

CoE operating model is designed for representation from all business units

Options for Structuring a CoE

Prior to designing the CoE, it is necessary to first define and articulate its mandate. This decision must be driven by leadership. Without clarity as to the goals and objective of the CoE—what it is the CoE is tasked with accomplishing—it will be difficult, if not impossible, to establish the correct structure and put the appropriate personnel in place.

There is no "right" answer. The CoE may be established with limited objectives in mind (for example, incremental process optimization within business units), or with a sweeping mandate such as helping to build a culture of continuous improvement throughout the organization. Without a clearly articulated and defined objective, confusion will hamper investment and improvement initiatives. Figure 14.5 shows the kinds of responsibilities that have to be handled for a successful Lean Six Sigma program; the question is whether the CoE should have the responsibility or the business units.

There are three basic operating models for the CoE, as shown in Figure 14.6.

In the *consolidated* model, the process improvement resources are sourced either from the business units or externally, and brought within the central CoE organization, which assumes P&L responsibility for the resources. Often, the resources will literally move desks to join the CoE at a central work location. Decisions, including resource funding and personnel decisions, process improvement priorities, and improvement approaches and standards, will be driven by the organization's central leadership team. In this case, there is standardization across business units, which allows for greater speed in funding and executing initiatives that span the enterprise. For this reason, the centralized model is more effective when the various business units are similar in nature.

In the *distributed model*, the larger organization has responsibility for maintaining only the most top-level of decisions (for example, which CoE methodology will be employed, or the purpose and technology behind organizational process repositories); other decisions are made at the business unit level. This model lends itself to organizations composed of very different business units, such as holding companies or companies where there is limited central authority, and the business decisions are loosely coordinated at the organization level. One downside of the distributed model is that it is more difficult to apply lessons learned and process best practices from one business unit to another. For this reason, it should be used in environments where there is little opportunity to capitalize on intellectual-scale economies across the organization, where a success in one area will likely have little transferability to another.

Figure 14.5
Responsibilities that must be assigned.

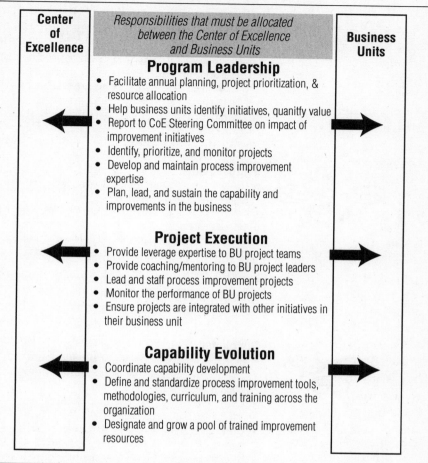

Center of Excellence	Responsibilities that must be allocated between the Center of Excellence and Business Units	Business Units

Program Leadership

- Facilitate annual planning, project prioritization, & resource allocation
- Help business units identify initiatives, quanitfy value
- Report to CoE Steering Committee on impact of improvement initiatives
- Identify, prioritize, and monitor projects
- Develop and maintain process improvement expertise
- Plan, lead, and sustain the capability and improvements in the business

Project Execution

- Provide leverage expertise to BU project teams
- Provide coaching/mentoring to BU project leaders
- Lead and staff process improvement projects
- Monitor the performance of BU projects
- Ensure projects are integrated with other initiatives in their business unit

Capability Evolution

- Coordinate capability development
- Define and standardize process improvement tools, methodologies, curriculum, and training across the organization
- Designate and grow a pool of trained improvement resources

The *representative model* may be the most confusing. There may be a natural tendency—in the interest of wanting to "split the middle," with respect to the operating models— to select this model in the interest of having to choose between consolidated and distributed structures. But do not choose this model just to avoid some tough decisions.

In a representative model, most of the process improvement resources will reside in the business units. As such, these resources will have a matrix reporting relationship with their business units and with the CoE. Typically, this means that the resources have a solid-line relationship into the business unit and a dotted-line relationship into the CoE. Regardless of the nature of

Figure 14.6
CoE operating models.

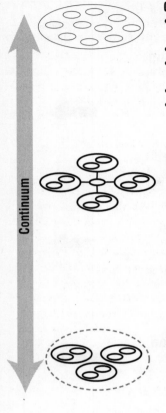

Continuum

Consolidated
- LSS resources are centrally located and fall under a central Center of Excellence P&L.
- More command and control to the central organization.
- Central authority makes decisions related to standards, functionality, funding, and change mangement.
- Information flows from the central body to business units.
- Centralization of resources allows for timely investment, resource decisions.

Representative
- Resources reside primarily within the business units, with a small core of central expertise.
- Governance body consists of representatives across the business units.
- Central body responsible for decisions related to degree of standardization and work jointly to capitalize on lessons learned.
- Strategic decisions guided by central authority, which LSS decisions made within business units.

Distributed
- Resources reside within the individual business units.
- Central body responsible only for overseeing the most top-level of decisions.
- Each business unit is responsible for its own process strategy and improvement approach.
- There is little or no information flow between business units.
- Each has awarenessof LSS Center of Excellence: rationale for adopting its methodology; how CoE supports organizational goals and objectives; scope and deployment timeline; how BUs can leverage the CoE.
- Maximizes individual business unit autonomy.

the reporting relationship, the resources will always remain physically located within the business units (that is, they don't move desks).

While most of the resources reside within the business units, there is still a "core" CoE within the representative model. This core is charged with coordinating and facilitating training, creating training curricula, monitoring and reporting of performance objectives (for example, dashboards to the steering committee), maintaining a knowledge exchange and/or process repository, providing LSS experts to mentor and coach project leaders, and providing deep LSS expertise for large-scale cross-enterprise initiatives.

The representative model is more appropriate for organizations with similar business units—like the consolidated model—but the enterprise is particularly concerned with maintaining business unit autonomy. Instances in which business units are operationally similar but with distinct business cultures may find that the representative model works best for them.

Providing CoE Oversight: The Steering Committee

Part of the infrastructure that helps to ensure that the CoE continues to be valuable to the organization is establishing a steering committee. The steering committee is normally composed of about 12 members (that's just an order of magnitude) and meets twice per quarter. It should have representation across all business units and include a committee chair (typically, the executive tasked with driving results from the CoE). The organization signals the relative importance of the CoE through the seniority of members of the steering committee and the frequency with which the steering committee meets.

The purpose of the steering committee is *not* to discuss the minutiae of individual initiatives or the prioritization of effort and resources; rather, the steering committee should be focused on enterprise-level performance of the CoE, and determining how to leverage its value across the organization.

WEAVING THE CoE INTO STRATEGIC PLANNING

In the past, one problem that many organizations ran into was having their Lean Six Sigma deployment become marginalized—viewed as something "extra" and not the "real work" of the organization. Organizations that let their deployments fall by the wayside are failing to appreciate just how much Lean Six Sigma can contribute to advancing their strategic goals.

The CoE can play an important role in making sure your organization fully leverages its Lean Six Sigma investment—if it is woven into your strategic and annual planning processes.

Usually the organization leadership will lay out the vision and longer-term objectives of the organization during the long-range planning cycle, which typically takes place every three to five years. Leadership will refine and update this vision during the annual planning process.

As the CoE matures, it often becomes an important part of this process. On one hand, the CoE helps to identify opportunities and prioritize projects, to optimize the efforts of finite resources. On the other hand, the CoE will ensure that leadership's strategic vision and objectives shape ongoing improvement efforts. The CoE should shape the organizational roadmap of LSS initiatives based on the input from the planning process. In this sense, the CoE is both an input to and output from the planning process. This alignment activity is often referred to as *strategy deployment*, as shown in Figure 14.7.

Figure 14.7
Alignment through strategy deployment: Strategy deployment is a management system to ensure that strategic breakthroughs are executed.

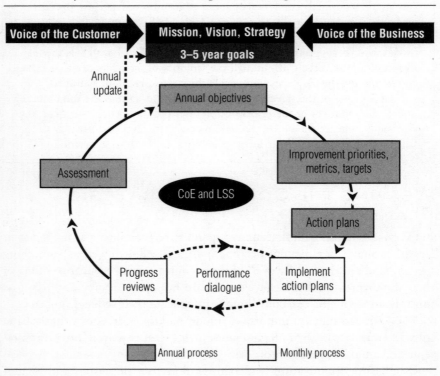

Upon completion of the annual planning process, business units will have objectives, targets, and priorities. To meet this end, the CoE is an important tool in effecting process reengineering solutions to business opportunities. The CoE, in large part through the champion forum, will help to prioritize LSS initiatives and allocate finite resources within and across the business units. The CoE is instrumental in helping the business units prioritize the roadmap and identify the upcoming intra- and interbusiness-unit LSS initiatives to meet the mandates set forth in the planning cycle.

The steering committee should leverage the CoE heavily to identify a metrics tracking plan. Too often, strategic plans are initiated without a mechanism for determining their relative success or failure. In this regard, the CoE should identify useful measurements and be the means by which these progress metrics are reported to the leadership. In practice, this means that the CoE will track the LSS initiatives in-flight within the organization, and identify the contribution of these initiatives to the overall strategic plan to the steering committee.

Leveraging the CoE as the primary cog in the execution of LSS initiatives to meet the strategic vision provides significant traction in the way of the sustainability of benefits. Far too often, organizations undertake improvement endeavors without a clearly articulated set of benefits. Upon completion of the initiative, the benefits are realized—but not sustained. To sustain benefits, it is essential that the organization understand the role of the process owners. By process owner, we mean a single point of contact—one owner—for generating improvement and leading the overall process. Process owners should own the predictive metrics that drive performance. This is a more advanced topic that goes beyond cost savings within a function but across core value streams of the business. The foundation that Lean and Six Sigma provide can make this a realistic future goal.

CONCLUSION

The invention of the Belt-based infrastructure now considered an integral part of Lean Six Sigma was a breakthrough in improvement methodology. Once that infrastructure was in place, it became much easier for companies to make sure that projects were selected based on their potential contribution to business goals, and that project leaders had the requisite problem-solving and project management skills to increase the odds of having fast, effective projects.

Even for all its benefits, however, the standard infrastructure does have limitations, especially as a company transitions from the early-launch stages to maintenance, where there is a greater need for coordination among, and alignment and sharing between, business units. That's where Centers of Excellence come in. They provide the mechanism for driving even greater levels of gains from Lean Six Sigma: driving replication; speeding up the learning curve; and constantly building institutional knowledge around where, when, and how to use Lean Six Sigma to your best advantage.

CHAPTER 15

GAINING NEW PERSPECTIVES ON DEPLOYMENT COST AND SPEED OPPORTUNITIES

With Anthony Curtis, Nolen Janes, Michael Mueller, Peter Gaa, and Rob Sharples

Ever since the economic collapse in 2008, our conversations with potential clients have taken on a new tenor: Those already embarked on a Lean Six Sigma journey wonder if there's more they could be doing. They tell us that they've trimmed all the fat they can. Those considering the journey wonder if Lean Six Sigma can make a big enough difference in performance—quickly enough—to help them survive this downturn.

In today's economy, long-term Lean Six Sigma deployments with three-year returns are difficult for leaders to accept. The volatility of the market today requires short-term gains while developing the flexibility for the long-term plan. The need is clear: Leaders desire faster break-even points and a positive return on the investment much more quickly than ever before.

One of the advantages of being in the consulting world is having the opportunity to work with leaders in diverse businesses as they adapt Lean Six Sigma to their organizations' unique environments. We also get to work with smart, observant colleagues. Together, these factors have given us insights how organizations can best take advantage of their Lean Six Sigma investments, and opened our eyes to new ways that Lean Six Sigma can help drive cost cuts and higher performance—ways that some businesses exploit but that many, many others overlook.

In this chapter, we'll cover some of the highest-leverage actions you can take to get more out of your Lean Six Sigma investment in the short term *and* position you for a stronger future. If you're doing some of these things already, that's great. But odds are good that some of these ideas will be completely new, and give you new perspectives on opportunities for cutting costs and improving speed in your organization.

LOOKING FOR FOCUS AND FLEXIBILITY IN DEPLOYMENT

After a recent major cash outlay to repurchase stock, a multibillion-dollar freight-hauling company wanted to use Lean Six Sigma to make operational improvements to help improve the balance sheet. However, despite needing "rapid returns," the company did not have the internal expertise to generate the kinds of cost savings it sought ($50 million within 12 months). Nor did it have the time to follow a traditional Lean Six Sigma deployment approach, where it might take as long as a year or two just to develop sufficient internal expertise, to carry it off without help.

For this company, the "right" deployment model differed from the standard model, in several key ways:

- Improvements were focused on the highest-cost issues (nonrevenue miles due to poor data accuracy, trailer management at terminals, trailer retention at customer docks, maintenance, and so on), rather than deployment of the methodology across the entire corporation.
- Teams were initially led by "hired hands" (external consultants); but gradually, internal staff took on more and more of the project management and problem-solving work, coached by the experts.
- Training was targeted at specific issues and team members.
- The company took advantage of every speed advantage it could, putting a priority on cost saving and early returns through a mix of Kaizens (see Chapter 7) and executive-sponsored projects.

Within three months of launch, this company had realized a 15-times return on investment, and was well on the way to achieving its goals.

Many companies today are in the same position as this hauling company, wanting more flexibility around Lean Six Sigma deployment. For this company, the need was to make substantial operational improvements and cost cuts very quickly, even though it did have a large number of trained Lean Six Sigma resources internally. Other companies have told us they either delayed or avoided deploying Lean Six Sigma—despite knowing they needed to make improvements—because they feared the up-front

investment of time and money required to develop the internal expertise required to pull off big successes.

Overall, we've seen five primary reasons why companies require greater
flexibility:

1. They have an important and/or urgent operational business issue that
   needs to be resolved *fast*.
2. They lack *sufficient* internal capability (LSS, problem solving, project
   management) to fix the issue(s).
3. They lack capacity (headcount) to fix the issue(s), even if they have
   the capability.
4. They want to see proof of the Lean Six Sigma concept before they
   launch a broader, transformational engagement.
5. They don't want a broad transformation that the traditional deployment produces (perhaps they are not large enough to support a cadre
   of LSS process improvement experts, or may have other priorities at
   the moment).

If your company falls into one of these categories, there is hope in the
next generation of Lean Six Sigma deployment models, which offers you
more options. Elsewhere in this book we've introduced several techniques
for shortening the time-to-payback for Lean Six Sigma deployment, including the Kaizen project model (Chapter 7) and the need to limit the number
of active projects. In the rest of this chapter, we'll look first at how to control the scope of a Lean Six Sigma deployment by focusing on strategic business issues, and then describe options around skill building that provide an
alternative to the traditional classroom training method often found in the
traditional Lean Six Sigma deployment model.

FOCUSING DEPLOYMENTS
ON BUSINESS ISSUES

The hauling company described earlier was in a position where it wanted to
make big gains, fast, in only a few areas of the company—the areas with the
biggest cost reduction opportunities. For that reason, we call the model it
used a *focused deployment*. Here is another example: A $5 billion distributor
of office products with more than 50 distribution centers and over 30,000
resellers required a more flexible approach, capable of delivering fast
results—initially built around a group of just four Black Belts. A small consulting team was deployed, which included experts in financial analysis,

business process architecture and Lean Six Sigma. The team deployed concurrently on four fronts, and within the first six weeks:

- Assessed and analyzed the organization's financial landscape (P&L and balance sheet) to identify and select the opportunities with the highest value and impact for the deployment of Lean Six Sigma project teams.
- Mapped the business process architecture, aligned the high-level processes to the financial levers, and identified opportunities to improve each of the enabling functions that support the primary customer-facing processes.
- Developed a deployment strategy and created a customized training program specific to the client's business environment and opportunities.
- Chartered and initiated projects with client-dedicated Black Belts, who also started their training.

Because of the fast pace, the Black Belts in training operated in an "apprenticeship role," learning and doing at the same time. This can be accomplished only when the training content is focused on the business topics and delivered in a nontraditional way. Instead of the typical five weeks of training delivered across four months, the Black Belts received one and a half days of training every other week, with the pace and content aligned to the progress of their projects.

As with the hauling company, the external consultants functioned in several roles:

- As masters, showing the apprentices how to do the project work (especially in the first four to six weeks as the Black Belts were learning more about Lean Six Sigma).
- As instructors during the training days.
- As coaches, to help Black Belts use the right tools and analysis to complete their projects.

Concurrently, customized training for the rest of the organization was developed and executed for leadership, project sponsors, and team participants. Specific training for team members was felt to be critical to equip team members with the tools and skills needed to accelerate project cycle times and shorten the time to realize economic benefits.

In addition, senior leadership worked on developing guiding principles and designing the infrastructure to support the processes, metrics, people, and rewards/recognition needed to continue working on process improvements and achieve the resulting gains.

The financial and business process analysis identified not only traditional Lean Six Sigma projects but a wealth of opportunity for the execution of Kaizens, as well. After a few months, and in response to these opportunities, the Black Belt training was further customized to provide the Black Belts the additional ability to execute Kaizen events.

An additional resource, highly skilled in the creative application of Kaizens, was brought in to coach and prepare the initial group of four Black Belts, as well as a second group of four individuals to focus only on executing Kaizen events.

Traditional Lean Six Sigma projects were focused on long-standing process opportunities, which had defied identification of true root causes and subsequent improvement. Kaizen teams focused on clearly defined and business-critical processes to accelerate business impact and include a wider range of associates in the process improvement process.

This innovative approach was highly successful for a number of reasons:

- It provided flexibility to a smaller organization that wanted to do all the same activities of a critical-mass Lean Six Sigma deployment. The firm used the voice of the customer (VOC) to understand its specific requirements and business environment, then tailored the structure of the deployment and training content to maximize application and accelerate benefits.
- The company conducted a financial and business process assessment to identify the key opportunities that linked to business and customer requirements for maximized results.
- It demonstrated flexibility and practicality to bring in additional resources at the right time, with specific skills aligned to opportunities as they developed.

Another Example of a Focused Deployment

A large biopharmaceutical company wanted to launch Lean Six Sigma within a specific business unit (the managed care government contracts organization). Operational effectiveness and efficiency had suffered in that area because of recent M&A activities. The company decided to see if it could

(continued)

(*continued*)
develop some basic Lean Six Sigma skills in that business unit and complete a set of pilot projects within just three months.

Because of the compressed timeline, the company worked with an external consultant to collaboratively design an LSS program office and deployment plan. It did not do any formal project selection up front, but did validate the existing, known opportunities with sponsors and process owners. A core group of six participants received just five days of training, then did a lot of learning "on the job," with close mentoring of the external consultants. Four projects were completed within the three-month timeline, with an aggregate impact of $400,000.

This pilot approach gave the company confidence that it could launch a broader Lean Six Sigma effort and achieve results quickly.

FLEXIBILITY IN BUILDING SKILLS

Focusing a deployment on a limited number of specific business issues is one way to speed up deployment and results. Other alternatives to the three- to four-month timeline required in the traditional Lean Six Sigma deployment model for training resources and generating results include:

- The "I do-we do-you do" skill development system
- Hiring a master consultant (sensei)
- Augmenting internal staff with outside resources
- Applied learning ("rapid path to results")
- Blended e-learning

Rapid Development of Internal Expertise: The I Do–We Do–You Do Approach

Continuous improvement programs traditionally have started with waves of 20 to 100 Belts (in some combination of Green and Black, typically) with multiple weeks of training. The training is usually held at the beginning of the project work. The plan is for Black Belts to complete their first projects in six months' time and Green Belts in four. The training not only can be out of sync with the project timelines, but the participants are often in different phases of their respective projects during the classroom training. The overarching desire of this deployment design is to build the necessary critical mass to push a continuous improvement culture throughout the organization. This approach has proven effective in many situations, but it is not always the best fit for the individual organization.

The principle behind this approach is the truism "learn by doing." The approach begins with traditional classroom training, either via a brief overview (one week) or the more robust Belt training (two to five weeks) on the LSS tools. As implied by the name, three phases follow this kickoff:

Phase I: "I do" Here, the expert LSS practitioner (from inside or outside the company) serves the primary role in leading a team, while the person in training is primarily an observer. The practitioner takes the lead role in facilitation and guides the counterpart's team through all the project's steps, from inception to successful implementation. The counterpart acts, primarily, as a "shadow," observing, learning, and becoming knowledgeable and more comfortable with the LSS tools.

Phase II: "We do" In this phase, the roles are reversed from phase I. The LSS expert becomes the shadow while the counterpart is now thrust into the lead role. Though in the shadows, the expert is very active in ensuring the project's success: meeting with the new team leader one-on-one, anticipating problems, helping to work through barriers. Part of the expert's role is to ensure that the counterpart is always viewed in the lead role, whether it be facilitating discussions, problem solving, assigning team roles, and so on. The expert watches for unplanned occurrences and any barriers to the project's success that the new lead might not be thoroughly competent to address.

Phase III: "You do" This phase is a replication of phase II except the expert is no longer acting as a shadow (and may not even be at the client site, if the expert was an outside consultant). The new team leader is flying solo, so to speak, to lead a new project and deploy the necessary Lean Six Sigma tools without an LSS Master Black Belt or Lean Master on-site.

At the conclusion of this process, the nearly trained team leader has a lot of real-world experience in the specific environment of the workplace, and will have gained a deeper understanding of cost reduction opportunities and other potential improvements.

When and How to Use the I Do–We Do–You Do Model   One advantage of the I Do–We Do–You Do model is that it provides an intense learning experience for the project leaders in training—allowing much greater access to expert advice and coaching than is customary in more traditional models. Results can also accrue quickly because each phase is nearly assured of success, thanks to the high level of involvement from an expert. From a business standpoint, there is also the advantage of knowing the outside expert is phased out of the process by design—giving you a more predictable sense of the time and expense of the engagement.

The downside is that the high demand on the expert's time limits the number of people who can be trained at any given time.

Therefore, our best advice is:

- Consider using this model whenever you have a limited number of high-potential, focused projects. It would be too limiting if you were trying to achieve broader organizational transformation.
- Pick high-potential people for the training. You want someone who will be driven to get the most out of this opportunity, both in terms of taking advantage of access to experts and in making sure the projects are successful. People who are critical thinkers and good communicators work very well.

I Do–We Do–You Do Case Study

We worked for a division of a heavy equipment manufacturer that repaired, replaced, and refurbished mining equipment, with locations across the United States and Canada and several other international locations. This division had operational goals to reduce cycle times, and it wanted to rapidly deploy education on and implementation of key Lean tools.

An example of how the division's deployment goals could be met quickly was the work we did at one warehouse, where we guided the staff through three sets of projects:

- In the *I do* phase—which lasted just two weeks—our consultants led teams that focused on applying Lean methods to better organizing a warehouse. The 5S method was used to clear the aisles of clutter, improve safety, organize and label materials, and so on. The estimated savings for the company was $270,000 per year, based on avoidance of warehouse costs, finding lost inventory, avoiding redundant costs, and accruing time savings (it was must faster to retrieve inventory).
- In the *We do* phase—lasting three weeks—our consultants guided warehouse personnel as *they* led projects, focused on the question, "How do we handle all of our newfound floor space and take inventory control to

the next level?" A key accomplishment was establishing a pull replenishment system. The impact was more than $290,000 per year in savings, which included reduced inventory carrying costs and further reductions in warehouse space needs.

- In the *You do* phase—which lasted five weeks—the newly trained internal resources expanded the application of lean methods to other areas of the warehouse (with minimal support needed from our consultants). A project in the shipping and receiving department delivered significant benefits to safety, flow and space utilization; a WIP project improved overall warehouse safety, housekeeping, organization, and space utilization. Total gains were estimated at $744,000 per year, from further reductions costs across the board (such as reduced inventory carrying costs).

In all, the launch of Lean Six Sigma in this warehouse lasted just 10 weeks and generated nearly $1.3 million in cost reductions.

Hiring a Master Consultant (Sensei)

By far the most common model of working with external Lean Six Sigma consultants in the United States is based around a relatively short-term relationship (a few months to a few years), during which time some number of consultants (typically 4 to 10) lead projects, provide training, and transfer skills to the hiring client. Once the skills and knowledge base are developed, the consultants leave.

By contrast, with a sensei model, a company or business unit develops a long-term partnership with someone who is considered a true master of the improvement methods most critical for that company. Typically, the sensei visits the company for one week every month over the course of many years (we've seen some relationships that lasted more than a decade). The sensei's role is to provide overall guidance for the deployment, though he or she does not usually get directly involved in leading projects other than to teach some skills to the client. The sensei does not teach or train the organization in the broad range of Lean Six Sigma tools, rather he or she teaches the organization how to think about the issues they face. The sensei will work either with leadership or build capability of a small team through a series of Kaizen events.

The sensei model has some limitations—primarily that it cannot help a company develop internal competence very quickly and requires an ongoing financial commitment to the sensei—but it can be very effective in some circumstances. For example, Toyota has used this approach over the past 30 years to develop capability within specific departments or within its supplier base. In general, it is most useful when your situation has some combination of the following characteristics:

- You need in-depth expertise in a limited area (and that expertise may not be in Lean Six Sigma analytics, but rather the specialty topics that provide the engine for your business).
- You have a limited number of easily identified cost drivers (versus having to do a lot of investigative research).
- You need a strong personality to counter an aggressive, hard-charging business leader.
- You do not need rapid results; rather, a reasonable rate of return over a moderate time horizon is acceptable.
- You would rather stretch the investment in Lean Six Sigma development over a period of years (versus hiring a team of consultants up front).
- You have already established a high level of internal capability and now just need periodic expert guidance, and appreciate having an outsider's view of the organization.

As the last bullet points out, using a sensei is not necessarily an either/or decision. It is very reasonable to decide that the first part of your journey will be guided by a team of consultants who rapidly establish a foundation, then have a sensei guide the rest of the journey.

Augmenting Internal Staff with Outside Resources

Inefficient procedures continue in many organizations because they seem unchangeable, remaining virtually unseen by those closest to the process. What is urgently needed are "aha!" moments—something that happens more reliably when the process is examined through the fresh eyes of an outside expert.

Experienced advisors can be brought in temporarily to jump-start an initiative or to fill in areas of the business where resources are constrained. While hiring consultants from outside the organization can add cost (assuming internal staffing levels remain constant), the benefit is the acquisition of trained and experienced LSS practitioners with fresh insights, who can hit the ground running and who have strong team-building skills.

As an example, a multibillion dollar transportation company was experiencing a severe cash shortage after the company was taken private. The company sought LSS talent from outside the organization to help the company identify promising areas to generate savings quickly. The outside consultants helped the company's business leaders identify targets for cost reduction, enhanced quality and speed, and additional revenues. The project execution team created a portfolio of several projects centered on the company's core service of freight delivery processes.

Two Kaizen events, led by the outside consultants, resulted in plans that would generate $1.5 million in savings, which would have been an excellent return. But in fact, in just three months, the company realized annualized cost savings of more than $14 million (Figure 15.1). This encouraged the pursuit of additional gains through LSS initiatives in the coming year, for a total of $50 million in savings by year two. Left on its own, without the

Figure 15.1
Example of cost reductions.

Portfolio of five high-level opportunities was identified to achieve more than $14M cost reduction in year 1 (see below) and $50M in year 2

Fuel optimization – $7M
Medium-sized cost reduction project focused on optimizing routing and improved processes to reduce fuel waste.

Fleet Management – $5.8M
Medium-sized cost reduction project focused on vehicle utilization. Increased turns from 2.25 to 3 per trailer per week.

Data accuracy project
Medium-sized project enabling process improvement across the board by understanding financial, utilization, and performance information, and identifying quck wins.

Trailer Management Kaizen – $1.2M
Kaizen project focused on optimizing trailer logistics; reduced empty trailer wait time from 62 to 12 minutes.

Truck Maintenance – $0.3M
Kaizen project reducing cycle time, particularly setup time, or maintenance on trucks.

available expertise of the outsiders, it is unlikely that the company could have identified these savings.

Applied Learning: Rapid Path to Results

Another model that offers flexibility in educating internal resources is *applied learning*, or as one of our clients dubbed it, the "rapid path to results." This approach yields high project team engagement, and drives for immediate project results. In the applied learning model, Lean Six Sigma tools and methodologies are introduced to participants in a just-in-time (JIT) manner and leveraged immediately on the business issue at hand. By targeting the training around practical application, the participants are more engaged, and project results are often realized immediately, as shown in Figure 15.2.

Figure 15.2
Impact of targeted, JIT training.

How Time Is Spent

Flexible JIT Training

Focused analytics and action = RESULTS

- Demonstrates action
- Shows rapid results
- Builds quick momentum
- Builds lasting gains

Under this rapid improvement/Kaizen-event-based format, new tools and skills are introduced to the participants and immediately applied to projects, under the watchful eye of an experienced practitioner. Training includes project identification and selection; project management; team dynamics; and the Lean Six Sigma tools and techniques necessary to successfully measure, analyze, improve, and sustain project results. The experienced practitioners stay with the project team throughout the life of the project and thus are able to answer questions and provide insights to participants on a continuing basis. This approach is highly effective in increasing skills development transfer, and the quick delivery of project results.

Applied Learning/Rapid Path to Results Case Study

Applied learning takes on many shapes and sizes. Often it includes (but is not limited to) multiple weeks of prework, two weeks of in-class training, skill application via Kaizens and/or Value Stream Assessment (VSA) sessions, and extensive out-of-class coaching by experienced practitioners. Through this process, the organizations' resources become qualified to lead similar follow-on events on their own. See Figure 15.3 for a generic applied learning roadmap.

A military support unit that had a need to improve their existing processes chose to apply Lean Six Sigma tools to their operations. The traditional Lean Six Sigma deployment model did not fit the unit's culture so they decided to implement a customized, applied learning model.

During the prework weeks, the most promising improvement opportunities (worst-performing processes) were identified and refined into a single project charter. The Kaizen leaders met with executive leaders, key stakeholders, and sponsors, to review the project charter and finalize the objectives for the first week of training. This approach was effective because of its flexibility and because it allowed leadership to develop a tightly scoped project that could be fully implemented and completed during the one-week training session. To ensure the week started off fast, data gathering, analysis, and logistical support for the session occurred prior to the kickoff.

The first training session was action-packed and focused on completing defined project objectives in *one week* through the introduction and use of basic Lean Six Sigma tools. This particular applied learning activity included:

1. *Value Stream Assessment*: participants developed a Shingo-style value stream map (Chapter 4) to use during the week to help analyze the process.

(continued)

(continued)

Figure 15.3
General roadmap for a rapid path to results model.

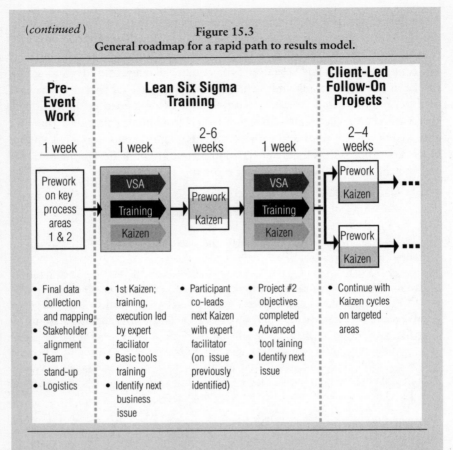

2. *Kaizen event*: Used to make immediate improvements. Participants built a "future state" value stream map, and implemented the new improvements and simulated changes to prove the concept.

During this first session, participants were taught, then applied, basic Lean Six Sigma tools, such as histograms, run charts, process capability, process constraint identification, and value-add/non-value-add analysis to their project. During the Kaizen, participants implemented actual process improvements that addressed the root causes of poor performance. The output of the Kaizen was a newly improved process and recommendations for improving a second process during the next training week.

The second in-class session followed the same format used in the first session. During this session, the more advanced Lean Six Sigma tools were introduced to the team. As the participants gained experience and confidence, they were encouraged to mentor project stakeholders on how to use Lean Six Sigma tools using the "I do–we do–you do" method. The output of the second week was the completion of the second project objective and additional project opportunity ideas for future Lean Six Sigma improvement projects/events.

At the end of these two weeks, this military support unit had:

- Completely remapped the core process of equipment repair.
- Built a new process that required just 6 steps in 6 days, compared to the starting point of 23 steps over 60 days (they could not be much more responsive to the units they supported).

Blended E-Learning

Several years ago, there was a backlash against the intensive—and extensive—classroom training that was built into standard Lean Six Sigma model. In a move to allow greater flexibility and autonomy in their approach to training, some companies switched almost entirely to an online or e-learning model, whereby employees were expected to complete a series of computer-based modules on their own.

"What these companies found was that work always trumped training," comments Doug Evans, a former colleague of ours who specialized in training development. "When employees tried to complete the modules while at work, they were constantly interrupted. Even employees with the best of intentions and eager to learn the material rarely completed the online training."

That's why the pendulum is swinging back in the other direction, producing what is now known as "blended learning" or "blended e-learning."

This approach is a combination of self-guided study plus interactive "live" classroom activities. People work at their own pace on modules that convey basic concepts, then attend classroom sessions where they get to apply what they learned under the guidance of an instructor.

Based on our experience, the self-guided portion of the training is best structured as a virtual classroom:

- The training is scheduled for a specific time, on a specific day.
- Participants "attend" a kickoff session via the Internet in the morning then work at their own pace on the designated modules for the day.
- There are two or more virtual check-in sessions during the day, at which time participants get to ask questions of the instructor.

"This approach requires the company to formally allocate the hours for the employee's training," says Doug. That sends a much different message about how important the education is to the company, versus expecting an employee to somehow squeeze in the training on his or her own time.

Scheduling the self-guided study for a particular day and time, having an instructor available throughout the day, and holding periodic check-ins has proven very effective.

"In theory, employees could work through the self-guided modules any time. But having a formal time allows me to work with the participants' managers or supervisors to make sure their 'real' work is covered and they can concentrate on learning," says Doug. (In fact, he strongly advises people to do the self-guided study from home, so they can avoid typical workplace interruptions.)

"Second," he adds, "a lot of people have trouble completing modules if they run into concepts they don't understand or questions they can't answer. Having check-ins allow people to get answers so they can finish the modules quickly."

After completing the online portion of the training, participants then come together for several days of actual classroom training, based on carefully constructed simulations.

This blended e-learning model has a number of advantages:

- *Improved skills transfer:* "Some people complain about having to attend classroom training, and others don't like the online part, but studies confirm that having both elements is the best way to transfer skills and knowledge," says Doug.
- *Stronger focus on what people really need to know:* The overall time spent in training is typically less with a blended approach than what the old classroom-only approach demanded (which was often 40 to 80 hours for Green Belts and twice that for Black Belts). The need to limit what people are exposed to has been a good thing, says Doug. "It's forced companies to be more deliberate about which topics are and aren't covered. Blended training is generally much better at focusing on concepts and skills that people need to apply right away."
- *Greater flexibility/lower cost:* In a blended e-learning model, participants only have to be in the same room at the same time for a fraction of the time required under the old models. That gives companies a lot more flexibility around timing, and avoids additional expenses around travel, for example. Plus, the overall training requirements are less for

both participants and instructors, which lowers the total cost of training substantially.

CONCLUSION

Given the pressures of today's economy, companies are very rightly looking for ways to improve the payback from their Lean Six Sigma investments. As you saw in this chapter, new methods are emerging that attack both sides of the payback question: the up-front cost (via compressing and targeting the training, for example) and the return (by making sure you're working on high-potential projects). Only you and your leadership can decide if any of these new options are right for your company.

No matter what, success via these newer paths will depend on the same factors as more traditional models: having highly engaged executives, linking project selection to a deep understanding of business priorities, and making sure your resources have the support they need to finish projects quickly.

CHAPTER 16

REENERGIZING A LEGACY PROGRAM

With Mitali Sharma, Jeff Howard, and Michael Mueller

About two years into its Lean Six Sigma deployment, a major national retailer was concerned because it was no longer seeing the big gains that were routine in the early days of the deployment. The early gains had been impressive, but since then economic returns had flattened out and interest in the program was waning. Still, with economic pressures increasing, the company thought it would be worthwhile to see if there wasn't something it could do to reinvigorate the deployment.

The first step was searching out the underlying causes for the lackluster performance. The company knew the problem wasn't with the methodology itself: Lean Six Sigma has been proven in practice time and time again. So there must be something in its deployment approach.

A close investigation revealed that the company had taken some shortcuts in its initial deployment, intended to make the program easier to digest by busy executives and staff. For example, a workshop for potential project sponsors had been pared down from the original one to two days to just a few hours. Stakeholders were selected without careful consideration, based on proximity to the CEO rather than an analysis of the political dynamics. A rigorous project selection process had been abandoned in favor of holding brief brainstorming sessions.

The consequence of these shortcuts was that the company had mediocre projects with ineffective sponsorship. It then faced two crucial questions: Should the Lean Six Sigma effort be rescued?

Answer: Leadership believed the need for cost savings and performance improvements was great enough to justify further investment.
If yes, had it done irreparable damage?

Answer: Leaders realized that although there was a perception problem—the poor performance in the past meant there was no strong incentive for managers to participate—the damage was not severe enough to warrant abandoning the effort altogether; but the effort needed to be repositioned.

The cure for this company was to start enforcing much more discipline around project selection and sponsorship. Leadership started by focusing on the areas where Lean Six Sigma had been successful already. Though that may sound counterintuitive—surely they should try to fix the sickest patients first?—it meant they were dealing with a receptive audience. Executive and managers were told that if they wanted to participate, they had to follow the discipline. Project sponsors had to be trained so they understood how to do that job well. Project selection had to be justified by better analytics and "size of prize" and extent of impact estimates.

These changes had immediate effects:

- The rate of return per Black Belt began to rise dramatically, meaning they were tackling larger, more important projects.
- The number of active projects began to rise. (Previously underutilized Black Belts were now getting the chance to pay back the investment in their training; but the company still paid attention to Little's Law to make sure that it didn't launch too many projects at the same time.)
- Project cycle time had already dropped 20 to 30 percent—for example, projects that might have taken four months in the past could now be completed in less than three.

For this company, given the history behind its deployment, the solution to its challenge was centered around having the discipline to pick the right projects, scope them appropriately, and support them with better-educated sponsors.

WHY DEPLOYMENTS LOSE STEAM

We've worked with a number of companies that saw impressive returns early on from their Lean Six Sigma efforts but then saw the rate of returns taper off or die completely.

Typical root causes we've seen are:

1. The LSS effort is focused too narrowly:
   - Within a building, call center, distribution center, or plant
   - Within a functional silo
   - On what is clearly visible
2. *Senior management's key measures not aligned with the improvement efforts.* Further, the measures tend to be only high-level and rear-ward-looking (sales, profits, and share price) and not include process-oriented and value-based metrics (Process Cycle Efficiency, overall asset effectiveness, customer satisfaction, lead times, customer service levels, learning cycles, key employee turnover, and so on).
3. *Critical relationships and interdependencies across the prime value chain are unknown or lack clear organizational ownership.* This ties to project selection and a robust project portfolio and requires a deep understanding of the key value levers in the business. This Prime Value Chain view, which leads to an understanding of where value is being created or destroyed in the business should ultimately drive the creation and prioritization of the project portfolio.
4. *A loss of focus/commitment, particularly among senior leadership (C-level and/or business-unit level).* Lean Six Sigma won't be on the agenda of executive meetings; leaders won't hold their direct reports accountable for results linked to Lean Six Sigma projects.
5. *Poor project selection and/or project pipeline management* Benefits associated with projects have declined due to poor execution, poor project selection, and a lack of maintenance of the project pipeline. (This is the case with the company whose story we feature in the text.) Often, there is overemphasis on Belt-led projects. Other opportunities, such as Kaizen events and broader, very high-impact strategic-level initiatives, are missed or ignored.
6. *Too much bureaucracy.* The infrastructure put in place to support the LSS program is more a hindrance than a help. The bureaucracy of complicated rules and excessive oversight slows down the work. To see if this is a problem, explore how the deployment is perceived by the business.
7. *Faulty resources selection.* Black Belt and Green Belt candidates are selected based on who is available, not who has the right skills and interest.

We've summarized these and other problems in Table 16.1 and described the kinds of solutions that have proven to work.

Table 16.1

Top 12 Symptoms of Deployment Trouble and Recommended Solutions

	Potential Problem	Root Cause	Proven Solutions
1	Organization views Lean Six Sigma as "flavor-of-the-month" initiative.	Multiple, past initiatives have been launched with a lot of fanfare and few results or long-term staying power. Why will this be different?	Demonstrate top leadership commitment; genuine leadership engagement and involvement is critical ("walk the talk").
			Select best people as Black Belts, Kaizen leaders and champions.
			Assign BBs to the most important problems in the business.
			Integrate LSS into the daily operation of the business
2	Results/benefits per project below expected levels	Poor project selection; poor project execution	Implement robust project selection process.
			Ensure adequate levels of project coaching to sponsors by George Group Program Manager and Master Black Belts.
			Execute disciplined tollgate review process—kill projects early, if necessary.
			Ensure effective team leadership training for Black Belts/Kaizen leaders.
			Ensure weekly engagement of project sponsors.

	Potential Problem	Root Cause	Proven Solutions
3	Lack of commitment to Lean Six Sigma	Lack of belief on part of individuals that LSS applies to their part of the organization; misconception about how Lean Six Sigma works or applies; perception that Lean is just a way to cut headcount.	Cascade leaders/sponsor workshops and awareness training throughout the organization.
			Provide specific project examples (George Group can provide hundreds of project examples in nearly any areas of the business) and/or external contacts to discuss applicability to specific areas.
			Drive a balanced portfolio of projects through effective opportunity identification and project selection ($X\%$ customer satisfaction, $Y\%$ cost reduction, and so on).
4	Failure to select the "best people" as Black Belts, Kaizen leaders, and champions	Managers would rather apply resources to their own highest priorities; select "experts" versus "future leaders"; lack of commitment	Drive alignment of priorities through the project selection process.
			Install robust Black Belt/Kaizen leader selection process
			See item 3.
5	Lack of confidence in results and organizational impact	Lack of insight into performance improvement at project level; lack of understanding of link to organizational benefits	Deploy detailed, conservative "rule book" or guidelines for tracking of project benefits and financial results.
			Train key members of organization to certify/validate results.
			Communicate successes.
			Track benefits at organizational level.

(continued)

Table 16.1
Top 12 Symptoms of Deployment Trouble and Recommended Solutions (*continued*)

	Potential Problem	Root Cause	Proven Solutions
6	Poorly written project charters (no clear definition, scope too large) lead to longer project cycle times due to increased time spent in the Define phase.	Lack of quality champion support during roll-out; champions not fully understanding their roles and responsibilities; lack of communication of the charter review process	Inspect and evaluate charters prior to assignment to Black Belts/Kaizen leaders Institute effective project sponsor and champion training. Allow enough time between project selection and project launch. George Group Program Managers and Master Black Belts provide mentoring to sponsors. George Group Master Black Belts focus on charters during coaching sessions.
7	Project charters not developed by project sponsors, but instead by Black Belts/Kaizen leaders, an indication of poor commitment because project sponsors do not actually "own" the projects	Sponsors are not trained; sponsors do not understand their roles and/or importance of their involvement in the charter process; champions are not actively engaged in the charter process	Ensure selection of projects relevant to organizational issues. Ensure the right sponsors are assigned to projects. Ensure sponsors are involved in opportunity identification. Ensure project sponsors are trained prior to sponsoring projects. Ensure George Group Program Managers and Master Black Belts are dedicating coaching time to project sponsors.

	Potential Problem	Root Cause	Proven Solutions
8	Overloading of project team member resources, leading to longer project cycle times	Desire to staff all projects with the best people, versus available people; failure to evaluate capacity	Design disciplined project launch process based on resource availability. Provide insight into projects-in-process.
9	Logistics associated with coordinating training events (materials, notifications, refreshments, and so on) not up to par	Speed of the rollout; lack of capacity; lack of defined process; lack of skills	Appoint skilled training coordinator. Develop robust training coordination process. Continuously evaluate and take action on feedback from students for continuous process improvement.
10	Failure to fill training classes	Lack of commitment; ineffective coordination of training events	See items 1, 3, and 9.
11	High Black Belt attrition	Lack of leadership commitment; lack of career path for Black Belts; failure to select "future leaders"	See items 1 and 3. Appoint HR/personnel resource to manage Black Belt Kaizen selection and transition back into the organization. Establish appropriate job descriptions and compensation levels. Develop robust selection and performance evaluation process.
12	No organizational buy-in into proposed project solutions	Lack of stakeholder involvement; lack of commitment to Lean Six Sigma	Ensure sponsors are actively engaged in project (MBBs and champions to inspect). Identify stakeholders during Define phase; involve throughout project, particularly during tollgate reviews See item 3.

Building a Steam Engine: Performance Management

Of all the problems just described that can happen with a Lean Six Sigma deployment, one of the worst is having projects that are not contributing enough to the metrics that top leadership cares about most: Economic Profit, costs, margin, shareholder value. (Or even just the perception that projects are not adding value; a case later in this chapter is from a company where the projects were doing well, but leadership didn't trust the numbers.)

As we've emphasized throughout this book, the absolute primary purpose for launching Lean Six Sigma and chartering projects in the first place is to create value that is important to the company. The best way to do that is by establishing a formal *performance management* system.

A performance management system defines:

- Metrics at every level of management, which are cascaded down from layer to layer.
- Specific responsibilities for each level of management for tracking, summarizing, and reporting performance at their level.
- Daily, weekly, and monthly review schedules: *what* should be looked at, *when*.

The work starts at the top, with leaders spelling out a vision for the future and developing an operating model that will be needed to support that vision. Typical questions include:

- What do we aspire to be (three to five-plus years)?
- How will we achieve that purpose?
- What goals do we set for success? What is the timing?
- How will we compete, grow, and differentiate ourselves?
- How must we operate to execute our strategy and achieve our business objectives?
- What principles will guide the change in operating model?
- What factors must be present for each capability to execute?
- What functional capabilities will be needed for execution?
- What will the process implications be?
- What individual capabilities will be needed: culture, skills, structure, behaviors, and performance measures?

The cascading begins by examining behaviors and how those are linked to current metrics. Executives should look at:

- *Business strategy:* To what extent do employees demonstrate understanding of how their day-to-day work and individual behaviors contribute to executing strategy?
- *Leadership:* What are leaders doing visibly and consistently to demonstrate the desired behaviors?
- *Talent and people:* How are performance management practices aligned with desired behaviors?
- *Processes and techniques:* How are processes aligned to desired behaviors?
- *Performance metrics:* What behaviors do our current metrics reinforce? Are they the right ones?

The answers to these questions will then set the foundation for putting each piece of the performance management system in place. The first step is specifying exactly which metrics will be tracked at each level, then setting targets for those metrics linked to the business goals that executives have outlined.

The next step is spelling out who is responsible for doing what with those metrics. For example, Figure 16.1 is a model for typical monthly review to be performed by executives:

Similar processes should be spelled out for each level. Table 16.2 for example, shows the plan for the level just below top executives.

Jumping down to the last layer in the system, Table 16.3 is the comparable plan for a frontline supervisor.

PROCESS OWNERSHIP: THE PARTNER OF PERFORMANCE MANAGEMENT

A global retailer kept wondering why certain kinds of problems appeared with its product repricing system. These included:

- Regularly seeing a large gap between labor hours allocated to stores to complete the repricing work and the actual hours consumed.
- Finding disconnects between the decision to change product price labels and store execution of those label changes (too many label changes, labels not always being changed for the right reason).
- Experiencing technology issues with the process, such as incorrect timing between label change requests and the generation of unnecessary labels.

Figure 16.1
Monthly executive performance management review

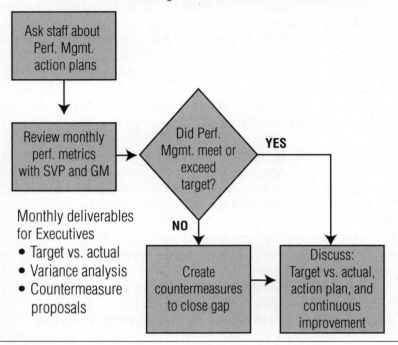

Performance Management Process for Executives

Table 16.2
Performance Management Plan at the General Manager/Senior VP Level

	Daily	*Weekly*	*Monthly*
Location	Review dashboard on walkaround for action items.	Review site trends with VP OPS coach and mentor.	Review trends with VP OPS and other GMs, leadership development.
Region	Observe VP OPS during review, coach, and mentor.	Observe VP OPS during status review, coach, and mentor.	Review show-to-show trends and across cities staff meeting.
Continuous improvement (CI)	Support broad-impact CI events with time and resources.	Identify broad-impact CI citywide and across cities.	Review with COO CI opportunities.

Table 16.3
Type/Frequency of Performance Management Activities for Frontline Supervisor

	Daily	Weekly	Monthly
Functions	Update information as needed during the week.	Review dashboard with full team and operations manager present.	Review in-site/ business-unit meetings trend, week to week.
Work area	Review dashboards at each staff meeting.	Roll up performance to the site meeting.	Review in-site/ business trend show to show.
Continuous improvement (CI)	Implement CI ideas from the team as they occur.	Identify CI opportunities that team can achieve.	Request support from site/business for larger opportunities.

These kinds of problems are symptomatic of a *lack of process ownership*: there was no clear owner of the repricing process, which meant *no single point of authority* for monitoring, improving, and sustaining that process.

Whereas performance management focuses on cascading value down through the existing organizational structure, process ownership is concerned with creating a system which involves people who are responsible for looking *across* functions. Both types of vision are needed to get the most from Lean Six Sigma deployments.

In fact, high-functioning process ownership is what links effective Lean Six Sigma deployment with overall operational effectiveness. A process owner is a person who responsible for the flow of work, whose line of sight cuts across functional boundaries, and who is focused on critical customer requirements.

We've talked throughout this book about the importance of shifting from a functional, or silo, view of an organization to a process view. To make that shift work, companies need to become more explicit about assigning process ownership, and establish a system that aligns individual process owners around enterprisewide strategic objectives. Problems and gaps around process ownership are common root causes we see with floundering Lean Six Sigma deployments.

Establishing a system of process ownerships requires business leaders to first adopt a macro view, to assess where "natural" process boundaries should exist, identifying the single person who will be in charge of each segment, and spell out the specific responsibilities for those roles.

If you have already begun incorporating process owners into your corporate structure but suspect that gaps may be contributing to deployment or operational problems, we recommend that you conduct an assessment focused on process ownership. You could, in fact, construct a maturity matrix that defines different levels of accomplishment around each function. You can then use the matrix to evaluate the status of your process ownership efforts. A sample of such a matrix is shown in Table 16.4. (Note: Categories not shown that we recommend including are: roles and

Table 16.4
Excerpt of Process Ownership Maturity Matrix

Stage Component	Beginning	Transitioning	Developed
Scope definition	Functional; silo-driven, without a view to the other functions linked in the overall process.	All functions required to meet customer requirements that are identified and known to each other.	Process scope is redefined to include the process flow required to meet customer requirements.
Customer insight	Customer feedback and metrics are gathered periodically.	Customer needs are expressed in terms of process requirements.	Customer needs are expressed in terms of process requirements, and periodically refreshed.
Right metrics	Basic metrics are in place.	Dashboards are refreshed to include key input and process metrics,	These input process metrics take precedence, link to enterprise goals, and are constantly monitored.
Portfolio management of improvement projects	Lack a complete view to all the projects being worked on in the organization; not sure if every project is tied to a critical business metric.	View to all projects being worked on in the functions, and an identified link to a KPI.	Projects in process are managed to maximize benefit capture; all projects are identified and selected based on the critical process metrics.
Link to bigger picture	Not a clear view on how the functional process links with fulfilling customer requirements and the overall process.	The end-to-end process for fulfilling customer requirements is identified and communicated.	Each person understands how his or her role is helping fulfill customer requirements in the overall process.

Figure 16.2
Process owner maturity rating. Preparing a diagram like this based
on your company's level of achievement in different dimensions of process
ownership can help give you an overall sense of progress, as well as
help identify target areas that need further development.

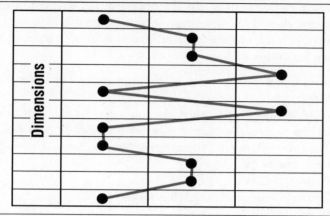

responsibilities, process documentation, improvement expertise, level of authority, incentives, systems, and leadership).

We usually create a visual map that summarizes the status of each component (see Figure 16.2). As with the overall maturity assessment, the purpose of a map like this isn't to suggest that anything less than a stage 3 is unacceptable; rather, it is to provide a starting point for discussions around whether being at a lower stage on any of the dimensions is holding the organization back in some way, which in turn can lead to plans to address the important gaps.

How to Reenergize a Deployment

Establishing a formal performance management system and clear process ownership are two of the best ways you can reenergize a Lean Six Sigma deployment. But there may be other underlying problems that are holding you back. So another dimension to putting the steam back in the value engine of your Lean Six Sigma deployment is doing an analysis of what is going well and what needs attention.

As with many things in life, often the people closest to a problem are unable to see it because they have become used to the status quo. Therefore, if your deployment is underperforming, it works best to have a neutral third party (or a team of outsiders) assess what's really going on behind the scenes. If you work for a large company or with a company with deep-enough manpower, and can afford to pull in a strong Lean Six Sigma leader or expert from another business unit who can be neutral, objective, and strong enough to be heard across the organization, that could work fine. Otherwise, you should strongly consider hiring someone from the outside.

Obviously, one job of the evaluator is to look at how the deployment is going, using indicators such as:

- How well the processes used to implement Lean Six Sigma are working:
  - A robust diagnostic approach, and a project identification and selection process that align project with your business's value agenda
  - The right balance of project types: Kaizen, Belt-led, strategic initiatives, and so on
  - Project reviews
  - Financial guidelines to track projects
  - Consistent use of toolsets
- Links to strategy
  - Projects aligned with overall enterprise strategy and to other initiatives
  - Level of engagement of project sponsors and process owners (it will be high if the projects are contributing to business objectives; low otherwise)
  - Deployment strategy implementation
- People involved in the deployment
  - Are roles and responsibilities clear?
  - Have job descriptions and career paths for Lean Six Sigma resources been documented?
  - Have rewards and recognition systems been developed?
  - What goes into team development?
  - How is the training and coaching perceived?
  - Are projects given sufficient leadership guidance?
- Degree that Lean Six Sigma has become embedded in the culture
  - Top-down commitment
  - Engaged management
  - Rigor and discipline to sustain the gains
  - Communication

It is equally important is to look at how far along the organization is in its journey to operational excellence. Only by looking at the organization as

Figure 16.3
Dimensions of operational excellence.

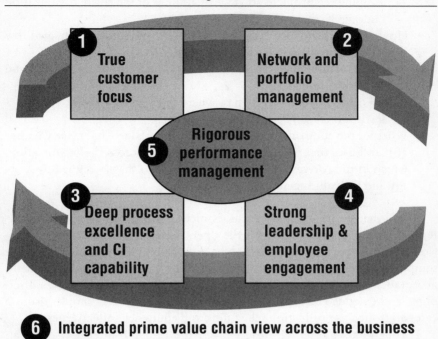

6 **Integrated prime value chain view across the business**

a whole can you identify places where Lean Six Sigma *could* be helpful but isn't being used. For this part of the evaluation, we look at six dimensions (see Figure 16.3).

The kinds of issues evaluators should look at include:

- Degree of true customer focus:
  — Does the organization understand what adds value from the customer standpoint?
  — Do offerings and customers generate economic profit?
- Status of network and portfolio management:
  — Ensuring segment/business unit strategies are synergistic
  — Understanding of the impact of portfolio complexity (see Chapter 10)
- Whether process excellence skills and knowledge are widely applied, or are restricted to formal Lean Six Sigma projects
- Is there strong leadership and employee engagement?

— How well is the company leveraging its human assets?
— Tapping the problem-solving capabilities of the entire organization
— Building lasting capabilities
- How well performance is consistently and continuously managed (see page 306 for more details)
  — Are executive-level goals driven down to the business unit and functional levels?
  — All metrics cascaded down to where the value is added
  — Institutionalized best practice sharing
- Whether the company understands its Prime Value Chain (see Chapter 10), and uses that to drive an enterprise view across the organization, which in turn drives a robust project portfolio that is aligned to strategy and the value agenda

A tool that we use to guide the assessment is a matrix that spells out different levels of maturity in both the operational and deployment dimensions. An excerpt is shown in Table 16.5. (Note: Categories not in the sample but that we recommend adding include: performance management, acceptance of the improvement discipline, problem solving, process discipline, and extended enterprise management; manufacturers should also use categories such as production scheduling and equipment effectiveness.)

Through data gathering, observation, and in-depth interviews, we can evaluate which stage is company is in on all the dimensions and indicate that on the matrix. The purpose is to think of this *not* as a report card, but rather as a starting point for discussions with the company leadership: "You're at stage 1 in Employee Engagement. Do you think that is holding you back in any way? Would there be advantages to moving to the next stage? If so, what would need to happen?"

The specifics here will naturally depend on what problems and opportunity you find, but common actions going forward include:

- *Starting with enterprise alignment.* The most common flaw in Lean Six Sigma deployments—and, in fact, throughout the organization—is the lack of strategic alignment. Aligning the entire enterprise around agreed-on priorities is a key lever for success: Knowing what is *most important* to the organization will shape decisions of every shape and size. The mechanics of alignment involved start with having centralized Lean Six Sigma program management: This is not about the reporting structure; this is about having an office, or even a person, that has oversight and responsibility to continually drive value

Table 16.5
Excerpt of an Operational Excellence Maturity Matrix

Component	Stage 0: Just Beginning	Stage 1: Taken First Steps	Stage 2: Beginning to Take Root	Stage 3: Operational Excellence Practices Embedded in Daily Work
Leadership Vision and Engagement	Leadership does not communicate vision to organization and does not visibly engage with employees.	Leadership shares vision (e.g., through newsletters) but does not actively engage with frontline personnel.	Leadership shares vision and is engaged in continuous improvement efforts.	Leadership is actively engaged in continuous improvement, clearly and regularly communicates vision and progress, and publicly recognizes and rewards progress.
Employee Engagement	Most employees work the minimum level that avoids termination.	Employees use their skills and experience in their work and generally appear engaged.	Employees actively drive change in the organization.	Employees align themselves to targets and generate value-generating improvement ideas.
Continuous Improvement Execution and Results	Continuous improvement execution is synonymous with capital projects.	Continuous improvement efforts exist but do not drive value for the organization, or value is not tracked.	Localized continuous improvement efforts (e.g., Kaizen events in some plants) and value are tracked locally or do not significantly impact bottom line.	Continuous improvement drives significant value throughout the organization and enables operations strategy.
Customer Focus	No knowledge of customer expectations or issues except among a small group of employees.	Customer focus limited to special requests and responding to complaints.	Regular communication with customers; joint problem solving.	Formal processes are in place to understand customer expectations, including those unstated; the customer is a partner in continuous improvement efforts.

generation. That office or person is charged with championing a strategic perspective to identify the highest-impact projects where executive direction might be most helpful.

- *Clearly identifying and prioritizing areas of concern and options for addressing those areas.* This works much like the project selection process described in Chapter 12: You look at all the opportunities you have, figure out whether they require a tactical solution (through some form of project) or leadership attention (to make strategic decisions), and develop a plan of attack.
- Adjusting the Lean Six Sigma deployment:
  - Establishing a consistent process for assessment, project identification, and prioritization within the businesses.
  - Adjusting resource training and deployment.
  - Using IT to set up better systems for project documentation, best practices sharing, project communication.
- Establishing a value tracking system (embedded in the performance management system).
- Implementing a program dashboard with metrics determined by the program leadership and the business leadership. Holding both the program and business responsible for the performance of the metrics.
  - Begin tracking both performance data and cultural indicators.

Case Study: Home Products Company

A building and home products company had been focusing on continuous improvement for more than two decades. It had established a formal Six Sigma program about a decade ago, and launched a few isolated Lean efforts during that time. But now management realized it was getting harder and harder to identify high-impact projects—and those they did launch were taking a year or longer to complete.

Rather than abandon its continuous improvement efforts, the company wanted to see what could be done to take it to an even higher level of performance. An investigation revealed that the opportunities lay in:

- Developing a more robust project identification process built around a more strategically aligned and value-based view of the company's project portfolio and stronger project portfolio management.
- Doing more to integrate its Lean and Six Sigma efforts, and put a greater emphasis on Lean.

- Shifting the continuous improvement culture and paradigm around overall project velocity speed to results.

As a consequence, the company designed and executed a Lean development and integration roadmap that leveraged Kaizens and Kaizen leader development and linked and sequenced projects to achieve bigger and faster effects with dramatic results: *more than $30 million in annualized real dollar benefits in less than six months.*

In addition, the company drove rapid and broad hands-on engagement at all levels: More than 1200 employees were *directly* involved in making improvements in year one. After just six months, the CEO commented that he could "literally feel the difference in the culture" on a daily basis.

Now, with a critical mass of trained Kaizen leaders able to lead four to six Kaizens a year, the company has dramatically shifted its paradigm around expectations for the scope of effort and speed of results. Furthermore, there is an almost obsessive focus on process improvement and attacking waste throughout the enterprise. Employees are continually asking: "Why do we do things this way?" and "How could we do it better/faster?"

Case Study: Service Company

A $6 billion service company that was best-in-class in its industry had year-over-year revenue growth for the past 50 quarters, paying dividends for 49 out of those 50. At one point, the company launched a major Lean Transformation effort, but two years in, leaders throughout the company expressed their disappointment at the lack of impact on business results or culture. (Ironically, they did, in fact, have quantified significant financial impact, but because they lacked financial rigor around qualifying and quantifying results, the cited benefits weren't believed.)

An evaluation of the company revealed several core problems:

- The participants had indiscriminately applied Lean tools and Kaizen methods, resulting in some improvement "events" that took 6 to 12 months to complete; teams struggled with data analysis because they lacked the Six Sigma tools.
- Executive engagement varied across the organization.
- A conservative fiscal culture affected how they quantified financial benefits.
- Project selection was still treated as a series of one-off events; there was no pipeline of high-potential projects.

(*continued*)

(*continued*)

This company saw that it would have to develop two core competencies to reenergize its improvement effort: integrate Six Sigma into its improvement methods, and develop a better system for project selection and monitoring. Within a year, the company completed a formal deployment planning process and trained 30 deployment champions in project selection. Those skills were put to immediate use to provide a mix of project types for the 50-plus Black Belts and 200 Green Belts trained by the end of tear two. By that time, the company had realized more than $50 million in type 1 and type 2 benefits.

CONCLUSION

With all the competing priorities that companies face these days, it's easy for improvement efforts to fall into a vicious cycle: the efforts lose focus, which means they lose impact, which means they drop lower on management's agenda and lose even more focus. The irony is that pushing to strengthen Lean Six Sigma is often the ticket to addressing other competing priorities.

To reenergize a Lean Six Sigma effort, you need to know where it has gone astray. Doing an assessment around the ingredients that contribute to a strong deployment is a first step. One key ingredient that is often lacking is making sure that improvement efforts are strongly linked to business priorities. A lack of strong process ownership may also be a contributing factor.

As demonstrated by the companies featured in this chapter, taking the time to reenergize a Lean Six Sigma deployment can pay off not only in terms of getting more back from the investment you've already made, but in generating significant savings—critical in these economic times.

Index